THE POETICAL WORKS OF ALEXANDER McLACHLAN

Literature of Canada

Poetry and Prose in Reprint

Douglas Lochhead, General Editor

The Poetical Works of

Alexander McLachlan

Introduction by E. Margaret Fulton

UNIVERSITY OF TORONTO PRESS

© University of Toronto Press 1974
Toronto and Buffalo
Printed in Canada
ISBN (casebound) 0-8020-2127-1
ISBN (paperback) 0-8020-6235-0
LC 73-82589

Literature of Canada 13
The Poetical Works of Alexander McLachlan was originally published in 1900 by William Briggs, Toronto. Of the poems included
in the appendix, 'Sabbath Morning's Soliloquy of an Ox' originally
appeared in *Poems*, published in 1856 by John C. Geikie, Toronto;
'Elora,' 'Old Canada; or, Gee Buck Gee,' 'The Old Settler's Address
to his Old Log House,' 'Going to the Bush,' 'Young Hoss,' 'The
Death of the Ox,' and 'Ontario' originally appeared in *Poems and
Songs*, published in 1888 by Rose Publishing Company, Toronto.

This book has been published with the assistance of a grant from
the Ontario Arts Council.

Preface

Yes, there is a Canadian literature. It does exist. Part of the evidence to support these statements is presented in the form of reprints of the poetry and prose of the authors included in this series. Much of this literature has been long out of print. If the country's culture and traditions are to be sampled and measured, both in terms of past and present-day conditions, then the major works of both our well-known and our lesser-known writers should be available for all to buy and read. The Literature of Canada series aims to meet this need. It shares with its companion series, The Social History of Canada, the purpose of making the documents of the country's heritage accessible to an increasingly large national and international public, a public which is anxious to acquaint itself with Canadian literature — the writing itself — and also to become intimate with the times in which it grew.

DL

Alexander McLachlan, 1818-96

E. Margaret Fulton

Introduction

That a volume of the poetry of Alexander McLachlan should be given a foremost place in the Literature of Canada: Poetry and Prose in Reprint series cannot be questioned. Douglas Lochhead in his introduction to one of the volumes of this series — Dewart's anthology, *Selections from Canadian Poets* — has focussed attention on the argument of Edward Hartley Dewart that 'a national literature is an essential element in the formation of national character.' If the statement was important in 1864 when the Canadian nation struggling to be born was composed of largely homogeneous ethnic groups, it is of even greater significance today, when so many of the Dominion's population are recent immigrants from many nations, who have only a very limited notion of what the Canadian 'national character' is, or of the identity they are seeking when they take out Canadian citizenship. Even many Canadians of the second or third generation have an equally vague notion of what Canada is all about. While background studies in history, politics, and sociology make a good attempt to overcome deficient knowledge of the past, these alone are not enough. They need to be supplemented with studies in the early literature of Canada; and foremost in any literature stands the work of the poets.

Dewart ranks Alexander McLachlan as a major early Canadian poet second only in importance to Charles Sangster. While much of his poetry may appear imitative and of a highly derivative nature, seen in its proper historic perspective it is more than just a pale reflection of the intellectual ideas permeating the thought of nineteenth-century British writers. Much of it is distinctly

Canadian, and no more graphic picture of the pioneer experience can be found than in McLachlan's poetry.

One could argue that there is no shortage of accounts of pioneer life in Canada. An abundance of letters, journals, and diaries of many early writers, such as Susanna Moodie and Anna Jameson, have authenticated and illuminated the struggles of the first settlers in the great forest-covered wilderness of Ontario. The poet, however, does more than record the hardships of the pioneer; he objectifies the struggle and invests it with a dimension beyond mere factual accounts. Despite the many imperfections in the verse of McLachlan, the reader finds this ontological factor. The spontaneity and sincerity with which he depicts the heroic struggles of the settlers in the new land cannot but stir a response even from the sophisticated modern reader.

Poetry should ennoble the reader. Dewart in his time challenged poets to aim for the very loftiest goal:

> Poetry fires the soul with noble and holy purpose. It expands and quickens. It refines the taste. It opens to us the treasures of the universe, and brings us into closer sympathy with all that is beautiful, and grand, and true. It sheds a new charm around common objects; because it unveils their spiritual relations, and higher and deeper typical meanings. And it educates the mind to a quicker perception of the harmony, grandeur, and truth disclosed in the works of the Creator.[1]

McLachlan took Dewart's challenge very seriously. His motivations for writing poetry were of the highest and yet the humblest. In line with the thinking of his times, he sought to do what Dewart required of the poet: he strove to ennoble and elevate the minds of that uneducated class of struggling men — the class to which he himself belonged — the mechanics, weavers, farmers, and labourers, who, seeing no hope of ever getting out from under the 'tyrant's yoke' in Scotland, left their beloved land of 'green glens' and 'Highlan' hills' to try, at least, to hew out in the Canadian wilds a better society for man.

Such a high purpose is not likely to be achieved with every poem a poet writes. Certainly McLachlan in a good many of his songs and ballads fails to inspire the reader. No great degree of critical acumen is required to disparage much of the poetry of McLachlan, which is marked by obvious imperfections of style. His predilection for end rhymes — many of them forced — becomes tedious and leaves him open to the charge of writing doggerel. His failure to vary from the iambic foot creates a further sense of monotony. Almost the only modification he practises is alternation between tetrameter and trimeter lines — a standard device he no doubt learned from the old hymn tunes and the Scottish psalter. The poet's innate sense of metaphor, however, does tend to compensate for the weaknesses of prosody.

The simple lyric 'Curling Song' is much more than a jingle about the joys experienced in the 'roaring rink,' whether in Scotland or in Canada. McLachlan was firm in his belief that man could move forward from a state of slaves and masters to form a new democratic brotherhood; and when he states that

...on the rink distinctions sink,
   An' caste aside is laid;
Whate'er ye be, the stane and tee
   Will test what stuff ye're made,

he has expressed a noble ideal through metaphor, in a manner which compares not unfavourably with that of Burns. Indeed it was commonplace amongst the contemporaries of McLachlan to refer to him as the 'Burns of Canada.'

Such praise the academicians of today would find extravagant. Obviously McLachlan lacked both the poetic talent and the vision of a Burns. Nothing of the 'Seer' or 'Prophet' characterizes him. He was neither a profound nor an original thinker and many of his poems seem but poor imitations of the poetry of the great eighteenth- and nineteenth-century British poets. In many lyrics, such as 'Man,' 'Who Knows,' 'God,' 'Infinite,' 'Awful Spirit,' 'Mystery,' and 'Stars,' McLachlan poses the great questions of ultimate meaning in life, and struggles with the concepts of deism and pantheism. Pope, Wordsworth, and Shelley had already dealt with these concepts, and so much more effectively that one might well ask, 'Why reprint or even bother to read McLachlan?'

The answer to this question can be found in Edward Hartley Dewart's introduction to this volume. When in 1900 Dewart and his fellow editors published this original edition of McLachlan's selected works they recognized what Emerson and Whitman had been writing about fifty to seventy years earlier in the United States: that if a nation is to survive politically and culturally it must be supported by a national literature. McLachlan's poetry begins such a national literature and whatever ineffectualities of style or content we find in his poetry, no one can deny that in many poems he does achieve that ontological sense — that extra dimension — which lifts the poem above mere sentimentality or banality. Further, throughout his poetry there is evidence of his possessing, as the *Guelph Evening Mercury* of 21 March 1896 stated in its obituary notice, 'a true streak of the poetic fire about him.'

Alexander McLachlan is completely representative of the waves of Scottish emigrants who, from the 1830s on, opened up and settled many of the western counties of Upper Canada — Canada West, as it was called from 1840 to 1867. These were the settlers who bent their political efforts towards creating a just and free democratic society, and who worked for the creation of a new nation — the Dominion of Canada. Tempting though it is to detail the poet's background and life, no need exists, for the biographical sketch included by the original editors of this volume in 1900 remains the best single source of information.

The Reform Bill of 1832 was a political triumph, but it did not end the economic disasters which were plaguing Britain. The working classes still had no alternative but to starve to death under miserable conditions in factory, mine, or farm, or to leave the country. Many chose to leave. McLachlan's father emigrated from Scotland to Canada in the 1830s and cleared a homestead in Peel County, but he died before he was able to bring his family to join him. Alexander, his only son, came in 1840, at the age of twenty-two, to claim his father's farm. Having received in Scotland only a limited formal education, he had worked as a weaver and been trained in tailoring. He knew first-hand the lack of opportunity in the old country and he could sing wholeheartedly with the other emigrants on board ship, 'Old England is Eaten with Knaves.' Yet in spite of the limited opportunities for advancement in his homeland his poetry records no bitterness, and poems such as 'Britannia' and 'The Anglo-Saxon' express only intense loyalty, and the hope that the wrongs will eventually be righted.

Ironically, conditions in Canada at that time were not such as to inspire fresh loyalty or optimism for the new land. Nevertheless, in 'The Genius of Canada,' 'The Men of the New Dominion,' 'Young Canada; or Jack's as Good's His Master,' and 'Hurrah for the New Dominion,' he makes clear his belief in and hope for his new country. He successfully works out a dual sense of loyalty and patriotism to the old and new lands. As the crown stood for nothing less than the decent and respectable public ideals of a democratic society, divided allegiance was not a problem in Canada in either the colonial or the early confederation periods. While singing the praises of a strong and independent Canadian nation, McLachlan would have that nation remain loyal to the British crown. 'Song' – a poem written especially for the Scottish Gathering in the Crystal Palace grounds, Toronto, 14 September 1859, but published also in *The Emigrant and Other Poems* – praises the simple, honest man of Scotland, 'A Highland Host in Canada' who must be ready at any time to rush to the support of 'brither Scots owre a' the earth,' and who must ever be 'faithfu' still to kirk and Queen.' This type of set piece indicates that McLachlan eventually came to see himself as a kind of poet laureate for Canada.

Certainly his attempts at pioneer farming were not of long duration. In the 1840s he had married his cousin Clamina, sold his father's farm in Peel County, and moved to a bush farm in Perth County. A delightful account of this type of youthful enthusiasm is recorded in the poem 'Going to the Bush' (see appendix p 425). For a few years McLachlan struggled on his bush farm; but burdened with young children (eleven in all) he went to the village of Erin in Wellington County, where he supported his family by tailoring, working as a mechanic, writing, and lecturing. What amazes us when we reflect on McLachlan's life is – to adapt Samuel Johnson's famous phrase – not that he wrote poetry badly but that, under the circumstances, he wrote it at all.

McLachlan's first volume – a slim one – *The Spirit of Love and Other Poems*, was published in 1846. The editors of 1900

xii

wisely included no selections from this early volume. The dedication lines are taken from Wordsworth and Shelley. The long title poem, 'The Spirit of Love,' is a thoroughly bad imitation of Wordsworth; but the idealism and the sincerity which mark his later more relaxed and natural style is apparent in spite of the stilted verse:

> So virtue, 'mid a world of crime,
> Anticipates the joyous time
> When Love with all her beams unfurl'd,
> Sun of the intellectual world,
> When by codes and creed unconfin'd,
> Shall shine o'er the wide realms of mind.

Considering that these lines were probably penned during the period when McLachlan, axe in hand, was hacking down trees and clearing land in Perth County, the wonder is that they are as good as they are. Has ever a poetic muse flourished in less propitious conditions!

In 1856, while still living at Erin, McLachlan published *Poems*, followed in 1858 by *Lyrics*, a copy of which he presented to William Lyon Mackenzie, suitably inscribed 'as a token of respect for the high patriotic purpose to which his life has been devoted.'[2] While many of the poems in these two volumes are nostalgic reminiscences of Scotland, a goodly number depict the Canadian scene. The dedication to Mackenzie indicates McLachlan's intense interest in the political and cultural life of the new nation. With the publication in 1861 of *The Emigrant and Other Poems*, followed in 1874 by *Poems and Songs* (from which two volumes most of the selections in the 1900 edition have been chosen) McLachlan had earned his reputation as the 'Burns of Canada.'

But was he really the Burns, or was he rather the Carlyle, of Canada? Certainly he wrote three poems in praise of Burns to one lauding Carlyle, and as already pointed out no one can fail to notice the influence of Burns on both his style and his two themes — the common man, and the democratic brotherhood.

In his life style, however, McLachlan seems to emulate Carlyle rather than Burns. An inveterate smoker but given only to occasional bouts of 'jollity,' he appears to have been as improvident as Carlyle, and as unsuccessful in prosaic pursuits. The poem 'Mammon's in the Way,' attacking 'all flunkeydom,' is a typical Carlylean attitude. Neither of these Scottish exiles — the Londoner or the Canadian — could ever be charged with letting 'Mammon' get in the way of his high purposes in life. In appearance, too, McLachlan — a tall and lean man — seems to have resembled Carlyle. In a fine painting hanging in the Orangeville Public Library one can detect behind a splendid beard the angular lines, the deepset eyes, and the noble brow which characterized Carlyle.

But the greatest similarity between the two Scots lies in the causes they championed. Dedicated to the amelioration of the conditions of the working classes, each strove to inspire all men with a higher sense of values. 'Up, and Be a Hero' is McLachlan's clarion call to the men of all ranks to work hard, to be independent, to be honest and true, and to believe in a supernatural power:

To the noble soul alone
Nature's mystic art is shown;
God will make his secrets known
    Only to the hero!

If thou only art but true,
What may not thy spirit do?
All is possible to you,
    Only be a hero!

Carlyle had taken very seriously his task of raising the 'British heathen' to nobler ideals by preaching the gospel of work, duty, and silent reverence for God. McLachlan reflects Carlyle's themes in his poetry. Like his fellow-Scot he undertook a series of lecture tours where he spoke to mechanics and tradespeople, as well as to the more educated classes. He, too, assumed the role of 'man of letters' in an effort to elevate the whole tone of man's thinking, and to raise the whole cultural level in Canada. Poems like 'Heroes,' 'Gladstone,' and 'Garibaldi' suggest the influence of Carlyle's *Heroes and Hero Worship;* and the subject for a lecture at Queen's College, Kingston, was 'Great Men.' Clearly McLachlan in his way was attempting to do for Canada what Carlyle with his lecture series was doing for England, and Emerson for the United States. If the reviews of the day are to be trusted, McLachlan was no less successful than either Carlyle or Emerson. Professor James George of Queen's wrote the following commentary:

> Those who had the opportunity of listening to the lecture of
> Mr McLachlan, on Wednesday evening, in the city hall, will not
> soon forget the high intellectual enjoyment they experienced.
> The subject chosen (i.e. 'great men') by the lecturer, is indeed
> a high one, and if handled by an ordinary man, would not only
> prove a failure, but could hardly be other than a miserable
> caricature. But Mr McLachlan is not an ordinary man — hence
> his audience saw no arrogancy in the choice of his high
> subject, just because there was no failure in the execution. It

was, indeed, treated throughout with the wisdom, knowledge, and taste of a master mind.[3]

Professor George was not alone in his high praise of McLachlan. The famous testimonial dinner of 28 April 1890, his friendships with two Fathers of Confederation, D'Arcy McGee and George Brown, and the fact that in the 1860s he was chosen by the immigration department of the government to give lectures in Britain encouraging emigration to Canada, all provide further evidence of his eminence as a distinguished and loyal Canadian.

As a poet, McLachlan attained a reputation both in Canada and beyond. Many of his poems appeared not only in Canadian publications but in the *Scottish American Journal*, the *Glasgow Citizen*, the *British Whig*, and other non-Canadian periodicals. As recently as 24 May 1968, the daily newspaper of his Scottish birthplace, *The Johnstone Advertiser*, ran a full-page article celebrating the hundred and fiftieth anniversary of the birth of McLachlan, the 'Patriot Poet of Canada' – an event which passed unnoticed in Canadian literary and cultural circles.

Is there need for a reprint of the poetry of McLachlan? The answer must surely be a categorical 'yes'! Once all the pejorative criticisms have been levelled – the imperfections of style, the derivative nature of the themes, the excessive Scottishness – the fact remains that in the bulk of McLachlan's poetry we hear a distinctively Canadian voice which moves not only the student of Canadian literature but any reader sensitive to the universal human struggle. It is not the voice of a Homer or Virgil or Milton or Shakespeare, but none the less a voice which helps to shape a national identity.

That McLachlan came to love the Canadian scene as much as the Scottish is clear in his poems 'The Maple Tree,' 'Indian

Summer,' 'October,' 'Whip-Poor-Will,' 'Elora' (a tribute to the Elora George in Wellington County) (see appendix p 428) and 'Ontario' (see appendix p 429). That he also believed implicitly in the challenge and the power of the new land to breed and foster the development of a nobler human being is apparent in 'Acres of His Own,' 'A Backwoods Hero,' 'Companionship in Books,' 'Dr Burns,' and 'The Backwoods Philosopher.' That he was — despite his early dabblings in deism and pantheism — committed to a basic belief in a personal God, whose gift of His Son, Jesus Christ, and the Holy Spirit provided the one eternal and unfailing source of strength for man, is clear in any number of poems; but the expression of such faith is perhaps most effectively shown in 'The Settler's First Sabbath Day,' in the fine portrait of 'Old Hannah,' and in 'The Man Who Rose From Nothing,' which states the simple creed 'Fear God and help the soul in need.' McLachlan's rejection of any narrow-minded theology is exemplified in 'John Fraser's Farewell to the Church of Scotland' and 'John Tamson's Address to the Clergy of Scotland.' Canada, the new land which gave an opportunity for a new type of political freedom, was equally to lead to a new style of religious freedom. The hypocritical theologies, the ties and bonds of the limiting and strife-producing orthodoxies of the old lands, were replaced in the new land with a unifying belief in a genuine Christian humanitarianism. Whatever the influences and subjects which shaped the poetry of McLachlan, he emerges as a genuine Canadian poet.

Our debt to Dewart and his assistants for their foresight in preserving McLachlan's poetry in the edition of 1900 as an integral part of the cultural developnent of Canada must be fully acknowledged. If the volume is to be criticized in any way it is because of the sin of omission rather than commission. The modern Canadian reader will find more of interest in the poems depicting the pioneer background than in the plethora of nostalgic Scottish reminiscences. It is easy to explain and to understand the biases directing the choices of the editors in 1900, but it is a great pity, from the point of view of the modern reader, not to have included more pioneer poems.

'The Death of the Ox' (see appendix p 431) if not a great poem is certainly a good poem, and one of intense interest. The old settler's monologue on the death of his trusty ox, Bright, gives in a few stanzas a better picture of the pioneer's life than dozens of letters written by those self-sacrificing, literate British women of the Anna Jameson variety. Something of the monologue style expressing man's sense of reliance on his animals is found in 'Auld Towser' and 'The Old War Horse'; but both poems lack the genuine pathos and the sense of communication which existed between the pioneer and his ox.

And thou wert so sagacious too, so sensible and shrewd,
And every word I said to thee, was fully understood.
No whip was e'er laid on thy back,
   nor blue-beech, never never!
While slaves and tyrants wrought and fought,
   we lived in peace together.

I've no doubt, but you learned some things,
   my poor old friend from me,
And many a silent lesson too, I also got from thee;
I ne'er could think thou were a brute,
   but just a silent brother!
And sure am I, to fill thy place I'll never get another!

Another unfortunate omission from this volume is the monologue 'The Old Settler's Address to His Old Log House' (see appendix p 434). Although somewhat sentimental, the old pioneer's reminiscences illustrate the passing of the era of the very early primitive struggles of the pioneer.

More regrettable even than the omission of the more serious pioneer monologues is the failure to include much of McLachlan's satire. His sense of irony is shown in many poems, such as 'Poor Donkey' and 'Go Into Debt'; and contrasting the somewhat lugubrious tone of many of the poems is the tone of biting, humorous satire which stamps a poem like 'Old Skinflint's Dream' as first-rate. Not all the settlers coming to the new world were noble Scots imbued with the highest ideals for man in his new society; a fair number of blackguards, knaves, and skinflints were also populating the Ontario counties. Again, one of the best of McLachlan's humorous satires is about an ox. In 'Sabbath Morning's Soliloquy of an Old Ox' (see appendix p 438) it is the ox's turn to pass judgment on his master. Unlike Bright, who had the good fortune to work with a fair and kindly master, this ox had got stuck 'beneath auld Jawbaw's heavy yoke,' and the only time he has to rest and ruminate on his sorry lot is when the old hypocrite takes a day off for church. The poem ends with a delightful reversal of roles when the ox thanks God that he is 'no' the brute' that his master is.

The fun and conviviality of the settler's lives is clearly depicted in 'The Picnic' and 'Sparking,' while 'Old Hoss' and 'The Age of Jollity' regret the passing of an idyllic age, and suggest that in the newer, more sophisticated state something of worth may be lost. This subject is more effectively dealt with in the humorous and lively satire 'Young Hoss' (see appendix p 444) obviously meant

xix

as a companion piece to 'Old Hoss,' but omitted from this volume.

In many poems McLachlan shows himself as adept in a Canadian backwoods dialect as in the Scottish. 'Old Canada; or Gee Buck Gee' (see appendix p 446) superbly satirizes all the new-fangled ways, and asserts that 'this edication's our undoin'.' McLachlan had striven to provide educational opportunities for the working class, but he had no intention of educating them off the land. Ironically, of his own family only one son farmed, and one daughter married a farmer. Three sons made their mark in medicine, and one daughter became a teacher. The old farmer who laments the state of the nation to his old ox Buck (the team-mate Bright is dead) sees clearly the danger of the tendency for too many to become 'Book Farmers' — no doubt specialists from the newly instituted Guelph School of Agriculture. While no reactionary, McLachlan, who has propounded a philosophy of honest toil, is surely sympathetic to the speaker's point of view when he says:

> I tell ye what! them and their books,
> Are getting to be perfect pukes;
> And sure enough this edication
> Will be the ruin of the nation;
> We'll not ha' men, it's my opinion,
> Fit to defend our New Dominion;
> Not one o' them can swing an axe,
> But they will bore you with the facts;
> I'd send the criters off to work,
> But that, by any means they'll shirk!
> Grandad to some o' them I be,

O, that's what riles and vexes me!
Ain't it a caution? — Gee Buck Gee!

So much for the educated ignoramuses — the specialists! What hope is there for the first century of the New Dominion if no one is left to farm the land and do the work; and what lesser hope for the second century if we do not even read our poets to discover what our heritage is?

Yes, indeed, 'ain't it a caution' that with all the education and supplies of books in the 1970s so little is known about McLachlan. Not even copies of all of his poems are accessible. For this reason grateful thanks must be given to Douglas Lochhead and to the University of Toronto Press for making available at least this 1900 volume of selected poems. It is to be hoped that some zealous Canadian scholar with a true pioneer spirit will soon undertake the arduous task of editing the complete works and of writing a full biography of so representative an early Canadian poet as Alexander McLachlan.

NOTES

1 Edward Hartley Dewart, 'Introductory Essay,' *Selections from Canadian Poets* (Montreal: John Lovell 1864), reprinted with an introduction by Douglas Lochhead, University of Toronto Press 1973, p xiii
2 The Toronto Public Library copy of *Lyrics* contains the inscription to William L. Mackenzie in McLachlan's handwriting.
3 Professor James George, in Henry J. Morgan, *Sketches of Celebrated Canadians and Persons Connected with Canada* (London: Hunter, Rose 1862) 756

Select Bibliography

Lyrics Toronto: A.H. Armour & Co. 1858
Poems Toronto: John C. Geikie 1856
Poems and Songs Toronto: Hunter, Rose & Co. 1874
The Emigrant and Other Poems Toronto: Rollo & Adam 1861
The Poetical Works of Alexander McLachlan Selected and edited
    with an introduction by Edward Hartley Dewart. Toronto:
    Wm. Briggs 1900
The Spirit of Love and Other Poems Toronto: J. Cleland 1846

Dewart, Edward Hartley *Essays for the Times* Toronto:
    Wm. Briggs 1898
Klinck, Carl F. *Literary History of Canada* Toronto: University
    of Toronto Press 1965
Logan, J.D. & D.G. French *Highways of Canadian Literature*
    Toronto: McClelland & Stewart 1924
Morgan, Henry James *Sketches of Celebrated Canadians and
    Persons Connected with Canada* London: Hunter, Rose
    & Co. 1862
– *The Canadian Men and Women of the Time* Toronto:
    Wm. Briggs 1898
Watters, Reginald Eyre, comp. *A Checklist of Canadian Literature
    and Background Materials 1628-1960* 2nd ed. Toronto:
    University of Toronto Press 1972

The Poetical Works of

Alexander McLachlan

EDITORS' NOTE

AFTER Alexander McLachlan's death, his daughter
Mary began to collect and arrange his numerous
poetic compositions, with a view to publishing a selection
of what might seem most worthy of presentation in per-
manent form.   Unhappily, death overtook her before she
could complete this work of filial devotion.   A few friends
of the poet, however, feeling that the work thus interrupted
should not be allowed entirely to fail, consulted together,
and made the selection here given.   Mr. McLachlan left a
very large amount of material in manuscript, all of which
has passed under review.   It is confidently hoped that the
present publication includes nearly all that he himself
would have wished to see in print.   The editors have not
attempted to do much more than select, punctuate for the
sense, and put here and there a few "finishing touches,"
large numbers of which were indicated by himself.   This
fact has restrained their hands : It was known that taking
liberties with his verse was something the poet resented.
He preferred to let his "wild, warbling measures rise,"
even when they transgressed the canons of prosody, for

example, whose laws he thought the crampings of an artificial school. He applied to Poesy the same rule that he applied to other productions, expressed in his own words (on *Music*) :

> " To gauge thee by reason
> Seems absolute treason."

The editors trust that their efforts in this first comprehensive collection of the writings of our earliest bard, with its accessories (Introductory Essay, Memoir, Notes, and Glossary), a rounding off, as it were, of his life and work, may deserve and receive appreciative commendation here and abroad.

TORONTO, CANADA,
    May, 1900.

CONTENTS

SONGS AND BALLADS

NATURE POEMS

4   *Contents*

IDYLS OF THE PIONEERS

SCOTTISH PORTRAITS

MISCELLANEOUS

SKETCHES FROM THE WANDERER

INTRODUCTORY ESSAY

—

BY REV. E. H. DEWART, D.D.

—

THE writers of a country who give literary expression to generous sympathy with what is good and true, who lovingly portray what is beautiful and grand in its scenery and significant in its history, and quicken the pulse of patriotic devotion and loyalty in the hearts of the people, are benefactors who deserve to be held in "everlasting remembrance." They may attract less attention and win less applause than warriors and politicians, whose lives are distinguished by more sensational features; but, though noiseless and often unacknowledged, their work exerts a greater moulding influence upon the thought and life of the nation. Among these benefactors the poets of a country must always have a prominent place.

Lord Macaulay's theory, that a semi-barbaric and unscientific age, in which the language is not sufficiently perfect to be the medium of acute distinctions and scientific definitions, is specially adapted to the production of poetry, and that it must die out when these conditions cease to exist, is open to unanswerable objections. It wrongly assumes that the proper subjects of poetry are fictitious legends, which require ignorance and credulity in those who read them. The great reviewer also overlooks the fact that a crude and imperfect language is not fitted to express the great thoughts and refined shades of meaning which are always found in the work of a great poet. Besides, there are at all times nations and communities that are ignorant, superstitious, and unscientific enough to satisfy fully Lord Macaulay's conditions; yet we never hear of any great original

9

poems being given to the world from such quarters. The fact that poets have flourished in all stages of civilization proves that the production of poetry depends far more upon the genius of the poet than upon the character of his environment.

All disparagement of poetry is based upon misconceptions of its true mission and character. Those who think the great questions of life are, "What shall we eat? and what shall we drink? and wherewithal shall we be clothed?" or who maintain that poetry cannot live in a scientific age, will naturally contemn poetry and all forms of art. But those who do this simply proclaim their incapacity to appreciate the thoughts and sentiments which constitute the main elements of the poet's message. Poetry is not an artificial invention. Like music and all forms of beauty, it appeals to faculties which our Creator has implanted in our nature. There could be no such thing as poetry, music, or the beautiful in art, if there was nothing in our nature that responded to these things. Let no one regard his indifference or contempt for poetry as an evidence of mental superiority. It is an imperfection which may be endured as a misfortune, but should never be flaunted as a virtue.

When I visited the picture galleries of Europe and looked upon the veritable works of Raphael, Titian, Leonardo da Vinci, Murillo, Rubens, and other old masters, I was most of all impressed by the wonderful genius that enabled these gifted souls to reproduce the visions of beauty that flashed through their brain, and leave them as a legacy to the world, to be seen and admired by future generations. So it is the peculiar glory of the poet that he has the power, not only to think great thoughts and vividly apprehend the grandeur and beauty of nature, but that in the exercise of his divine art he can cause others to see through his unscaled eyes, and feel in some degree what he has felt in those exalted moods, in which he "clothes thought and language with the hues of every holy thing." We all know how scenes and events which the poet has enshrined in song are lifted into an undying light, and have an interest for us that but for the poet they would never have possessed.

Alexander McLachlan deserves grateful recognition and a place of honor among our Canadian poets, not only for the good work he has accomplished, but also because of the stage of our country's history and the circumstances in which that work was done. The period in which he wrote entitles him to rank as one of the pioneer bards of British Canada who have laid the foundations of our poetic literature in the face of many discouragements. One is not surprised that men of leisure, the hothouse plants of literary culture, nurtured from early youth on the poetry of Greece and Rome, as well as that of Britain and America, should in due time blossom into verse of proper form. But when one who had not the advantage of such prompting inspiration, but who was through life hampered and repressed by constant care and toil, in spite of all this "lightens his labors with songs" in various moods, and leaves a large and worthy contribution to the poetic literature of his country, we cannot but feel that he never could have done this had not the instinct of the born poet been irrepressibly strong within him. But for this these lyrical outpourings of the heart would never have been produced. They were evidently written to give expression to sentiments that would not be suppressed. McLachlan eminently fulfilled the description of Longfellow's ideal poet,

> " Whose songs gushed from his heart,
> As showers from the clouds of summer,
> Or tears from the eyelids start ;

> " Who, through long days of labor,
> And nights devoid of ease,
> Still heard in his soul the music
> Of wonderful melodies."

In my "Selections from Canadian Poets," published in 1864, speaking of McLachlan, I said : "It is no empty laudation to call him 'the Burns of Canada.' In racy humor, in natural pathos, and in graphic portraiture of character, he will compare favorably with the great peasant bard.   In moral grandeur and beauty he strikes higher notes than ever echoed from the harp of Burns."   Many will deem this too strong.   Perhaps it is. Ardent admirers of Burns may think it out of place to institute any comparison with the immortal author of "The Cottar's Saturday Night."   Yet I still think that there are stanzas in this volume that justify the last remark in the sentences I have quoted.   At any rate, without questioning the superior genius of Burns, it will not be denied that the two poets have a good deal in common.   This is not the result of any conscious imitation on the part of McLachlan.   Though, doubtless, his admiring sympathy for Burns had a great influence over him, the similarity to which I refer was mainly caused by their minds being cast in a similar mould.   They were animated by the same democratic spirit.   They had the same reverent esteem for simple manhood, regardless of all outward distinctions ; and the same unspoiled love of Nature and insight into her inner meanings.

In many of his poems our Canadian bard shows that at times he stood face to face with "the burthen of the mystery" of life and human destiny.   In truth we may say, it somewhat unduly overshadowed his whole existence.   If he selected lowly themes, it was because he discerned truth and beauty, not visible to ordinary eyes, in the simplest things of common life. He could say as truly as Wordsworth himself,

> "Thanks to the human heart by which we live,
> Thanks to its tenderness, its joys and fears,
> To me the meanest flower that blows can give
> Thoughts that do often lie too deep for tears."

The most distinguishing characteristic of McLachlan's poetry is his intense feeling of regard for the common people.   Whatever concerns human beings enlists his earnest sympathy, because he has "faith in the Fatherhood of God and brotherhood of man."   His simple and lucid style, his warm brotherly sympathy with all who toil or suffer, and his honest hatred of all oppression and injustice, make him pre-eminently the poet of "the common people." In ringing words which all can understand, he voices the thought and feeling of the great toiling democracy. For this cause, as well as for his extensive treatment of Canadian subjects, whether he conforms in all respects to the canons of the critics or not, this volume should be favorably received and widely perused by the people of Canada. Among our intelligent working men and women it should have an extensive circulation. Though he is keenly alive to the ills that darken and embitter so many lives, his ideas of the dignity of labor and the superiority of honest worth to all material prosperity, and his faith in the ultimate triumph of the right, are adapted to inspire his readers with courage and patient hope in breasting the currents of un-propitious fate.

Like many others, had McLachlan written less, and given more time and thought to polishing and perfecting the language in which he expressed his thoughts, it would have been better for his fame as a poet. He was too often satisfied with putting the passing thoughts that occupied his mind into easy, homely rimes. The ardent love which he cherished for Scotland, his native land, colors most of his writings. Even in poems on other themes, written in Canada, a place is found for references to the scenery and memories of the land beyond the sea. However others may regard this, it will hardly be deemed a fault by Scotsmen.

It would be a thankless and superfluous task for me to point out the pieces in this volume which I regard as specially excellent. Every reader will judge for himself as to what he may deem the best. There are, however, some poems which specially illustrate our author's genius. If he has mainly chosen homely and common subjects, his fine ode on *God* shows that he can fitly treat the loftiest theme. In this piece there is elevation of thought, sublime imagery, and a rhythmic music which makes a pleasing harmony between the sense and the sound. This adaptation of the metre to the theme is a feature of many of the poems. In *May* there is a dancing, sparkling gladness, in keeping with the joyousness of the season and scenery it describes. In his poem on Burns (p. 397) there is a mastery of the Scottish dialect, and a felicitous indication of the distinguishing features of the poet's character as revealed in several of his poems. In *Britannia* sententious expression and patriotic fire are blended. The immortal British names cited in the poem fitly lead up to the ringing climax :

> " These are the soul of thy renown,
> The gems immortal in thy crown,
> The suns that never shall go down,
> Britannia ! "

In the portraits of *David*, *Carlyle*, and *Gladstone*, as well as in other pieces, the style sometimes drops into the homely, and the language is not always what would be called poetic. Yet there are quaint turns of thought, that have in them an element of surprise and striking fitness and force. I have spoken of McLachlan's power to penetrate the crust of outward appearances, and unveil the meaning hidden from common sight at the heart of things. This is strikingly illustrated in that fine lyrical miniature, *Old Hannah*. An aged widow sitting at her cottage door is a common enough object. But in the poem the harmony and beauty of the surrounding scenery, the glimpse into the widow's sad life history, and the revelation of the inner faith that gave peace in old age and bereavement, invest the picture with a meaning and interest which make it an instructive religious lesson, and a treasured memory. The same insight is seen in *Martha* and other pieces. Not only are positive elements of character unveiled, the absence of such qualities is made to tell an interesting story. *Neighbor John* is made to interest us, because of his not possessing qualities that he ought to have possessed :

> " His only joy since when a boy,
> Has been to plod and moil,
> Until his very soul itself
> Has grown into the soil,

" He has no visions, hears no voice
　To make his spirit start ;
The glory and the mystery
　Ne'er settled on his heart.

" Talk not of old cathedral woods
　Their gothic arches throwing ;
John only sees in all these trees
　So many sawlogs growing."

It must be gratifying to every lover of his country to note the signs of a growing interest in our Canadian literature ; though there is still room and need for improvement with regard to the extent of this interest. If I have not referred in these introductory remarks to the Canadian poets of the present day, this is simply because I have been directing attention to a new edition of the poems of a poet of the last generation. Sangster, McLachlan, Heavysege, Kirby, Chapman, MacColl, Reade, Sweeney, McGee, W. W. Smith, and Mrs. Leprohon, Mrs. Moody, Miss Murray, Miss Helen M. Johnson, Mrs. Faulkner, Miss Vining (Mrs. Yule) and others of their period, may be regarded as the vanguard of our poetic writers. But I am glad to pay my hearty tribute of recognition to the value and excellence of the contributions to our poetic literature by our poets of a later period, such as Mair, Campbell, Roberts, Cameron, Lampman, Carman, the two Scotts, Miss Machar, Miss Crawford, Mrs. Curzon, Mrs. Harrison, Miss Pauline Johnson, Miss Wetherald, Mrs. Blewett, Mrs. McLean, and several others worthy of "honorable mention." They have worthily carried forward the banners of literary progress which had fallen from the hands of our earlier bards. Their work is full of promise for the future. Interest in what they have accomplished will not lessen our interest in those whose work was done in earlier and ruder times.

If McLachlan's graphic descriptions of the scenery and rural life of Canada in *The Emigrant*, and other poems, ought to interest all Canadians, it is equally true that his loving and appreciative references to "Caledonia, stern and wild," should give his poems a special claim to the regard of all Scotsmen and Scottish-Canadians.

2

FARM RESIDENCE OF ALEXANDER M'LACHLAN

From a pen-and-ink sketch by Arthur Cox, A.R.C.A.

BIOGRAPHICAL SKETCH

A LEXANDER M'LACHLAN, the Scoto-Canadian poet, was born in 1818 in Johnstone (" the Brig o' Johnstone"), Renfrewshire, Scotland. His father, Charles McLachlan, was an intelligent, well-informed mechanic, possessed of considerable literary ability, who took part in the temperance and Chartist agitations of his time, as did, too, the subject of this sketch. Charles McLachlan, with his brother Daniel and the latter's wife and children, came to Canada in the thirties, and were among the earliest pioneers in the township of Caledon, Peel county, Ontario. Both sought to become Canadian farmers. Charles had left his wife and children in Scotland till he could clear land and establish a home for them. This accomplished, he sought and obtained employment as a machinist at Paterson, N.J., on his way back *via* New York, intending to bring his wife and four children to his new Canadian home; but death overtook him at Paterson.

The poet's mother was Jane Sutherland, daughter of Alexander Sutherland, a native of Sutherlandshire, in the Highlands, and a Cameronian covenanter, of which descent the poet was proud. This grandfather, described as a rigid Calvinist of the old school, now became the head of his widowed daughter's household with her young family of four, of whom the poet was the third child and only son. She and her second daughter remained in Scotland till 1859, when they came to Canada, where the mother, taking cardiac dropsy, died suddenly in 1860, at the poet's home. The two other daughters had come to Canada early in the forties. All three married farmers in Brant county, Ontario, reaching the same years as the poet, and dying in the order of their birth.

When his mother and her young family were thrown on their own resources, young McLachlan worked in a cotton factory, and when old enough became apprentice to a tailor in Glasgow. In 1840 he came to Canada and took possession of his father's farm, but sold it in 1841. He married Clamina McLachlan, commemorated in his poem *Clamina*. She is the daughter of his uncle Daniel, and survives him. In 1844 he bought a bush farm in Downie township, Perth county. In 1847 he removed to another in the township of North East-hope, in the same county. He cleared about twenty acres, but finding that he was no farmer, sold it, and in 1850 bought an acre in Erin township, Wellington county, removed to it, and lived there till 1877, devoting himself to tailoring, reading, writing, and lecturing. His lectures were commonly under the auspices of Mechanics' Institutes. In 1862 he was appointed government lecturer and emigration agent for Canada in Scotland. This appointment came through his personal friend and brother poet, Hon. Thomas D'Arcy McGee, then a member of the Canadian cabinet. Among admirers at this time was the late Prof. George, vice-Principal of Queen's College, Kingston, Ont., to whom the volume published in 1861 was dedicated. The present Principal, Dr. Geo. M. Grant, but at a later date, also appears among those who paid their tribute of praise.

In 1872-73 some friends and admirers of his poetic gifts took up the project of a suitable pecuniary testimonial to him. A considerable amount was subscribed. Then the publication of a new volume of his poems was projected, and appeared in 1874. By consent of subscribers to the testimonial fund, the cash collected was paid as a guaranty to its publishers.

In 1877 he moved to a farm in Amaranth township, Dufferin county, seven miles west of Orangeville, the county seat. The farm-house and surroundings have been painted by his artist friend, Mr. Arthur Cox, Toronto. The picture is in possession of Mr. James L. Morrison, Toronto, who has kindly permitted its reproduction for this volume. An enlarged painting of this was bought by the well-known clothier, Philip Jamieson, and for years was displayed in his shop, corner of Queen and Yonge Streets, Toronto, but was destroyed in the Simpson fire. This farm was managed for several years by his son Malcolm, then by his youngest son, Alexander.

During these years on the Amaranth farm the project of a testimonial fund was revived by admirers. The idea appears to have started with Alex. McNabb, Esq., of Ozone, Texas, formerly police magistrate in Toronto.* He was soon seconded in this by Messrs. J. L. Morrison and Arthur Cox, already mentioned, and by Messrs. James Bain, Jr., Alex. Fraser, M.A., and Wm. Adamson. They induced Mr. David Boyle, Ontario's archæologist, and others, too numerous to mention, to lend a hand. Associated as secretary was Geo. Kennedy, LL.D., of the Ontario Crown Lands department, Toronto. The vigorous push of these men was a mainspring which soon resulted in a collection intended to bring comfort to his declining years. From far and near contributions were received, amounting to $2100, which, as an investment in trust, was presented to him at a public banquet at the Walker House, Toronto, 28th April, 1890. His friend, David Walker, was both caterer and host. Mr. Morrison was in the chair and made the presentation. The list of subscribers deserves reproduction here, but want of space forbids.

The death of his farmer son, Alexander, in March, 1895, broke up the farm management, though continued for that season. Late in 1895 the poet bought a home—a substantial brick house on Elizabeth street, Orangeville,—removed there and died in it, quite unexpectedly, 20th March, 1896. His remains rest in Greenwood Cemetery, two miles west of Orangeville. To commemorate him a modest monument is to be erected there in the summer of 1900.† The spot, a fairly

---

* A poetic epistle to Mr. McNabb was the last piece of work undertaken by the subject of our sketch. He lived to produce a fragment only, not printed herein.

† The Secretary-Treasurer of the Monument Fund is Dr. Alex. Hamilton, 57 Harbord Street, Toronto, who will receive offerings.

ideal one, is an eminence overlooking the road running north. It has been neatly kept and is adorned with flowers he loved. Certain gloomy forebodings (in *Cartha Again*) are thus unlikely to prove prophetic :

> " In a grave in the forest, when life's journey's past,
> Unknown and unhonor'd, they'll lay me at last ;
> Abune me nae blue-bell nor gowan shall wave,
> And nae robin come to sing over my grave."

Of his eleven children, ten—five sons and five daughters—reached maturity. His relict, one son, a practising physician in Michigan, and four daughters survive. Two other sons became physicians. The eldest daughter married a farmer ; three single daughters are at home. Mary, the second daughter, was a teacher, and became, at her father's request, his literary executor. She had put his literary remains largely in shape for this publication when death supervened, 10th February, 1899, leaving that work to Mr. W. J. Clark, barrister, Toronto, who has left selecting, editing and arranging to five other hands, not unsympathetic, it is trusted.*

To the foregoing, a curt recital of bare facts, the reader may wish to have color added by brief pen-pictures of a few scenes as they passed before the subject of this sketch in his life-panorama. They are drawn by one who has distinct recollections of him from 1853 :

(*a*) His childhood was spent (" when George IV was king ") in the fertile and populous valley of the Clyde. Looming up on the northern horizon, as one looked across that noted stream from the garden of their house, could be seen the peak of Benlomond, often mentioned or implied in his verse. The Cart (poetic Cartha) is a stream draining a large district south of it into the Clyde. Of its two branches, the Black Cart and the White Cart, one is crossed by the "Brig o' John-

---

* The editors are (in alphabetic order of their surnames): W. P. BEGG, D.D., Massena, N.Y.; DAVID BOYLE, Ph.B., E. H. DEWART, D.D., A. HAMILTON, M.A. M.D., GEO. KENNEDY, LL.D., the last four of Toronto.

stone." Paisley is on the Black Cart. The Gryffe, a clear stream, the water supply of Paisley, was tributary to the Cart. From the centre of the Clyde rises a perpendicular rock, Dumbarton or Balclutha, crowned with Dumbarton Castle, a stronghold of the Britons. In the district are many ruins, some of which are noted in *The Sempill Lords*, and in *Paisley Abbey* and others near and farther afield. Near by was Elderslie, the seat of Scotland's hero leader, Sir William Wallace, and near which was the Wallace oak, even then falling to decay. He has told us (in *The Spirit of Love*) that this oak was familiar, and

> " A thousand times beneath that tree,
> O Freedom, I have worshipped thee ;
> And then I deemed the very sod
> Was sacred where my hero trod.
> Oh, yes, it was my first of joys,
> When, a troop of wild school-boys,
> In mimic warlike pomp array'd,
> We fought the Southron 'neath thy shade,
> And sang, while to the charge we led,
> ' Scots wha hae wi' Wallace bled.' "

There, too, were rife stories such as that commemorated in *The Warlock o' Gryffe*, and such doings as *Auld Granny Broon* gives voice to, for

> " She howff'd by the Locher's lood fa', "

the Locher Falls being then a picturesque scene. The air was thick with a thousand other legends of tradition and superstition, among a people to whom fairies, ghosts, hobgoblins and witches still played great parts in the *rôle* of popular mythology. As Sir Walter Scott has put it :

> " Old tales I heard of wo or mirth,
> Of lovers' sleights, of ladies' charms,
> Of witches' spells, of warriors' arms,
> Of patriot battles, won of old
> By Wallace wight and Bruce the Bold."

With this background, foreground and surroundings, young McLachlan seems to have passed a happy childhood free from care, in rural districts, the suburbs of bustling industry, near the hum of manufacturing centres. Excursions with play-fellows must have been varied and frequent, for his verse shows him familiar with wild-flowers, birds, and Nature in her every mood. In this way it became true of him that

> " The child is father of the man,"

and inspired him to

> " Sing the lays
> Of Scotia's bonnie woods and braes,
> Of hoary hill, of dashing stream,
> Of lonely rock where eagles scream,
> Of primrose bank and gowany glen,
> Of broomy knowe and hawthorn den,
> Of burnside where the linnet's lay
> Is heard the lee lang summer day."

(*b*) The period of his youth, until he was twenty-two, in 1840, was a time of unrest and agitation. He remembered the political stir culminating in the Reform Bill of 1832. Temperance agitation, notably that of Father Matthew in Ireland, had its counterpart in Britain. Denunciations of taxes on cereal food-stuffs, known as the Corn Laws, filled the air, and Ebenezer Elliot's rimes fired the popular heart. Chartism, analogous to the strikes and labor agitations of a later day, was in full swing. Distress in the manufacturing districts, notably those of Manchester and Glasgow, contributed largely to peopling Ontario with swarms of immigrants from all parts of the British Isles in the quarter century following 1825. Young McLachlan was now brought to face the realities of life, and would seem not only to have been moved by these agitations but to have taken some part in them. Some poetic effusions, appended to his first publication in 1846, show the outcome of his muse on this line in the years preceding 1840. When quite young he was accustomed " to spout " (that is, recite) his verses to his com-

panions, voicing the rights of the common people against the
aristocracy.   The vein of democracy which runs through his
compositions had a natural origin in this way, at this time, in
these surroundings.   His grandfather, whom he described as a
bigot in opinion, but with that sterling force of character and
moral rectitude noteworthy as the product of Scotland for
centuries, was, as we have said, a covenanter.   This brought
forcibly to the young poet's mind aspects of religious fervor
and zeal.   He often said that it was hearing the Psalm,

> " By Babel's stream we sat and wept
> When Zion we thought on,"

as interpreted by the covenanters and applied to themselves in
their struggles, that first stirred his imagination and awoke
early glimmerings of the poetic faculty.   Much under the
influence and teachings of his stern old grandfather, for whom
he had great love and admiration because of the integrity of
his character, the elder's bigotry and intolerance produced
reaction in the mind of the younger, and drove him to question-
ings which landed him in skepticism as to a future life that cast
a shadow over his middle life, but which was removed in
later years.   *A Grandfather's Blessing*, in the first part of *The
Emigrant*, Section vi., is simply the address of this grandfather to himself on leaving for Canada, aged twenty-two.

(c) Early manhood finds him for ten years struggling to
clear bush farms in Canada, facing sterner realities of life
owing to the untimely death of his father.   Here were the
scenes of the pioneer's life.   He not only sees them, but takes
part in them.   The ax, the plow, the flail or thrasher, the ox-
yoke, the logging-bee, the "raising" of house or barn, *The
Fire in the Woods*, the cow-bell, *The Log-Cabin*, the straw-
stack, the wail of *Whip-poor-will*, the merry whistle of the
quail, "Bob White," the cheering spray of natural music from
a rising *Bobolink*, that sprightly Ariel the *Humming-Bird*, howling wolves, bounding deer, bears, and Indians—all are parts
of new scenes.   He is now making a "clearing"—"the sky

keekin through "—in two counties of a well-wooded country with its accompaniments of sawlogs and sawmills, lumber and stumps—fitter nurse of muscle and sunburn than of poetic natures. His muse has vividly portrayed much of all this in *The Idyls of the Pioneers*, especially in *The Emigrant*. But we need not, should not, and shall not, spoil the reader's appetite by any foretaste.

(*d*) McLachlan's middle life, the quarter century ending in 1877, exhibits him on our canvas more as a man of letters.   In this time he published four volumes* of poems, and undertook a series of public lectures that made him a somewhat familiar figure in the Canada West of the time.   Development was now the order of the day.   Population was becoming thicker, towns were springing up, stages between them were giving way to railway trains, the roughness of pioneer life was yielding to objects of taste and refinement.   People were still vigorous because less pampered.   McLachlan planned *The Emigrant,* but stopped short in executing that ambitious plan, composing so much only as the reader will find in succeeding pages. †
Had he but entered more fully into the spirit of Columbus's new world, and especially the marvellous new world of the closing half of the nineteenth century—if he had finished *The Emigrant, con amore* and *con spirito*—he might have ranked as a father of our literature, much like Chaucer in another and not

---

* The publications preceding this present volume are described thus :

1846. *The Spirit of Love and Other Poems.*   Pamphlet, 36 pages, 16mo. Printed by J. Cleland, Toronto.

1856. *Poems.*   192 pages, 12mo., cloth.   John C. Geikie, Toronto.

1858. *Lyrics.*   151 pages, 12mo, cloth.   A. H. Armour & Co., Toronto.

1861. *The Emigrant and Other Poems.*   236 pages, 12mo, cloth.   Rollo & Adam, Toronto.

1874. *Poems and Songs.*   223 pages, 8vo.   Hunter, Rose & Co., Toronto.

1888.   Ibid., Second Edition, Rose Publishing Co., Toronto.

All are to be found in the Public Library, Toronto.   The volume of *Lyrics* (1858) therein was " presented to William L. [Lyon] Mackenzie, as a token of respect for the high patriotic purpose to which his life has been devoted, by the author."

† The pioneer and his times is a theme too often shunned by our versifiers. Recently, however, Dr. O'Hagan has given an instalment in *Songs of the Settlement and Other Poems.*   70 pages, 16mo.   William Briggs, Toronto, 1899.

wider field.   He rose imperfectly to the occasion largely from
being imperfectly appreciated by the people of his day, and,
lacking encouragement, he remained a Scottish bard of the
first half of his century, rather than a Canadian bard of the
second half, the bard of a glorious dawn in our country's
literature.   A struggling life and missed opportunities often
go together.   Do readers ask further explanation?   Well,
McLachlan lacked a Mæcenas ; with one, he would have had
the key-stone to a strong arch.   He had his early volumes
printed (not published—a very different thing), in Toronto, a
place then almost as far out of the way as Alaska is now.   He
essayed to be his own publisher, but lacked the executive ability
and tact for successful publication.   There was then no wealthy
class, there was no middle class.   The struggling pioneer appreciated the gristmill, the sawmill, the stump-machine, the stone-
boat, and

"Oxen terrible to haul,"

but poetry was to him no indispensable desideratum.

(*e*) The evening of his life was the eighteen years after 1877,
spent on the Amaranth farm, he being nearly sixty years of age
when he went there.   His literary life left him far from independent.   Sons and daughters had grown up.   Half of them
remained with him, a solace, help, and support.   He still
wooed the muses.   *Grip*, the Canadian *Punch* of that day,
had him for a time as a regular paid contributor of verse, often
illustrated by the pencil of its remarkable humorist-cartoonist-
editor, J. W. Bengough.   Mr. James L. Morrison must have
put his hand to the plow in this phase of McLachlan's public
appearance.   Many effusions, unpublished otherwise, first
appeared in *Grip's* columns.   Most of these had the democratic
ring.   His earlier sympathy with Chartism now found vent
in favor of Labor.   Dr. A. M. Stewart, the publisher of that
widely and well-known New York weekly, *The Scottish-Ameri-
can*, often furnished him this as a suitable avenue for putting
his verse in print from time to time.   At one time or other he
was much gratified and encouraged by personal commenda-

tions of his verse, as from Sir Archibald Alison, the historian of Europe, and many others of trans-Atlantic fame. Leaders in American literature recognized his genius by public and private greetings. His papers show many autograph letters from such men as Thoreau, and the poets Ralph Waldo Emerson, John G. Saxe, Longfellow, Dr. Oliver Wendell Holmes, John G. Whittier, and James Russell Lowell. Now and then he visited Toronto and other places, where he got warm receptions, for he was known as one who made and kept friendships.

(*f*) In personal appearance, McLachlan, while not tall, was above the average, his weight medium, his eyes blue, his hair dark turning to grey without baldness, his temperament nervo-bilious. He was good company, full of anecdote and repartee, loved a joke, appreciated humor, told a good story well, spoke with unmistakable Clydesdale accent, and loved the solace of tobacco. In later years his trend was to the slender, rather than the portly, build. He held that the names *McLachlan*, *McNachtan*, etc., should have their middle syllable pronounced as *lack*, *knack*, etc., but with, of course, the guttural for *ck*.

(*g*) In his poem *Companionship in Books* he gives expression to the companionship and elevating influence of the few good books found in pioneer life. His later life had better variety and a good assortment. One of his editors remarked that "McLachlan was strong in the weird," resembling in this respect the Ettrick Shepherd. The weird in Shakspeare suited him most. He would recite parts of *Hamlet*, *Othello* and *Macbeth*, with the power of becoming the character he acted, so that it was fascinating to listen to him. He often expressed the wish that he had become an actor, and might have done so but that he knew it would have broken his mother's heart. Scott he thought next to Shakspeare in delineation of character. Coleridge he admired much, and could recite the *Ancient Mariner*. The reader may in many places in his compositions trace the influence of Scott and Coleridge especially, as of others herein named. Shelley's *Skylark* and *Cloud* were great favorites. He voiced admiration of Burns in four poems, two of which are herein. Hogg he admired for his imaginative powers, and thought the literary world had not done him justice. He found Wordsworth's quiet contemplation soothing and refreshing, returning to him often and ever. After Carlyle's great prose epic, *The French Revolution*, burst like a meteor on the world, the Chelsea sage found in him almost a worshipper. He complained, though, that Carlyle gave him no help to solve the riddle of existence. Of that he got more satisfaction from Ruskin and Emerson. The latter more than any other influenced him, leading him out of doubt and perplexity into an atmosphere higher and purer, by helping him to recognize God in man. He said that Carlyle and Emerson had done a great work for mankind. Carlyle, with eloquent pen, had aroused the world to existing evils and to ponder on them. Emerson showed the sacredness of life and infinite possibilities for good in man if he listened to the God within him. He was a great admirer of Tennyson and Longfellow.

(*h*) As to his philosophy of life, his system (or lack of system) was not well defined. It is left to the reader to reach his own conclusions as to that, for it is felt that it was wavering and uncertain. Inclined to speculation, yet not well-grounded in laws of natural forces and phenomena, he grasped vainly after ultimates. At one time he thought highly of Swedenborg. He was ever more inclined to mysticism or metaphysics than to physics or materialism. As to his belief in a future existence, we leave him to speak for himself in his *Elegy* on the death of a favorite son, John :

> "Farewell, my beloved one ! we'll meet yet again
>   In a higher and holier sphere,
> Where the myst'ry of sorrow, the meaning of pain,
>   And death's mighty mission's made clear.
> We'll meet in the land where are no sable suits,
>   No grinding of heart and of brain,
> And this tearing affections e'en up by the roots
>   Shall lacerate never again."

In conclusion, it may be in order to indicate what niche in the temple of lyric poets should be assigned McLachlan, and who are in his immediate surroundings to invite comparison. Rev. Dr. Dewart, in his Introductory Essay (pp. 11, 12), has seen fit, justly we think, to adhere to his judgment, formed thirty-six years ago, that our author compares favorably with Burns, in whose favorite metre a good deal of his verse appears, so rendering comparison the more easy. The writer has evidence that other contemporaries shared and endorsed Dr. Dewart's opinion as to favorable comparison with Burns. In addition to the opinions and examples cited by Dr. Dewart, we may say that the two *Dreams* (Hawkie's and Skinflint's) have very much the tone of the Ayrshire bard. In some epistles to friends he is even more happy, and strikes a higher and a purer note. As a writer of songs and ballads, now herein classed together for the first time, McLachlan shows remarkable power. In patriotism or love of motherland he is even more pronounced than Burns. In his octosyllabic metres he has not the Homeric fire of Scott, nor does his canvas glow with word-pictures in action like that wizard's, but he comes more fitly into comparison with Longfellow, whom he resembles a good deal. In quiet contemplation and in moralizing he reminds us of Cowper and Wordsworth, both of whom he surpasses. His ardent love and worship of nature is akin to that of Wordsworth, but he clothes natural scenery and phenomena (especially the starry heavens, the sun, and the seasons) with a spirituality—a pervading Intelligence, a guiding Glory—and a fire hardly equalled in English literature. The pieces we have ventured to class as Nature Poems are likely to become his more enduring monuments.

Prologue

TO THE POET

On the occasion of his reception by the Toronto Press Club, 19th March, 1887.
Written and read by his friend David Boyle.

Maist fowk, I think, 'll think wi' me
That sin' Jacques Cartier sailed the sea
　Lang syne frae auld Saint Malo
(Weel bent to gie his friens frae France
I' this new lan' a siccar stance),
　Fu' mony a mensefu' fallow
　Has focht wi' tree, an' stump, an' stane,
　To gar the yirth yield routh o' grain.

An' mony (gowd an' siller gowkit)
Hae deep doun i' her hurdies howkit;
　A wheen, forbye, wi' timmer dealins
　Hae won themsels weel-stockit mailins.
Some mair, wi' gab an' cutty harns,
Seem'd whalpit 'neath gey canny starns ;
　For ane an' a' hae hain'd bawbees,
　Or gawsie pooches tell big lees.

Abune a' sic (owre douce an' blate)
Some twa'r 'hree chiels held heicher state,
　Wha scriev'd an' sang, an' sang an' scriev'd,
　That dreichsome dargs micht be reliev'd

Wha wrocht to see the bonnie day
Whan ilka law wad mean fair play
  To rich and puir, to big an' wee,
  That a', i' fac', micht brithers be.

But they've ne'er been wi' siller fash'd,
Their screeds hae aft been sairly snash'd
  Tho' aye they scrieve an' tug awa
  To saften Faither Aidam's fa'.
Sic like are ye—McLachlan, frien'—
  A poet pawky, canty, keen;
  We're prood to see ye here the nicht,
  Fameeliar speerit o' the licht.

Lieve lang; gie's dawds an' whangs o' rime
That winna dee wi' lapse o' time—
Humanity's great creed haud fast:
"We're a' John Tamson's bairns at last."

THE POETICAL WORKS

OF

ALEXANDER McLACHLAN

HEROES

ALL hail to the chiefs of thought,
   Who wield the mighty pen
That light may at last be brought
   To the darken'd souls of men !—
To the gifted seers who preach,
   To the humble bards who sing,
To all the heads that teach
   In Truth's enchanted ring ;

To the soldiers of the right,
   To the heroes of the true,—
Oh ! ours were a sorry plight,
   Great conquerors, but for you !
Oh, ye are the men of worth !
   Oh, ye are the men of might !
Oh, ye are the kings of earth !
   Your swords are Love and Right.

'Tis not at the beat of drum
   Earth's great ones all appear :
At the nation's call they come,
   But not with sword and spear.

Then hail to the brave who lead
    In the humble paths of peace !
To the hearts that toil and bleed
    That wrong may sooner cease !

Oh ! what are the robes we wear,
    Or the heights to which we climb ?
'Tis only the hearts we bear
    Can make our lives sublime ;
'Tis only the good we do
    That lives throughout all time ;
'Tis only the faithful few
    Who reach the heights sublime.

Then hail to the chiefs of thought
    Who wield the mighty pen
That light may at last be brought
    To the darken'd souls of men,—
To the soldiers of the right,
    To the heroes of the true,—
Oh, ours were a sorry plight,
    Great conquerors, but for you !

BRITANNIA

ALL hail, my country ! hail to thee,
        Thou birthplace of the brave and free,
Thou ruler upon land and sea,
                Britannia !

No thing of change, no mushroom state !
In wisdom thou canst work and wait,
Or wield the thunder-bolts of Fate,
                Britannia !

Oh, nobly hast thou play'd thy part !
What struggles of the head and heart
Have gone to make thee what thou art,
                Britannia !

Great mother of the mighty dead !
Sir Walter sang and Nelson bled
To weave a garland for thy head,
          Britannia !

And Watt, the great magician, wrought,
And Shakespeare ranged the realms of thought,
And Newton soar'd, and Cromwell fought,
          Britannia !

And Milton's high seraphic art,
And Bacon's learning, Burns's heart,
Are glories that shall ne'er depart,
          Britannia !

These are the soul of thy renown,
The gems immortal in thy crown,
The suns that never shall go down,
          Britannia !

Oh, still have faith in truth divine !
Still sacred be thy seal and sign,
And pow'r and glory shall be thine,
          Britannia !

THE ANGLO–SAXON

THE Anglo-Saxon leads the van,
   And never lags behind,
For was not he ordain'd to be
   The leader of mankind ?
He carries very little sail,
   Makes very little show,
But gains the haven without fail,
   Whatever winds may blow.

He runs his plow in ev'ry land,
   He sails in ev'ry sea,
All prospers where he has a hand,
   For king of men is he.
He plants himself on Afric's sand,
   And 'mong Spitzbergen's snows,
For he takes root in any land,
   And blossoms like the rose.

Into the wilderness he goes,
   He loves the wild and free,
The forests stagger 'neath his blows—
   A sturdy man is he.
To have a homestead of his own,
   The giants down he'll bring—
His shanty's sacred as a throne,
   And there he'll reign a king.

For let him plant him where he may,
   On this you may depend,
As sure as worth will have a sway,
   He's ruler in the end.
For he believes in thrift, and knows
   The money-making art ;
But tho' in riches great he grows,
   They harden not his heart.

He never knows when he is beat,
   To knock him down is vain,—
He's sure to get upon his feet,
   And into it again.
If you're resolved to be his foe,
   You'll find him rather tough ;
But he'll not strike another blow
   Whene'er you call "Enough!"

His is a nature true as steel,
   Where many virtues blend,
A head to think, a heart to feel,
   A soul to comprehend.

I love to look upon his face,
Whate'er be his degree,—
An honor to the human race,
The king of men is he.

———

COWARDICE

THERE'S somewhat that's lurking unseen,
A phantom that folks are afraid of;
Oh! what does this cowardice mean?
Oh! what kind of stuff are men made of?

There's Sandy, six feet in his socks,
Yet tales of his childhood enslave him,
And he sits with his soul in the stocks,
In spite of the reason God gave him.

Yes, tho' he's six feet and twelve stone,
Poor fellow, we will not upbraid him,
For ah! he has never outgrown
The suit that his grandmother made him.

E'en men who would evil assail,
For whom death itself has no terror,
Before Madam Grundy grow pale,
And bow at the shrine of old Error :

And kneel to the thing they despise,
And bow to the veriest follies,
And prop up the temple of lies
As if 'twere the Holy of Holies.

Afraid of what people would say,
They give themselves up to deceiving.
Come forth in the light of the day,
And stand by the truth ye believe in.

And ye shall be strong in the right,
  Tho' fanatics hate and abhor ye,
For ye shall have angels of light,
  And the shield of truth hanging o'er ye.

Be hooted and hiss'd by the mob,
  From post unto pillar be driven,
Be sneer'd at by every snob :
  Of such is the kingdom of heaven.

WHERE'ER WE MAY WANDER

WHERE'ER we may wander, whate'er be our lot,
    The heart's deep affections still cling to the spot
Where first a fond mother with rapture has prest,
Or sung us to slumber in peace on her breast ;

Where Love first allured us, and fondly we hung
On the magical music which fell from her tongue.
Tho' wise ones may tell us 'twas foolish and vain,
Yet when shall we drink of such glory again ?

Where Hope first beguiled us, and spells o'er us cast,
And told us her visions of beauty would last,
That earth was an Eden untainted with guile,
And men were not destined to sorrow and toil ;

Where Friendship first found us, and gave us her hand,
And link'd us for aye to that beautiful land,—
Oh ! still shall this heart be, and cold as the clay,
Ere one of their features shall from it decay.

O Fortune, thy favors are empty and vain !
Restore me the friends of my boyhood again—
The hearts that are scattered or cold in the tomb,
Oh, give me again in their beauty and bloom !

Away with Ambition ! it brought me but pain ;
Oh, give me the big heart of boyhood again !
The faith and the friendship, the rapture of yore,
Oh, shall they re-visit this bosom no more ?

LIFE'S CONTRADICTIONS

THIS life is a drama, a great panorama,
    With strange alternations of joy and of woe ;
Or are we but dreaming, and things only seeming ?
    For, save that we're ignorant, what do we know ?

We're strange contradictions : our loves turn afflictions,
    Our sweetest affections are scourges of flame ;
There's strength in our weakness, there's pride in our
        meekness,
    And near neighbors always are glory and shame.

Lovely humanities bloom among vanities,
    Beamings of peace 'mid our tumult and strife ;
Spiritualities close by realities,
    Oh, who can read us the riddle of life ?

And mere brute unreason comes duly in season,
    As sure as the dewdrops and flowers of spring ;
And Reason, astounded, stands dumb and confounded,
    She out of the stern facts no reason can wring.

Behold the oppressor, the wrong's stern redresser,
    The bane and the antidote both at a birth.
Is nothing disjointed ? are all pre-appointed,
    The saints and the sinners, the saviors of earth ?

Oh, whence, and oh, whither have we been sent hither,
    Without chart or compass the track to pursue ;
Cast on a wild ocean of endless emotion
    To buffet the waves with this terrible crew ?

We journey as strangers this desert of dangers,
  And, 'mid all our knowledge, is this all we know ?
The road's long and dreary, we're wayworn and weary,
  We vanish, and who can tell whither we go ?

———

TO A BEAUTIFUL CHILD

AH, lovely child, with face so fair,
    And rippling streams of sunny hair,
And spirit all untouch'd by care ;
    While Hope and Joy,
As in a trance of glad surprise,
Look out from thine enraptured eyes,
    My happy boy.

The world to thee is fresh and new,
As beautiful with early dew
As when the first pair wander'd through
    Their glorious Eden,
Ere yet the serpent had beguil'd,
Or driv'n them to the desert wild,
    All sorrow-laden.

Life's still to thee a vision bright,
And earth an Eden of delight,
A thrill in ev'ry sound and sight,
    Each touch a joy ;
And ev'ry little bird that sings,
And all the flow'rs are heav'nly things,
    My happy boy.

Thy world is spirit-haunted still,
The valley green, the murm'ring rill,
The solemn wood, the great old hill,
    The tow'ring pine ;
And all the rivers, as they roll,
Are ever ringing through thy soul
    A song divine.

Let Science reason and define ;
A deeper instinct, child, is thine,—
Thy intuitions are divine.
    Unschool'd by art,
Or the frivolities of time,
Thou still canst feel the beat sublime
    Of Nature's heart.

Thou still canst talk with flow'r and tree,
And still the mountains nod to thee ;
And through thy soul the great old sea
    Still heaves sublime !
And Awe and Wonder, hand in hand,
Still lead thee through this magic land,
    This vale of Time.

And Charity, all void of art,
Has built her temple in thy heart,
Where selfishness has ne'er a part ;
    And long may'st thou
Live but by sympathy and love,
And intuitions from above,
    As thou dost now.

And may no sceptic, weak and blind,
Have pow'r to blight thy youthful mind
With hateful thoughts of human kind,
    Thy peace destroy,
And dwarf thy spiritual stature,
With blasphemies of Man and Nature,
    My hopeful boy.

His gospel is of sin and shame—
That men love only pow'r and fame,
That Friendship's but an empty name,
    That Love is lust ;
And men are but a herd of knaves
That crawl into their worthless graves,
    Dust unto dust.

May never Bigot get control,
To fix his shackles on thy soul,
And turn earth to a dismal hole
        Where Love's unknown,
And ev'ry heart is rank and foul,
And God with an eternal scowl
        Is looking on.

Such blasphemies are a disgrace ;
Such libels on the human race
Make God-like Reason hide her face
        In grief and shame,
And wring from ev'ry manly breast
A sacred, solemn, sad protest,
        In God's great name.

While others wealth and honors chase,
Tho' poverty stare in thy face,
Strive thou to elevate our race
        From sin and guilt ;
Dare to be honest, and despise
The tow'ring monument of lies
        Fashion has built.

Still dote on Nature's ev'ry feature,
Love and revere thy fellow-creature,
Have Faith in God, and Man, and Nature,
        And look above !
Get knowledge, but get something more,
Something to worship and adore,
        And love, still love.

MAN

COME forth, ye wise ones—ye who can
  Decipher Nature's mystic plan—
Come, sound me but the depths of man.

What am I ? and whence have I come ?
No answer save a dreary hum—
Oh ! why, ye wise ones, are ye dumb ?

What is this house in which I dwell ?
Alas ! alas ! there's none can tell ;
Oh, Nature keeps her secret well !

And all I hear, and touch, and see,
Time and creation, are to me
A marvel and a mystery !

Great Ruler of the earth and sky,
Oh ! from my spirit's depths I cry,
Almighty Father, what am I ?

And what is all this world I see ?
Is it what it appears to be,
An awful, stern reality ?

And are these men that come and go,
Or but the shades of Joy and Woe,
All flitting through this vale below ?

And what is Time, with all her cares,
Her wrinkles, furrows, and grey hairs,
The hag that swallows all she bears ?

The mystic where, the when, the how,
The awful, everlasting now,
The fun'ral wreath upon my brow ?

And for what purpose am I here—
A stranger in an unknown sphere—
A thing of doubt, of hope, and fear—

A waif on time, all tempest-tost—
A stranger on an unknown coast—
A weary, wand'ring, wond'ring ghost?

Didst thou not, Father, shape my course?
Or am I but a causeless force—
A stream that issues from no source?

Ah, no! within myself I see
An endless realm of mystery,
A great, a vast infinity!

A house of flesh, a frail abode,
Where dwell the demon and the God;
A soaring seraph and a clod;

The hall of the celestial Nine,
The filthy sty of grov'lling swine,
The animal and the divine;

Creation's puzzle, false and true,
The light and dark, the old and new,
The slave, and yet the sovran, too;

Angel and demon, Nero, Paul,
And creeping things upon the wall,
I am the brother of them all.

A part of all things, first and last,
Link'd to the future and the past,
At my own soul I glare aghast.

A spark from the eternal caught,
A living, loving thing of thought,
A miracle in me is wrought!

A being that can never die,
More wonderful than earth and sky,
A terror to myself am I.

My spirit's sweep shall have no bound.
Oh ! shall I sail the deep profound,
A terror with a glory crown'd ?

When from this dust and darkness free,
All glorified, shall these eyes see
The All in All eternally ?

————

A DREAM

Dreams are the mirror of the mind,
We see ourselves in dreams.

I SAT myself down by a lone mountain stream
　　Which hurried away to the sea ;
Around me the rude rocks of ages were strewn,
　　Above me an old willow tree.

The waters came dashing adown the rude rock,
　　Till exhausted and foaming they fell ;
And bubbled a moment within the dark pool,
　　Then gladly sped on through the dell.

I gazed on the tumult, the strife, and the foam,
　　And the bubbles that pass'd like a dream ;
In aerial beauty they bounded along,
　　In the light of the laughing sunbeam.

I thought of existence, its tumult and strife,
　　Of time's rapid, turbulent stream ;
And long, long I ponder'd the meaning of life,
　　When thus a voice spoke in my dream :

" Launch'd upon an unknown river,
   Hurrying to an unknown sea,
Without compass, sail, or rudder,
   What a hapless crew are we !

" Deeps, infinite deeps, before us,
   Ruin riding in the wind,
Cloudy curtains hanging o'er us,
   And eternities behind.

" Onward, onward, ever onward,
   Full in sight of that dread sea ;
Not a beacon-light to cheer us,
   Not a single star.   Ah, me ! "

An old man approach'd, as the voice died away,
   And sadly he look'd in my face ;
He lean'd on his staff, and he shook his locks grey,
   As he hopelessly talk'd of our race :

" With light and with darkness we're compass'd about ;
   The clearer our vision, the darker our doubt.
The knot of our destiny will not undo ;
   The bars of our prison we cannot get through.

" We grasp at lov'd shadows—while grasping they're flown—
   The fruit of our knowledge is still the unknown ;
We scale the blue summits, for which we have long'd,
   To sit down and sigh for the regions beyond.

" A longing still haunts us wherever we go,
   And knowledge increases the weight of our woe ;
And all that we cling to is fleeting as breath,
   And life is the valley and shadow of death. "

He rose to depart, and he heav'd a deep sigh,
   While o'er us there hung a great cloud ;
But deep in its bosom there beam'd a bright eye,
   And a sweet voice kept chanting aloud :

" The heav'ns will not unveil themselves,
   Yet mortal eyes may see
In mortal frames the budding flow'rs
   Of immortality. "

The cloud slowly vanish'd, and where it had hung
  There stretch'd out a beautiful blue,
And e'en from the rude rocks a welcome was rung,
  As an angel's form rose to my view.

Her face had the sadness that's sister to joy—
  It was not the sadness of thought ;
Her voice was sweet music, without earth's alloy,
  And these were the tidings she brought :

  " Life's the great mystery, deeper than death—
  Infinite history, woven of breath.
  Death but deciphers the pages of time ;
  Mortal, do thou make their meaning sublime."

The bright blue all faded, and quickly I found
  I still was alone by the stream ;
The willows above me, the mountains around,
  Yet scarce could believe all a dream.

ON THE DEATH OF ———

L AY him by the mountain torrent,
    Where the lofty cedars wave,
That the winds may wail his requiem,
  And the birds sing o'er his grave.
His warm heart is cold as ashes,
  And his radiant eye is dim,
And the voice of praise or censure
  Falls alike unfelt by him.
He is free from pain and sorrow,
  And the burdens that he bore,
And the wrong and the injustice,
  They can wring his heart no more.

As a pilot on life's ocean
  He was not devoid of skill,
But the adverse winds of fortune
  'Round his bark were roaring still.

He has tasted of the anguish
  Which the gen'rous spirit feels,
Striving after pure ideals,
  With starvation at his heels.
If his bark was sorely shatter'd,
  Think but of the storms he past,
Point not to the batter'd bulwarks,
  If he's safely moor'd at last.

Quick, impulsive, was his nature,
  Yet he sorrow'd to give pain;
He had foes, for he was rather
  Apt to speak the truth too plain.
When he witness'd an injustice
  He could not control his tongue—
Call it weakness, half his sorrows
  From this noble weakness sprung.
Yet he lost no jot of courage
  Striving 'gainst the wind and tide,—
Oh, his very heart grew bigger,
  Fighting on the weaker side.

Where conformity was wanted,
  Somehow he could not conform,
He would choose his path, and tread it,
  Even through the thunderstorm.
Are ye right because ye never
  Step from off the beaten way?
Are all those that tempt the thicket
  Ever hopelessly astray?
They must try the wilds untrodden,
  They must tempt the stormy sea,
Who would bring us joyous tidings,
  Who would make us wise and free.

Like ourselves, he had some frailties
  Better he had been without,
But upon his truth and honor
  Malice could not fix a doubt.

They are firm that never falter,
  They are very wise indeed,
Who have ne'er pursued a phantom,
  Never lean'd upon a reed.
Charity for human frailty
  Never, never yet was wrong;
Straight they are that never stumble,
  Clemency becomes the strong.

Oh ! he bore a buoyant spirit
  Poverty could not destroy,
All the leanings of his nature
  Ever were to light and joy.
Happy, smiling human faces,
  Charity's thrice-blessed words,
Fell upon his heart like sunshine,
  Or the song of summer birds ;
Then the sallies of his humor,
  Genial as the summer rain—
No, we'll never, never listen
  To such gust of soul again.

Tho' his heart had specks of darkness,
  There were gleams of the divine ;
Mem'ry wipes the failures from it,
  Locks it in her sacred shrine ;
Hangs it in her halls of twilight,
  Yea, to make the darkness bright,
Like a lovely star to twinkle
  Ever on the vault of night ;
Severs it from dust and ashes,
  Frees it from the dross of clay,
Death and time and love and sorrow
  Washing all its stains away.

4

WHO KNOWS?

THE night was dark, the winds were out,
    The stars hid in the sky,
The mousing owl too-hoo'd aloud
    The wan moon rushing by.
I sat there in my lonely room,
    The children all asleep;
Ah! there they lay in dreams at play,
    While I nurst sorrows deep.

I ponder'd long this weary life;
    I cried, " Is 't as it seems,
Or sail we here in phantom ship,
    In search of vanish'd dreams,
From deep to deep, from doubt to doubt,
    While Night still deeper grows?
Who knows the meaning of this life?"
    A voice replied, " *Who knows?*"

Shall it a myst'ry always be?
    Is none to lift the veil?
Knows no one aught of land we left,
    Or port to which we sail?
Poor shipwreck'd mariners, driv'n about
    By ev'ry wind that blows,
Is there a haven of rest at all?"
    The voice replied, " *Who knows?*"

" Why have we longings infinite,
    Affections deep and high,
And glorious dreams of immortal things,
    If we're but born to die?
Are they but will-o-wisps, that gleam
    Where deadly night-shade grows?
End they in dust and ashes all?"
    The voice still cried, " *Who knows?*"

Its hopeless tones fell on my heart,
  A dark and heavy cloud ;
The great horn'd moon look'd down on me
  In terror from its shroud.
It plainly said, " Ye're orphans all,
  Is there no balm for woes ? "
The screech-owl cried, the night wind sigh'd,
  Alas, alas, " *Who knows ?* "

I pray'd for light that weary night,
  I question'd saint and seer ;
But demon Doubt put all to rout,
  Kept ringing in mine ear :
" Your life's a trance, a mystic dance,
  And round and round ye go ;
Ye're poor ghosts all at spectral ball,
  And that's the most ye know.

" Ye dance and sing in spectral ring,
  Affrighted Nature raves ;
The screech-owls cry, the night-winds sigh,
  The dead turn in their graves.
Ye come like thought, ye pass to naught,
  And what surprises most,
'Mid your ghostly fun there's hardly one
  Believes himself a ghost !

" Oh ! thought is sad, 'twould make you mad ;
  'Tis folly to weep and rave ;
So follow Mirth around the earth—
  There's naught beyond the grave.
Your hearts would sink, dared ye to think,
  So dance with death at the ball ;
And round ye go till cock shall crow,
  And that's the end of all."[1]

---

[1] Small figures refer to Notes. (See p. 403.)

FATE, A FRAGMENT

The following stanzas form the concluding part of a poem entitled "Fate, A Fragment," inscribed to Dr. Patullo, Brampton, later of Toronto, and published in full in 1856.

The poem begins with an assertion by a Mortal, to the effect that a firm purpose and a determined will can rise above earth's cares and troubles. As a curtain is withdrawn, a Spirit bids him look. He sees a great temple, in which is a judge seated on a throne, marking something in a large book at the bidding of an unseen dictator. Outside the temple, demanding admittance, is a vast crowd of every kindred and creed. He sees one admitted whose face is haggard and sorrowful, who asks if his name is in the book.

The Oracle (or Judge), answering in the affirmative, inquires, "What further wouldst thou ask of me?" He describes the hopeless and miserable condition to which Doubt has brought him, and wishes to know whether behind the Veil in the future there is not something which Death cannot destroy. Then Hope would return.

The quotation begins with the Oracle's answer :

Oracle

THOU in thy ignorance must wait :
　　Tears, prayers, cannot alter Fate ;
Behind the veil no eye may see—
Such is the will of destiny.
But on its folds behold a sign—
A crown, a cross, a face divine.
If thou from doubt and death wouldst flee,
Forget thy proud philosophy,
And climb the hill of Calvary.

Mortal

Like a shadow he has gone,
While the aisles these notes prolong.

First Voice

Not in Science, not in Art,
Hides the balm for wounded heart;
We are bound until made free
By the great Humility.

Knowledge is the tree of woe—
All your fathers found it so ;
All Philosophy is vain,
Be a little child again.

Second Voice

Who would not exchange for the visions of youth
  The wisdom we gather with years?
Oh, who has not learn'd, 'tis a sorrowful truth,
  That knowledge is water'd in tears.

Third Voice

Without the great temple the nations await,
In wonder and awe, the decisions of fate :—
Admit the strange mortal that's next at the gate.

Hosts of shadows lead him on
To the footstool of the throne ;
Some in mirth and mockery,
Some in sad sincerity.
There, as in a trance, he stands,
With rapt look and folded hands ;
While voices round him, clear and cool,
Proclaim him but a dreamy fool.

Oracle

Mortal of the breathing air,
What is thy peculiar care?—
Is it hope, or doubt, or fear,
Or what passion, brings thee here?

Poet

I've sought thy great temple, for I am opprest ;
A wish, a great longing, will not give me rest ;
The great face of Nature is awful to me—
A woe and a wonder in all that I see.

The grey clouds that wander, the infinite blue,
The great silent visage that's aye looking through,
The leaves of the forest, the waves of the sea,
The hills and the valleys—are calling on me ;
They beckon me to them, as if they would tell,
The secret they've guarded for ages so well.
The seen and the unseen, the wonderful whole,
Awake thoughts which trouble and torture my soul ;
And, sleeping or waking, they will not depart—
They'll march forth to music, or tear out my heart.

I'd speak what the spirit had spoken to me,
For a priest, and a prophet, a poet, I'd be ;
I'd emulate gladly the great that are gone—
Unveil to the world its soul in my song.

I'd be as the bards, the great minstrels of yore,
For big human hearts in their bosoms they bore ;
They pour'd forth their numbers, unfetter'd by art,
And found a response in the great human heart.
I've never heard aught in our smooth, polish'd tongue
Like the rudely sublime strains my old mother sung.
Their awful simplicity I'd fain make my own,
Their great naked virtue revive in my song.
I'd question the past till its secret I'd wring,
And from the far future glad tidings I'd bring ;
I'd summon the dead from their silent domain,
Sage, hero, should act o'er life's drama again ;
The poor humble hero in song I'd enthrone ;
The great hearts that struggled, yet perish'd unknown,
I'd conjure again from their unhonor'd graves
To shame our lax age and its time-serving slaves.
And yet in my song hate could scarce find a place—
Despite of its errors, I still love our race ;
The lowly, the lofty, the lordly, the small,
Poor, rich, wise and foolish, I feel with them all.
I fain would do something for those gone astray,
Tho' 'twere but to sing of a happier day.

Confusion's around us, the time's out of tune ;
The heart asks for concord, the only blest boon ;
We've wander'd from nature, we worship cold art,
And, striving to fly from, we torture the heart ;
And its silent sorrows appeal to my string—
How happy could I but a soothing tone bring !
Its mirth and its madness, its joy and its woe,
Its great gusts of sadness which will overflow ;
Its deep aspirations for that blessèd clime
Which lies 'yond the regions of death and of time ;
Its infinite longings, its hopes and its fears,
Its doubts and its darkness, its smiles and its tears—
I'd treasure them all in my heart and my brain,
And brood, like the spirit, o'er chaos again.

Oracle

Poets are the pets of Nature :
Lovingly she forms each feature.
Well she knows men would revile her,
So she brings the reconciler,—
Yea, for the great love she bears him,
In her roughest mood she rears him ;
Heavy burdens she lays on him,
Care and sorrow heaps upon him ;
Fills him with celestial fires,
And with herds of low desires ;
Now an angel she will start,
Now a naked human heart—
Lets a thing of flesh and sin,
Or a soaring seraph, in ;
Now she lights his eye with gladness,
Now with melancholy madness ;
Now through hell's confines he's driven,
Now he cleaves the vault of heaven ;
Now shudders at the damnèds' cries,
Now drinks the airs of Paradise ;
Until his joys, his agonies,
Start into wizard-melodies ;

Till his tones, his words of wonder,
Catch the spirit of the thunder,
And in melody sublime
Sweep adown the straits of time.

Canst thou for the muse's sake
Suffer wrong and scorn and hate ?
Is to thee her meanest tone
Dearer than earth's proudest throne ?
For her canst thou suffer want ?
For her fight with sin and shame,
E'en without the hope of fame ?
Canst thou bear, e'en by the good,
To be wrongly understood ?
Canst thou hear, with judgment cool,
Wise men stamp thee but a fool ;
Painted puppies of a day
Scorn thee for thy poverty ?
Hear, then, 'mid the scorn and laughter
Of thy time, the " Hail hereafter."

OLD HANNAH

'TIS Sabbath morn, and a holy balm
    Drops down on the heart like dew,
And the sunbeam's gleam like a blessèd dream
    Afar on the mountains blue.
Old Hannah's by her cottage door,
    In her faded widow's cap ;
She is sitting alone on the old grey stone,
    With the Bible in her lap.

An oak is hanging above her head,
    And the burn is wimpling by ;
The primroses peep from their sylvan keep,
    And the lark is in the sky.

Beneath that shade her children played,
　But they're all away with Death,
And she sits alone on the old grey stone
　To hear what the Spirit saith.

Her years are past three score and ten,
　And her eyes are waxing dim,
But the page is bright with a living light,
　And her heart leaps up to Him ·
Who pours the mystic Harmony
　Which the soul alone can hear !
She is not alone on the old grey stone,
　Tho' no earthly friend is near.

There's no one left to love her now ;
　But the Eye that never sleeps
Looks on her in love from the heavens above,
　And with quiet joy she weeps.
For she feels the balm of bliss is poured
　In her lone heart's sorest spot :
The widow lone on the old grey stone
　Has a peace the world knows not.

A WRECK

A NDREW was erst the village pride :
　　Oft 'neath the yew tree's shade
Both old and young with rapture hung
　On wondrous words he said.
Now in the public bar he stands,
　In a dizzy, drunken crew,
A lounging sot, in thread-bare coat,
　His elbows peeping through.

How changed since when he touch'd our hearts,
　As if with magic wand !

We thought that he would one day be
    A wonder in the land ;
For while he spake the ages all
    Seem'd open to his view—
This gibb'ring sot, in thread-bare coat,
    With lips of livid hue.

And from the wreck of old belief
    What wondrous forms he drew !
And how he wrought disjointed thought
    In pictures strange and new !
Who could have deem'd this mournful change
    Would e'er have come to pass—
A seedy sot, in thread-bare coat,
    Alas ! and yet alas !

Is this the man of loving heart,
    Which knew no crook nor wile ?
For he was free as man could be
    From ev'rything like guile ;
His sense of moral worth remains,
    Yet he does the thing that's mean—
A sneaking sot, in thread-bare coat,
    He sinks to the obscene.

He still presents the lordly brow,
    The great black, flashing eyes,
But wan despair is seated there,
    " The worm that never dies."
The princely port, the regal air,
    The stately tread, are gone—
A palsied sot, in thread-bare coat,
    To the grave he staggers on.

The ghost of former self will come,
    And try to break his chain ;
He'll curse the cup, he'll give it up,
    Yet seek it once again.

How mournful are his gibes and jeers,
How sad to hear him sing—
That joyless sot, in thread-bare coat,
That God-forgotten thing !

The dreams of boyhood haunt him still,
They come but to annoy ;
He fills the cup, he drains it up,
And laughs, the ghost of joy !
The wreck of richly-laden souls
Is a dire and fearful thing :
Oh ! shun his lot, that sinking sot,
Whose dying dirge we sing.

———

A VISION

Inscribed to Alex. McLaren, Esq., Rockside, Caledon,
Peel County, Ontario

Behold, the Dreamer cometh

IS THIS world, with all its wonders,
Our whole life, a passing dream—
Shadows we, that unto shadows
In a death-like grapple seem ?

What's this mighty maze of being ?
Tell me, sages, if you can,
What is light, and what is darkness ?
Tell me what is meant by man ?

To illuminate our dungeon
All your striving is in vain ;
Of themselves the sunbeams enter—
Of themselves pass out again.

We have all our times and seasons,
   When the brooding spirit sees
Over ages, over æons,
   Into the eternities.

When the clouds which mar our vision
   Melt like morning mists away,
When the past and unborn future
   Meet upon the brink of day.

Tired, weary with conjecture,
   On a stilly Sabbath night,
Clear as sunshine on my spirit,
   A strange vision did alight.

I beheld a mighty ocean,
   Thickly strewn with wrecks of time,
And the fleet of death discharging
   Its sad cargo from each clime.

Of the dead within its bosom,
   Kingdoms—continents—I saw,
Heap'd in regular confusion,
   As a peasant piles his straw.

Here an earthquake-swallow'd city,
   And a field of battle there ;
Still the spectres eyed each other
   With a horrid wolfish glare.

Long I gazed in silent horror,
   Fix'd as if by death's decree ;
For a myriad eyeless sockets
   All were fasten'd upon me.

But the spirit spake within me,
   Saying : " What hast thou to fear ?
Not for empty, idle horror
   Hast thou been admitted here.

" Mortal, cast thine eye far upward ;
    While thou breathest mortal breath,
Vain's thy hope of penetrating
    The infinite depths of death."

I beheld the cloud of being
    Rise like vapor from the main ;
Rolling o'er its awful bosom,
    Sink into its depths again.

As it rose, that cloud was braided
    With a lovely rainbow ray ;
As it fell, the glory faded,
    Blending in a solemn grey.

And the spirit spake within me,
    Saying : " That which thou dost see
As shadow o'er death's gulf, is Time,
    The rainbow of Eternity."

Ages, with their weary burdens,
    While I gazed, came rolling home ;
Still another and another
    Melted in the deep like foam.

Myriad human forms and faces
    Look'd out on me through the gloom,
Individuals, empires, races,
    On their journey to the tomb.

Now a face divinely human,
    'Mid a group of children seen ;
Now a blood-bespatter'd visage,
    Horrid as a demon's dream.

Some, pursuing their own shadows,
    Vanish'd quickly from my sight ;
Others, grasping shining baubles,
    Soon were swallow'd in the night.

Now the ringing laugh of gladness,
    Now the short, sharp shriek of woe ;
Joy and sorrow, mirth and madness,
    Hurrying to the gulf below.

Yet, with an appalling sameness,
    Aye the ages roll'd along ;
Over each a voice kept singing
    Poor humanity's sad song :

"An infinite dome, o'er a world of wonder,
An eye looking down on the poor dreamer under.

An ocean of wrecks, and beyond it our home ;
Each wave as it breaks leaves us whiter with foam.

A marriage to-day, and a fun'ral to-morrow,
A short smile of joy, and a long sigh of sorrow.

A birth and a death, with a flutter between,
A lamp and a breath—tell me, what does it mean ?"

Then arose, as if in answer,
    From the great deep, voices three,
Pealing till they woke the awful
    Echoes of eternity :

First Voice

Roll, roll, roll,
    With thy burden of hopes and fears ;
Toil, toil, toil,
    In thy garden of blood and of tears.

On, on, on,
    Tho' weary, way-worn and opprest ;
Long, long, long
    Is the Sabbath of peace and of rest.

Second Voice

Eternal, oh, eternal,
  The spirit's range shall be ;
Her heavy mantle she but casts
  Upon the deep, deep sea.

Immortal, oh, immortal
  The glad triumphant strain,
Soon as the spirit leaves the realm
  Of sorrow, death, and pain !

Third Voice

Day dawns from the deepest shadow,
  Flow'rs above corruption bloom ;
Joy springs from the breast of sorrow,
  Life immortal from the tomb.

Hope and fear are aye united,
  Love and wretchedness are twain,
Hearts are by affection blighted,
  Only in a world of sin.

And the spirit stirr'd within me,
  As the voices died away ;
Suddenly Time's rainbow vanish'd,
  And the dead cried out, " 'Tis day."

Morning in the east was dawning,
  Earth-born sounds fell on mine ears,
And the awful vision vanish'd
  In a flood of human tears.

THE POET TO THE PAINTER

Dedicated to Arthur Cox, A.R.C.A., Toronto

Invocation to the Arts

HAIL to each high ideal art,
　　At whose command things base depart,
While beauteous forms to being start
　　In the dark mind,
Leading the earth's sad troubled heart
　　Its rest to find.

The early truth-seekers

For truth the olden masters wrought,
The false with pen and pencil fought,
The lessons of creation taught
　　In limn or line,
Embodying their inner thought
　　Of things divine.

Their motive

To rouse the soul to higher flights,
To taste of holier delights,
And raise to spiritual heights
　　Unthinking men,
They spent laborious days and nights
　　With brush and pen.

Their power

Poet or Painter can descry
In common things that round us lie
What these in spirit signify,
　　And to them give
The deep, intense humanity
　　By which they live.

The Painter's inspiration

The Painter is a soul possest,
With demons stirring in his breast :
No passing moment do they rest,
　　But strive until
The colors have in joy expressed
　　The spirit's will.

His privilege

And he is one who hears and sees
Great Nature's wondrous mysteries,
The everlasting harmonies
    That sweep along,
Then carols forth in ecstasies
    His painted song.

The Poet's inspiration

The Poet is a soul sincere
To whom all living things are dear,
While wisdom, love, and hope, and fear,
    Like stars that shine,
Surround him with an atmosphere
    Of thoughts divine.

His inner struggles

Yet one, alas! who cannot sleep,
Striving to climb the eternal steep,
And a communication keep
    With the unseen;
Still hearing deep call unto deep,
    What doth it mean?

His night vigils

And wisdom—which is but the spoil
Of all life's weary stain and toil—
For her he burns the midnight oil
    When fancies throng,
Pouring his bursting heart the while
    Into his song.

His reward

Yet still, anon, he, startled, hears
The very music of the spheres
Burst in on his enraptured ears!
    While a great train
Of prophets, poets, saints, and seers
    Join in the strain.

The lament

But we have to lament that here
Genius is in an alien sphere ·
Her song, alas! but few revere
    Or understand.

5

She wanders like a pilgrim drear
In a strange land—

Genius
unnoticed

A land where undevelop'd souls
Are drifting round in listless shoals ;
Who, tho' the wave of beauty rolls
So very near,
In spirit distant as the poles,
See not, nor hear.

Beauty
discarded
for gold

For them the daisy blooms in vain ;
Unnoticed is the violet's stain ;
The mountain but obscures the plain ;
And the green field
Is lov'd but for the golden grain
That it doth yield.

Nature
wantonly
desecrated

Thus in our grand old solemn woods,
Green temples of the solitudes,
The worshipper of self intrudes
But to profane—
Where still the mighty mother broods
He seeks but gain !

Nature's
highest repre-
sentation of
the Divine
neglected.

How few will leave the busy mart
To see the orb of light depart,
Or from their couch of slumber start,
Ere yet 'tis day,
To hive the sunrise in the heart
And bear't away.

The Painter's
prayer.

Oh ! for a draught of spirit wine,
Distill'd by the immortal Nine,
In which the virtues all combine—
That deathless draught !
That nectar from the cup divine
By Genius quaff'd !

The Poet's
prayer

Oh ! for the magic power that brings
From out the secret deeps of things,
The soul that mounts on living wings,
    From time set free—
That through creation soars and sings
    Eternally.

The power
must be a
gift

Be ours the gift—heaven's highest dower—
This sense of spiritual power
That falls like an inspiring shower,
    Above all law,
Before which Intellect doth cower
    In wondering awe ;

The gift not
transferable

The gift some simple peasant caught,
Who toil'd not in the mines of thought ;
The art in vain by Science sought
    But to destroy ;
The thing that never can be taught—
    Creation's joy !

Motive for
hope

And who can tell but that we two
May hear a voice from out the blue,
Or see a form of beauty new
    To paint or pen,
To be God's record of the true
    For other men ?

Motive for
action

Then let us strive with all our might
To scale the spiritual height,
And kindle on its crest a light
    To shine afar,
To be to wand'rers in the night
    A guiding star.

GAUN HAME

OH, dry the saut tear frae thine e'e, Mary!
    Oh, dry the saut tear frae thine e'e!
And look not sae sadly on me, Mary,
    Oh, look not sae sadly on me!
There's Ane that will aye be thy stay, Mary,
    Thy wounds He will tenderly bind;
They'll all pass away like the wind, Mary,
    They'll all pass away like the wind!

It's no' me that's deein ava, Mary,
    Its no' me that's deein ava:
It's but the worn clay drappin aff, Mary,
    It's but the auld house gaun to fa';
It's but the caged bird gettin free, Mary,
    That soon will soar singin awa';
It's no' me that's deein' ava, Mary,
    It's no' me that's deein ava.

This tenement's gaen to decay, Mary,
    I feel as if 'twerena the same;
I'm sick o' this cauld house o' clay, Mary,
    I weary to win awa' hame.
Oh! sweet shall oor meetin' be there, Mary,
    Nae sigh o'er the sorrowfu' past;
The hame where the hert's never sair, Mary,
    And wrangs are a' richted at last.

And there we'll be aye young again, Mary,
    The fields will forever be green;
And nae lang regrets o' oor ain, Mary,
    And death never enter the scene.
I've them wi' me ye canna see, Mary,
    I feel the firm grip o' a haun';
Tho' a' here is darkness to thee, Mary,
    They're leadin me into the dawn.

The dear anes that left us lang syne, Mary—
    Ah, left us oor wearifu' lane,
But never were oot o' oor min', Mary—
    Are a' comin' roun' me again.
Ah! there's oor ain Willie and Jean, Mary!
    And wi' them a bricht-shinin' train,
Wha say through their pityin' e'en, Mary,
    Ye winna be left a' your lane.

Then dry the saut tear frae thine e'e, Mary,
    Then dry the saut tear frae thine e'e!
And look not sae sadly on me, Mary,
    Oh! look not sae sadly on me.
The grief that is turnin' thee grey, Mary,
    Nae doubt for some good is design'd,
'Twill all, like the wind, pass away, Mary,
    'Twill all pass away like the wind.

MUSIC

HAIL, Music! all hail!
        Earth's languages fail
To tell what thou tellest to me!
        O spirit divine,
        Space cannot confine,
All hearts are led captive by thee!

    At a mortal's command,
    From the mystical land
Where the spirit of Harmony dwells,
    And the great river starts
    That flows through all hearts,
Thou com'st with thy magical spells.

    To celestial spheres,
    Seen by sages and seers
On the rush of thy magical tide,

I am borne over time
To the regions sublime,
Where the mighty immortals abide.

Oh, the cankers of time,
In that passion sublime,
Are swept with earth's grossness away ;
We rise to a glory
Where hearts grow not hoary,
And taste not of death and decay.

Thou language of angels !*
Hosannas ! evangels !
The great Hallelujahs are thine ;
The great storms of gladness,
The glorious madness,
That make us poor mortals divine.

So holy and pure,
I can hardly endure
The glory that circles me round !
Yet forever I'd dwell
In this heavenly spell,
This infinite ocean of sound.

No logic can grasp thee !
Love only can clasp thee !
For wholly celestial thou art !
To gauge thee by reason
Seems absolute treason,
All hail to thee, Queen of the heart !

TO AN INDIAN SKULL

AND art thou come to this at last,
    Great Sachem of the forest vast?
E'en thou, who wert so tall in stature,
And model'd in the pride of nature!
High as the deer thou bor'st thy head;
Swift as the roebuck was thy tread;
Thine eye, bright as the orb of day,
In battle a consuming ray!
Tradition links thy name with fear,
And strong men hold their breath to hear
What mighty feats by thee were done—
The battles by thy strong arm won!
The glory of thy tribe wert thou—
But where is all thy glory now?
Where are those orbs, and where that tongue
On which commanding accents hung?
Canst thou do naught but grin and stare
Through hollow sockets—the worms' lair—
And toothless gums all gaping there?

Ah! where's that heart that did imbibe
The wild traditions of thy tribe?
Oft did the song of bards inspire,
And set thy very soul on fire,
Till all thy wild and savage blood
Was rushing like a foaming flood;
And all the wrongs heap'd on thy race
Leapt up like demons in thy face,
As, rushing down upon the plain,
Thou shout'st the war-whoop once again,
And stood'st among thy heaps of slain.
What tho' to thee there did belong
A savage sense of right and wrong,
In that thou wert alike, indeed,
To those who boast a better creed;

Repaid thy wrongs with blood and gall,
And triumph'd in thy rival's fall,
Like any Christian of us all.

Like me, thou hadst thy hopes and fears ;
Like me, thou hadst thy smiles and tears ;
Felt'st winter's cold and summer's heat ;
Didst hunger, and hadst weary feet ;
Wert warm'd by kindness, chill'd by hate,
Hadst enemies, like all the great.
Tho' thou wert not in type a dove,
Yet thou hast felt the thrill of love !
Oh, thy Winona, was she fair ?
And dark as midnight was her hair ?
Thy wigwam, was 't a sacred place ?
And dear to thee thy dusky race ?
Ah, yes ! thy savage imps were dear,
And they would climb thy knees to hear
And drink thy tales with greedy ear.

What tho' a wild, rude life was thine,
Thou still hadst gleams of the divine—
A sense of something undefined—
A Presence, an Almighty mind,
Which led the planets, rock'd the sea,
And through the desert guided thee.
The dark woods all around thee spread ;
The leafy curtains overhead ;
The great old thunder-stricken pine,
And the cathedral elms divine ;
The dismal swamp, the hemlock hoar ;
Niag'ra's everlasting roar ;
The viewless winds, which rush'd to wake
The spirit of Ontario's lake—
Did not their mighty anthems roll
Through all the caverns of thy soul,
And thrill thee with a sense sublime,
With gleams of that eternal clime
Which stretches over Death and Time ?

And oft, like me, thou'dst ask to know
Whence came we, whither do we go?
A marvel 'twas, poor soul, to thee,
As it has ever been to me.
From the unknown we issued out,
With myst'ry compast round about;
Each, with his burden on his back,
To follow in the destin'd track:
With weary feet, to toil and plod,
Through Nature, back to Nature's God.
Mine was the cultivated plain,
Thine the leafy green domain;
Thine was a rude, unvarnish'd shrine,
In form thy idols were not mine;
But, ah, mine were as strange to thee
As thine, my brother, are to me!
And yet they differ'd but in name,
And were in truth the very same.

Dreams of the hunting field were thine—
What better are these dreams of mine?
Ah, my red brother, were not we
By accident compell'd to be
Christian or savage? We, indeed,
Alike inherited a creed—
We had no choice what we should be;
Race, country, creed, were forced on thee,
Red brother, as they were on me!
Then why should I have lov'd thee less,
Or closed my heart to thy distress,
Red Rover of the wilderness?

Soon must we go, as thou hast gone,
Away back to the Great Unknown,
Where, elevated above doubt,
We, too, shall find the secret out:
Then may'st thou, the uneducated,
Be found the least contaminated,
From civ'lization's trammels free,
Who knows, poor soul, but thou may'st be
Exalted higher far than we?

SIR COLIN; OR, THE HIGHLANDERS AT BALAKLAVA

THE serfs[2] of the Tsar know not pity nor mercy,
  And many a turban is roll'd on the plain;
Like dust the poor sons of the prophet are trampled,
  And, Allah, il Allah! they'll shout not again.

Sir Colin! Sir Colin! why stand ye thus idle?
  Yon dark mounted masses shall trample thee o'er;
Sir Colin! Sir Colin! thy moments are number'd—
  The hills of Glenorchy shall know thee no more.

Why wakes not the pibroch thy fathers have sounded,
  Which roused up the clansmen in battles of yore?
Till downward they swept, like the tempests of Avin,
  Or demons all dashing with dirk and claymore?

Thy band shall be hack'd like the stripes of the tartan:
  McDonald! McDermid! to glory, adieu!
Gregalich! Gregalich! the shade of thy hero
  May blush for his sons, by his own Avon Dhu.

Hush! hark! 'tis the pipes playing " Hollen MacGaradh,"
  The spirit of Fingal at last has awoke—
Yet motionless all, as the giant Craig Ailsa—
  While the foam-crested billows rush on to the shock.

The horsemen of Russia roll nearer and nearer,
  Now slacken a moment, now sweep to the shock;
One terrible flash—'tis the lightning of Albin!
  One peal, and the tartans are hid in the smoke.

Now Duncan! now Donald! the mettle you're made of,
  In this awful moment, oh, may it prove true!
Be thy spirit as firm as the rocks of Saint Kilda,
  Thy swoop like the eagles of dark Benvenue.

2 See note at end.

It is not the deer ye have met on the heather—
  That is not thine own Corrybrechtan's[3] loud roar !
Triumphant emerge from that dark cloud of thunder,
  Or die, and behold the red heather no more.

The cloud clears away—'tis the horsemen are flying !
  All scattered like chaff by the might of the Gael ;
One long yell of triumph, while bonnets are waving,
  And " Scotland forever ! " resounds through the dale.

GARIBALDI

O SONS of Italy, awake !
    Your hearths and altars are at stake !
Arise, arise, for Freedom's sake,
    And strike with Garibaldi !

The Liberator now appears,
Foretold by prophets, bards, and seers—
The hero sprung from blood and tears,
    All hail to Garibaldi !

Let serfs and cowards fear and quake !
O Venice, Naples, Rome, awake !
Like lava from your burning lake,
    Rush on with Garibaldi !

Up and avenge your country's shame,
Like Ætna belching forth her flame,
Rush on in Freedom's holy name,
    And strike with Garibaldi !

'Tis Freedom thunders in your ears ;
The weary night of blood and tears,
The sorrows of a thousand years
    Cry " On with Garibaldi ! "

------

3 See note at end.

The Roman Eagle is not dead ;
Her mighty wings again are spread
To swoop upon the tyrant's head,
   And strike with Garibaldi !

The land wherein the laurel waves
Was never meant to nourish slaves ;
Then onward to your bloody graves,
   Or live like Garibaldi !

WOMAN

WHEN my gloomy hour comes on me,
   And I shun the face of man,
Finding bitterness in all things,
   As vex'd spirits only can ;

When of all the world I'm weary,
   Then some gentle woman's face,
Coming like a blessèd vision,
   Reconciles me to our race.

All the children of affliction,
   All the weary and opprest,
Flee to thee, belovèd woman,
   Finding shelter in thy breast.

While we follow mad ambition,
   Thine is far the nobler part,
Nursing flowers of sweet affection
   In the valleys of the heart.

Man can look and laugh at danger,
   Mighty with the sword is he ;
But he cannot love and suffer,
   Pity and forgive, like thee.

Blessed ministers of mercy!
  Hov'ring round the dying bed,
Come to cheer the broken hearted,
  To support the drooping head.

Oh, my blessings be upon you,
  For beneath yon weary sky
Ye are ever bringing comfort
  Unto sinners such as I.

When the most have but upbraidings
  For the guilty, erring man,
Ye speak words of hope and mercy,
  As dear woman only can.

When my weary journey's ending,
  When my troubled spirit flies,
May a woman smooth my pillow,
  May a woman close my eyes.

———

MARTHA

IN a sweet secluded nook,
  Down beside the quiet brook,
There an humble cabin's seen
Peeping from the ivy green,
While a great elm bends above it,
As it really seem'd to love it.
There old Martha lives alone,
But tho' to the world unknown,
There's a heart that's truly human
In the breast of that old woman!
Oft I seek that quiet place
Just to look upon her face,
And forget this scene of care,
Where men palter, curse, and swear;

And the demons all are rife,
In the never-ending strife
For the vanities of life.

What a world of love there lies
Mirror'd in her deep blue eyes !
What a ray of quiet beauty
They throw round each daily duty !
How it is I cannot tell,
Yet I feel the magic spell
Of the quiet Sabbath grace
Always breathing from her face ;
And her voice, so calm and clear,
Lifts me to a higher sphere,
And unlocks my spirit's powers.
Gentle thoughts spring up like flowers ;
Gems deep hidden in my heart
Into life and being start ;
When that saintly face I see,
Heav'n and immortality
Aye grow clearer unto me.

She's acquaint with sin and sorrow,
Knows their weary burdens thorough,
And her hearth is a retreat
Of sad hearts, of weary feet ;
And while others find but flaws,
Quoting still the moral laws,
She but thinks of what is human,
Loves them all, the dear old woman !
Time, which makes most heads but hoary,
Changed hers to a crown of glory.
Many, ah ! many a benediction
From the children of affliction,
Blessings from the haunts of care,
Nestle 'mid the glory there ;
And she always seems to me
An embodied prophecy
Of a better world to be.

THE STAMP OF MANHOOD

COME, let us sing to human worth,
   'Tis big hearts that we cherish,
For they're the glory of the earth
   And never wholly perish.
All Nature loves the good and brave,
   And show'rs her gifts upon them ;
She hates the tyrant and the slave,
   For manhood's stamp's not on them.

Thine eye shall be the index true
   Of what thy soul conceiveth ;
Thy words shall utter firm and few
   The things thy heart believeth ;
Thy voice shall have the ring of steel ;
   The good and brave will own thee ;
Where'er thou art each heart shall feel
   That manhood's stamp is on thee.

And if stern duties are assign'd,
   And no one near to love thee,
Be resolute, nor look behind—
   The heav'ns are still above thee.
And follow Truth where'er she leads,
   Tho' bigots frown upon thee ;
Thy witnesses will be thy deeds,
   If manhood's stamp is on thee.

Let hope around thy heart entwine,
   Thy loadstars love and duty,
And ev'ry word and deed of thine
   Will be embalm'd in beauty ;
And goodness from her highest throne
   Will blessings pour upon thee ;
Thee Nature's soul will love to own,
   If manhood's stamp is on thee.

MAMMON'S IN THE WAY

HE who attempts to right a wrong,
    E'en in our boasted day,
Has need of faith and courage strong,
    For Mammon's in the way.
If with a wrong that's liv'd too long
    You hint what you would do,
Be sure at once both knave and dunce
    Will quickly turn on you.

The gods will try you in their schools,
    With deep humiliations;
Let loose upon you all the fools
    With horrid imprecations.
Some old iniquity ye'd crush
    That's been a plague for years?
Lo! what a host of hornets rush
    All buzzing 'bout your ears.

And Ignorance and Impudence
    Will in their wrath belie you,
All flunkeydom in anger come
    To insult and defy you;
For if you would do any good
    To our benighted race,
Look out for base ingratitude,
    For insult and disgrace.

You're told reform will ruin bring;
    And every precious dunce
Will prove that 't is a wicked thing
    To cease to steal at once;
The devil is to go ahead,
    The world in bondage stay,
Because some coward is in dread
    That Mammon's in the way.

But he's the hero who can brook
  The insult and disgrace,
And yet has nerve enough to look
  The devil in the face.
Be sure you're right, and then proceed
  To sweep the pest away ;
Those very men that now condemn
  Will in the end hurrah.

Time on his route wheels things about :
  Those that to-day look grim
Will be the very first to shout
  " We aye believ'd in him !"
Then never faint in self-restraint,
  Nor yield to passion's heat ;
'Tis not by roughs and fisticuffs
  That Mammon can be beat.

THE OLD RUIN GREY

THE old ruin grey is mould'ring away,
  And the rank weeds around it entwine ;
The old wind alone knew the glory now gone,
  And it sighs o'er the long-perish'd line.

No one in the dell its hist'ry can tell,
  Or why it was built on the steep ;
They only do know it was great long ago,
  And now it's a pen for the sheep.

The fox makes its lair, and the fowls of the air
  Seek shelter within its old halls ;
The bluebell so meek, the foxglove and leek,
  Are peeping from out its old walls.

6

Thus old Ruin drear claims all that we rear,
  When but a few years hurry by ;
Man's proud works are vain, but the old hills remain
  O'erhung by the great silent sky.

It is little we know but the old tale of woe :
  " We are the poor sons of a day,
And the baubles we chase, yea, our name and our race,
  Must pass like the old ruin grey."

———

THE SEER

THE temple was a ruin'd heap,
  With moss and weeds o'ergrown,
And there the old Seer stood entranced
  Beside the altar-stone :
Time's broken hour-glass at his feet
  In mould'ring fragments lay ;
And tombstones, whose old epitaphs
  Were eaten all away.

He pointed ever and anon,
  His gaze was fixt on air,
While thus he talk'd to shadowy forms,
  Which seem'd to hover there :

" On, on to regions lone
  The generations go ;
They march along with mingled song
  Of hope, of joy, and woe.
On, on to regions lone,
  For there's no tarrying here ;
The hoary past is join'd at last
  By all it held so dear.

" There, there, on edge of air,
  How fleetly do they pass:
I see them all, both great and small,
  Like pictures in a glass.
Long, long this crowding, motley throng,
  Of ev'ry creed and clime,
With hopes and fears, with smiles and tears,
  Of the young and the olden time.

" Round, round on this earthly mound,
  The laden ages reel ;
No creak, no sound, but ceaseless round,
  To Time's eternal wheel.

" There, there, with long grey hair,
  Are patriarchs of our race ;
A glory crowns each hoary head,
  They pass with solemn pace.
Earth, earth, there were men of worth
  When they were in their prime,
With less of art, and more of heart,
  A happy golden time.

" There, there are ladies fair
  That danced in lordly hall ;
The minstrel grey, whose simple lay
  Brought joy to one and all.
Fleet, fleet were your fairy feet,
  And ye knew the joy of tears,
While minstrels wove old tales of love,
  With hopes, with doubts, with fears.

" There, there, still fresh and fair,
  I see them march along,
The bowmen good, the gay green wood,
  I hear their jocund song.
See, see how the green oak tree
  With shouts they circle in ;
The stakes are set, the champions met,
  The merry games begin.

" Round, round, on their earthly mound,
    The laden ages reel ;
No creak, no sound, to the ceaseless round
    Of Time's eternal wheel.

" Hold, hold, ye were barons bold !
    I know by the garb ye wear,
The lofty head, the stately tread,
    The trusty blades ye bear.
Where, where are your mansions rare,
    The lordly halls ye built ?
Gone, gone, how little known
    Your glory or your guilt !

" Away, away, as to the fray,
    Ah ! there they madly rush,
And in their path of woe and wrath
    A dark, deep, purple blush !
Here, here, like Autumn sear,
    The hoary palmers come ;
Their tales they tell of what befell—
    The list'ning groups are dumb.

" Round, round, on their earthly mound,
    The laden ages reel ;
No creak, no sound, but ceaseless round,
    To Time's eternal wheel.

" Lo ! lo ! what splendid woe
    Your rearward host reveals !
It marches there with its golden care,
    To sounds of steam and wheels.
Speed ! speed ! oh, Guile and Greed
    Are sure a monstrous birth ;
Let wan Despair weave fabrics rare,
    And Gold be God on earth.

" Oh ! oh ! what sigh of woe
    Is from its bosom roll'd !

What faces peer, like winter drear,
  'Mid the glitter and the gold !
Still, still, 'mid all this ill
  Are souls with touch sublime,
Who nobly strive to keep alive
  Hopes of a happier time.

" Round, round, on their earthly mound,
  The laden ages reel ;
No creak, no sound, but ceaseless round,
  To Time's eternal wheel.

" Hail ! hail ! ye shadows pale,
  For ye were men of thought ;
The crags were steep, the mines were deep,
  Where painfully ye wrought.
Speak ! speak ! why your secret keep ?
  This mystery I'd know—
Say, what is breath, and life, and death ?
  And whither do we go ?

" Still, still, no word ye will
  Vouchsafe my greedy ear ;
The crags are steep, the mines are deep,
  And I can only hear :
" ' On, on, ev'ry age has gone,
  Its burden on its back;
Despite our will, for good or ill,
  We follow in the track.'

" Round, round, on their earthly mound,
  The laden ages reel ;
No creak, no sound, but ceaseless round,
  To Time's eternal wheel."

THE RUINED TEMPLE

FAR in a deep secluded dell,
    Where very few intrude,
Where bubbled still the " Holy Well,"
    A ruin'd temple stood ;
Used by the shepherds as a fold
    When winter seals the sod,
Yet countless generations old
    Went there to worship God.

How wearily the wind did moan,
    'Mid ruin and decay,
Where still a sacrificial stone
    Among the rank grass lay.
The holy fire had all burnt out—
    The vital spirit gone—
And all was darkness, dread, and doubt,
    Around that altar-stone.

I sat me down in that lone place
    To muse upon decay,
The changed conditions of our race,
    And faith that's growing grey ;
Weird faces seem'd to flit around
    That ancient altar-stone ;
There might be nought, yet still methought
    I was not all alone.

And in my contemplations deep
    Hours must have pass'd away—
Perchance there fell on me that sleep
    Of which the poets say :
" We drink from out a magic cup,
    From fountains never dry,
Which lock the outer senses up,
    And ope the inner eye.

" Tho' memory may not retain
   A shred of what we see,
What was is written on the brain,
   What is, and what shall be."
And in my reverie or dream
   For light, more light, I cried :
" O truth, with thy celestial beam
   Let me be satisfied."

The beacon-lights, our guides of yore,
   Have one by one gone out,
And left us, 'mid the tempest's roar,
   In darkness and in doubt.
Tho' stubbornly men close their eyes,
   Yet still 'tis plain to me
The anchors old have lost their hold—
   We're drifting out to sea.

No wonder with foreboding fears
   We hear the tempests roar ;
The pole-star of a thousand years
   Can be our guide no more.
What millions of the good and brave
   For light, more light, have cried ;
Yet went down to the yawning grave
   With souls unsatisfied.

I'd pray'd for light both day and night,
   But I'd had no reply ;
Then did I hear close by mine ear
   A whisper'd " Look on high."
And instantly a holy light
   Through all the ruin shone,
But so bewild'ring to my sight
   I scarce could look thereon.

The tide of time seem'd backward roll'd,
   Once more 'twas holy ground,
And all the generations old
   Were gathering around.

At length with trembling joy and awe,
　Upon the altar-stone,
A heav'nly being there I saw,
　Majestic and alone.

And from a lyre in his right hand
　Leapt forth a thrilling strain,
While still anon the spectral band
　Join'd in the deep refrain.
Oh, could I, could I but rehearse
　The song as it was sung,
The song of Truth—immortal Youth,
　Forever fair and young—

A song that in my heart doth live
　With its majestic roll,
To you, alas ! I can but give
　Its sense, but not its soul.
But tho' that song I cannot sing,
　Yet, like a mighty river,
Its tones shall roll, and heave my soul,
　Forever and forever.

————

CHANGE

OH ! how wondrous are the changes
　　Ev'ry day and hour we see;
Things to make us ask in wonder,
　" Wherefore ? and oh ! what are we ? "
Things more wonderful than fiction,
　Or the poet's wildest dreams;
Things enough to make us question
　If this world is what it seems.
　　　Change! change ! surpassing strange !
　　　What fearful changes come!
　　　The stars grow pale; the prophets fail;
　　　The oracles are dumb.

Men come forth in strength rejoicing,
   And they bid the world take note
Of their comings and their goings,
   And the mighty works they've wrought.
Deeming that they are immortal,
   How like gods they walk the scene !
Time looks in, and, lo! they vanish—
   Rubb'd out as they ne'er had been.
      Change ! change ! surpassing strange !
       Their pomp, their pow'r, their glory
      Are all forgot—were, and are not—
      The old eternal story.

Nations spring as 'twere from nothing,
   And are mighty in their day—
But to wax and wane and crumble,
   And to nothing pass away.
Great Niag'ra, with his thunders,
   And the tow'ring Alps sublime,
Earth and sky, with all their wonders,
   Bubbles on the flood of time.
      Change ! change ! surpassing strange !
      Can such things surely be
      All hurried past, and lost at last
      In Death's eternal sea ?

Oh ! Creation's but a vision
   Seen by the reflective eye ;
But a panoramic pageant
   Pictured on the evening sky.
There is nothing here abiding—
   There is nothing what it seems ;
Airy all, and unsubstantial,
   Wavering in a world of dreams.
      Change ! change ! surpassing strange
      Is time's eternal chorus !
      We hardly know the road we go,
      Or the heavens bending o'er us.

Shall we give ourselves to Pleasure ?
  Drench with wine the brow of Care ?
That were but the coward's refuge,
  But a hiding from Despair.
Shall we wed us to Ambition,
  Led by Fame's alluring round ?
Ah ! alas, their promis'd glories
  End but in a grassy mound.
      Change ! change ! surpassing strange !
       There's nothing sure but sorrow ;
     And we must bear our load of care,
      Nor dream of rest to-morrow.

Shall we put our trust in knowledge
  Men have garner'd here below ?
Ah, the fruit of all their labor's
  But a heritage of woe.
Oh ! the sum of all the knowledge
  Garner'd underneath the sky
Is that we are born to suffer,
  Is that we are born to die.
      Change ! change ! surpassing strange !
      Our knowledge comes to naught,
     And we are fool'd and over-ruled
      By ev'rything we sought.

POVERTY'S COMPENSATIONS

OH, I am poor, and very poor !
  But why should that distress me
Since Hope, through all my poverty,
  So often comes to bless me ?
If I have not the joys of wealth,
  Neither have I its troubles,
And all its outward shows I deem
  But empty, idle bubbles.

A full purse and an empty heart
   Quite often go together;
What signifies our fields' increase,
   If our affections wither?
I never was so hard beset
   As to forget the features
Of Justice, Mercy, and the rights
   Of my poor fellow-creatures.

There is no station in this life
   That is from ills exempted;
Virtue would be an easy thing
   If we were never tempted.
Then why should I afflict myself
   About mere worldly riches,
If I've a heart that's free from care,
   And ne'er with envy itches?

The blue vault's hanging o'er my head,
   Green mother-earth is under;
Above, beneath, on ev'ry side,
   A mystic world of wonder.
Have I not in this threadbare coat,
   And in this lowly station,
Caught tones of rapture trembling from
   The harp of God's creation?

Can gold assist me to divine
   The actual from the seeming,
Or from each mighty symbol wrest
   Its everlasting meaning?
No; but for me the mighty dead
   Unfold their living pages,
And I'm permitted to commune
   With prophets, bards, and sages.

Yes, they, the really truly great,
   Kings, potentates, excelling—
Without the pride and pomp of state—
   Come to my lonely dwelling;

And their society has been,
  'Mid sorrow and privation,
A joy which took away the sting
  From woe and tribulation.

Then let us with a thankful heart
  Accept what God has given,
And with the cank'ring love of gold
  Ne'er may our hearts be riven ;
And let us try to love our God
  And our poor fellow-mortals :
Such is the wealth acceptable
  At highest heaven's portals.

———

DAVID, KING OF ISRAEL

COME and look upon this picture,
    Thoughtfully those features scan :
There he sits, the bard of Scripture,
  Not·an angel, but a man.

In his hand the harp that often
  Thrill'd the shepherd in the glen,
And has now supreme dominion
  O'er the hearts and souls of men—

That same harp which charm'd the demon
  In the darken'd soul of Saul ;
And has sooth'd the troubled spirit
  In the bosoms of us all.

Human nature's strength and weakness,
  Hope and heart-break, smiles and sighs,
With a world of joy and sorrows,
  Mirror'd in those deep-blue eyes,

'Tis a face that, somehow, tells us
　　God hath made us all the same—
Of one blood and heart and nature,
　　Diff'ring but in creed and name ;

All that has been done or suffer'd,
　　All that has been thought or said,
Israel's strength, and Israel's weakness,
　　Summ'd up in that lordly head.

Yet, curtail'd, hemm'd in, and hamper'd,
　　He could only utter part
Of the great infinite message
　　That was lying on his heart.

'Tis a face supremely human,
　　Brother to us, ev'ry one,
For he oft had sinn'd and sorrow'd,
　　Just as you and I have done.

Yet it tells a tale of struggle,
　　Of a life-long, weary fight,
Wrestling foemen all the day long,
　　Wrestling phantoms all the night.

Fighting with infatuation,
　　Scorning the degrading chain ;
Hating sin, yet rushing to it,
　　Rising, but to fall again ;

Always sinning and repenting,
　　Promising to sin no more ;
Now resisting, now consenting,
　　Human to the very core.

Now he deems himself forsaken,
　　Feels that he's a poor outcast ;
But tho' he should die despairing,
　　He will struggle to the last.

He has felt the soul's upbraiding :
  Conscience oft has made him smart
Until pain, and shame, and sorrow,
  Leapt in lyrics from his heart.

From the depth of his affliction
  To Jehovah he would cry,
Who, in love and pity, rais'd him,
  Set him on a rock on high ;

Gave him gleams of worlds transcendent,
  Brighter than the rainbow's rim ;
Touch'd his harpstrings with the raptures
  Of the soaring seraphim.

Like the mighty waters gushing
  Is the torrent of his song,
Sweeping onward, roaring, rushing,
  Bearing human hearts along.

Then, anon, like gentle dew-drops,
  Falls that spirit, sweet, serene,
Peaceful as the quiet waters,
  Fragrant as the glades of green.

Then what living gusts of gladness
  Startle the enraptured ear,
While a tone of human sadness
  Makes the sweetest strain more dear.

Not the rapt and holy prophet,
  Not the pure in ev'ry part,
But the sinning, sorrowing creature,
  Was the " man of God's own heart."

His was love surpassing tender,
  And God gave it as a sign,
That the heart that is most human
  Is the heart that's most divine.

UP, AND BE A HERO

UP! my friend, be bold and true,
　　There is noble work to do ;
Hear the voice which calls on you,
　　"Up, and be a hero ! "

What tho' fate has fixed thy lot
To the lowly russet cot,
Tho' you are not worth a gro't,
　　Thou may'st be a hero !

High heroic deeds are done,
Many a battle's lost or won,
Without either sword or gun—
　　Up, and be a hero !

Not to gain a worldly height,
Not for sensual delight,
But for very love of right,
　　Up, and be a hero !

Follow not the worldling's creed ;
Be an honest man, indeed ;
God will help you in your need,
　　Only be a hero !

There is seed which must be sown,
Mighty truths to be made known,
Tyrannies to be o'erthrown,
　　Up, and be a hero !

There are hatreds and suspicions,
There are social inquisitions,
Worse than ancient superstitions ;
　　Strike them like a hero !

In the mighty fields of thought
There are battles to be fought,
Revolutions to be wrought ;
    Up, and be a hero !

Bloodless battles to be gain'd,
Spirits to be disenchain'd,
Holy heights to be attain'd ;
    Up, and be a hero !

To the noble soul alone
Nature's mystic art is shown ;
God will make his secrets known
    Only to the hero !

If thou only art but true,
What may not thy spirit do ?
All is possible to you,
    Only be a hero !

ROBERT BURNS

HAIL to thee, King of Scottish song !
    With all thy faults we love thee,
Nor would we set up modern saints,
    For all their cant, above thee.
There hangs a grandeur and a gloom
    Around thy wondrous story,
As of the sun eclips'd at noon,
    'Mid all his beams of glory.

A marvel and a mystery !
    A king set on a throne
To guide the people's steps aright,
    Yet could not guide his own.

A marvel and a mystery!
A strange, a wondrous birth—
Since Israel's king there has not been
Thy likeness upon earth.

For thou wert the ordain'd of Heaven,
Thy mission's high and holy;
To thee the noble work was given
To lift the poor and lowly.
Thy words are living, soulful things,
Around the world they're ringing;
Hope's smiles they bear, and ev'rywhere
Set weary hearts a-singing.

Untutor'd child of Nature wild,
With instincts always true,
Oh, when I'm weary of the saints
I turn with joy to you!
The bigot and the blockhead still
Are at thy mem'ry railing,
Because thou wert a son of Eve,
And had a human failing.

A benefactor of our race,
Yet on the face they strike thee,
And, like the Pharisee of old,
Thank God they are not like thee.
Well, let them rave above thy grave,
Thou canst not hear their railings;
We take thee to our heart of hearts,
With all thy faults and failings.

For they were human at the worst—
True hearts can but deplore them—
The faults from which great virtues spring,
We throw a mantle o'er them.
And loving souls in ev'ry place
Still hail thee as a brother;
Like thee, thou glory of our race,
Where shall we find another?

7

GLADSTONE

HAIL to the man, of men the chief!
   He tow'rs above our time,
Like to the peak of Teneriffe,
   Majestic and sublime.

He treads the path the great have trod,
   Retains, 'mid jeer and ban,
Faith in the Fatherhood of God,
   And Brotherhood of man;

One of the high, heroic souls,
   That God appoints to find
A pathway for humanity
   Upon the march of mind;

That put traditions to the rout—
   What need they be afraid of?—
And turn our idols inside out,
   And show what rags they're made of;

Whose thoughts are falling down in showers
   The masses to awaken,
And principalities and powers
   To their foundations shaken.

He hears within the high command,
   With his own soul engages,
From tyrannies to rid the land,
   And right the wrongs of ages.

This "Grand Old Man" has blown a blast
   That's waken'd in affright
The spectres grim, the things aghast,
   Of Chaos and old Night.

Tho' oft a mark set up for hate,
  He's at this very hour
Great Britain's only truly great
  And stanchest living power.

The heights of fame oft he did scale,
  Unspoil'd by adulation ;
Now, unalarm'd, he walks the vale
  Of deep humiliation.

What matters who may bless or ban,
  By whom he's lov'd or hated?
To-day, to be the "Grand Old Man,"
  To-morrow, execrated.

But even in the darkest day
  He flinches not from duty,
And aye's attended by a ray
  Of truth and moral beauty—

A beauty, an urbanity,
  In all that he doth teach ;
The music of humanity
  Is ringing in his speech ;

Above the pall that hangs o'er all
  We hear his ringing voice ;
Above the din of selfish sin
  We hear him and rejoice.

Such men are never vanquish'd, tho'
  From pow'r they may be hurl'd ;
Their motto still, as on they go,
  Is "Truth against the World."

THE SPIRITS OF THE PRESS

HARK ! 'tis the spirit of the age
    That doth in song address
The heroes of the printed page—
    The spirits of the press.
Great change is coming over things—
    All hail the dawning light !—
A voice throughout creation rings :
    "Arise ! defend the right ! "

Then at the summons, oh, awake !
    And may ye live to see
Ontario, beside her lake,
    Great, glorious, and free.
Tho' in our time the love of gold
    Has grown a social blight,
Yet be ye neither bought nor sold ;
    Still dare defend the right !

In moral manhood be ye strong,
    For ye were meant to be
The friends of right, the foes of wrong,
    The guards of liberty.
In freedom put your hope and trust,
    Nor envy social height ;
Heroic souls upon a crust
    Have battled for the right.

And no great deed was ever done
    In mere pursuit of pelf ;
The greatest battles ever won
    Are triumphs over self.
But caste and creed now spread abroad
    A mildew and a blight,
And even in the name of God
    They trample on the right.

He's but a knave—a party slave,
    To aims heroic blind—
Who'll meanly strive to keep alive
    The hatreds of mankind.
Leave party slurs to hungry curs
    Who're paid to bark and bite !
Trade not for gain your heart and brain,
    But dare defend the right.

Intolerance is want of sense ;
    Judge people by their deeds ;
For Mammon's tools make wise men fools
    By playing on the creeds.
And what tho' mere time-servers sneer,
    Do ye the truth indite ;
And ev'ry good man must revere
    Defenders of the right.

——— *178682*

MEMORIES OF SCOTTISH LITERATURE

An Address to a Scottish Thistle in Canada

L OV'D badge o' my country ! ah, why art thou here,
    Sae far frae auld Scotland, the land we love dear ?
This is not our country, we're exiled afar
Frae mighty Benlomond and "dark Lochnagar."

.   .   .   .   .   .

What a host o' Scots worthies, the living and dead,
Hae crown'd wi' a glory our auld mother's head !
With sigh sympathetic they ilk ane appear,—
I see them, lov'd thistle, approaching us here.

Tho' I ne'er saw them living, I ken them richt weel ;
I know the lov'd face o' each leal-hearted chiel.
Ha ! there the great minstrel, the soul of the north,
Wi' smiles, tears, and tempests, stalks sturdily forth.

.   .   .   .

He brings Highland Mary in beauty array'd ;
Death steals not that beauty, it never can fade :
Like a vision of Eden, thro' good and thro' ill,
That form and those features hae haunted me still.

　　　·　　　　·　　　　·　　　　·　　　　·

But see, belov'd thistle, e'en Scott in his joy
Comes on wi' his troopers and dauntless Rob Roy ;
There, steel-cover'd barons and grim kilted thanes,
And tall plaided chieftains, and royal grand-dames ;

There, kings wi' their sceptres, blue gowns wi' their bags,
High pedigreed damsels, and auld wither'd hags ;
And puir hunted " Hill-folk " wha fought not in vain—
There, Burley and Bothwell are at it again !

There, " Meg," as she tauld the auld laird o' her wrangs,
Or pour'd out her sair heart in wizard-like sangs ;
There, tiltings and tourneys, and forays and feuds,
And robbers and reavers amang the green woods ;

And fox hunts and fule hunts, and tyrants and slaves,
And half hearts and haill hearts, and true men and knaves ;
A won'erfu' world, that was a' dead and gane
Till the wizard o' Waverley woke it again.

Another, lov'd thistle, to whom thou wert dear
As licht to the lovely, approaches us here :
'Tis canty auld Christopher,[4] blithest o' a',
Weel kent by his ain ringing, laughing hurrah.

Here comes a small band with a deep-measured tread,
Stern, earnest as that which at Loudon Hill bled :
Its leader stalks forth wi' a sad, solemn smile—
The shade o' the mighty immortal, Carlyle.

And yonder, great Chalmers, the second John Knox,
Whose sentences fell like Fate's terrible shocks :
His large human nature no nation could bind ;
His love o' the thistle was love o' mankind.

The vision has vanish'd, the shadows are gane,
And yet, belov'd thistle, we arena alane :
These are the immortals that never depart ;
They fade to grey visions, but dwell in the heart.

THE HALLS OF HOLYROOD

The *British Workman* offered a prize, open to the world, for a
suitable poem.   This one obtained the prize.

HERE let me sit, as ev'ning falls,
    In sad and solemn mood,
Among the now deserted halls
    Of ancient Holyrood ;
To think how human pow'r and pride
    Must sink into decay,
Or, like the bubbles on the tide,
    Pass, pass away.

No more the joyous crowd resorts
    To see the archers good
Draw bow within the ringing courts
    Of merry Holyrood.
Ah, where's that high and haughty race
    That here so long held sway ?
And where the phantoms they would chase ?
    Pass'd, pass'd away !

And where the monks and friars grey,
    That oft in jovial mood
Would revel till the break of day
    In merry Holyrood ?
The flagons deep are emptied out,
    The revelers all away ;
They come not to renew the bout—
    Where, where are they ?

And where the plaided chieftains bold
 That round their monarch stood?
And where the damsels that of old
 Made merry Holyrood?
And where that fair, ill-fated Queen?
 And where the minstrels grey
That made those vaulted arches ring?
 Where, where are they?

Tho' mould'ring are the minstrels' bones,
 Their thoughts have time withstood;
They live in snatches of old songs
 Of ancient Holyrood.
For thrones and dynasties depart,
 And diadems decay,
But these old gushings of the heart
 Pass not away.

———

CARTHA AGAIN[5]

OH! why did I leave thee?   Oh! why did I part
 Frae thee, lovely Cartha, thou stream o' my heart?
Oh, why did I leave thee and wander awa'
Frae the hame o' my childhood, Gleniffer an' a'?
The thocht o' thee aye mak's my bosom o'erflow
Wi' a langing that nane save the weary can know;
And a' fortune's favors are empty and vain,
If I'm ne'er to return to thee, Cartha, again.

When I hear the soft tone o' my ain Lowlan' tongue,
Ance mair I'm a laddie the gowans among:
I see thee still winding thy green valley through,
And the Highland hills tow'ring afar in the blue;
But the lintie, the lav'rock, the blackbird, an' a',
Aye singing, "My laddie, ye've lang been awa'."
Nae wonder I sit down an' mak' my sad mane—
Am I ne'er to behold thee, sweet Cartha, again?

When I hear the sweet lilt o' some auld Scottish sang,
Oh, how my bluid leaps as it coorses alang !
The thumps o' my heart gar my bosom a' stoun',
My heid it grows dizzy and rins roun' an' roun' ;
My very heartstrings tug as gin they would crack,
And burst a' the bonds that are keepin' me back ;
But then comes the thocht, here I'm doom'd to remain,
And ne'er to return to thee, Cartha, again !

In a grave o' the forest, when life's journey's past,
Unknown and unhonor'd they'll lay me at last ;
Abune me nae bluebell nor gowan shall wave,
And nae robin come to sing over my grave.
But, surely ! ah, surely ! the love o' this heart
For thee, lovely Cartha, can never depart ;
But free frae a' sorrow, a' sadness and pain,
My spirit shall haunt thee, dear Cartha, again.

WEE MARY

FAREWEEL ! my wee lassie, fareweel !
    Thou wert dear as the licht to mine e'e ;
And nae ane can ken what I feel
    In this sorrowfu' pairting wi' thee.

A welcome wee stranger thou wert,
    But thou didstna bide lang wi' us here ;
Thou cam'st like the Spring to my hert,
    But thou left it all wither'd and sear.

Ah, Mary ! I canna but weep,
    For my hert was sae wrapt up in thee ;
Fain I'd think thou art gane but to sleep,
    And thou'lt toddle again to my knee.

Oh, thou wert a beam of delicht
    Which sae lighted my hert up wi' joy !

I ne'er thocht thou'dst fade frae my sicht,
  Or death would e'er come to destroy.

And the bairns are a' greetin' for thee,
  For they've lost their wee playmate an' a' ;
And Johnnie creeps up on my knee,
  And he asks if ye'll aye be awa'.

What tho' to forget thee I try,
  And the words that thou lispit to me ;
The streams o' this hert winna dry,
  And a' nature's the mem'ry o' thee.

The sweet little birdies that sing,
  And the innocent lamb on the lea,
The bonnie wee flow'rs o' the spring,
  Are a' but faint shadows o' thee.

I WINNA GAE HAME

I WINNA gae back to my youthfu' haunts,
  For they are nae langer fair :
The spoiler has been in the glades sae green,
  And sad are the changes there ;
The plow has been to the very brink
  O' the lovely Locher fa',
And beauty has fled wi' the auld yew tree
  And bonnie wee birds awa'.

Young Spring aye cam' the earliest there,
  Alang wi' her dear cuckoo,
And gentle Autumn linger'd lang
  Wi' her lanely cusha-doo ;
And peace aye nestled in ilka nook
  O' the bonnie gowany glen,
For it's always Sabbath amang the flowers,
  Awa' frae the haunts of men.

How oft hae I paused in thae green retreats
  O' the hare and the foggy-bee,[6]
While the lintie lilted to his love
  In the budding hawthorn tree ;
And the yorlin sang on the whinny-knowe
  In the cheery morn o' spring,
And the laverock drapt frae the cloud at e'en
  To fauld up her weary wing ;

And the mavis sang in the thorny brake,
  And the blackbird on the tree,
And the lintwhite told his tale o' love
  Far down in the gowany lea ;
And the moss and the cress and the crawflow'rs crept
  Sae close to the crystal spring,
And the water cam' wi' a lauchin' loup,
  And awa' like a livin' thing.

And it sang its way through the green retreats,
  In a voice sae sweet and clear,
That the rowan listen'd on the rock,
  And the hazel lean'd to hear ;
And the water-lilies rais'd their heads,
  And the bells in clusters blue,
And the primrose cam' wi' her modest face
  A' wet wi' the balmy dew ;

And the hoary hawthorn hung its head,
  As lapped in a blissfu' dream,
While the honeysuckle strain'd to catch
  The murmurs o' that stream ;
And the buttercup and the cowslip pale
  To the green, green margin drew ;
And the gowan cam' and brocht wi' her
  The bonnie wee violet blue.

And the red, red rose and the eglantine
  And the stately foxglove came,
And mony an' mony a sweet wee flow'r
  That has died without a name ;

While the burnie brattl'd down the brae
  In her ain blithe merry din,
And leapt the rock in a cloud o' spray,
  And roar'd in the boiling linn.

And churn'd hersel' into silver white,
  Into bubbles green and gay,
And rumbled roun' in a wild delight
  'Neath the rainbow's varied ray ;
And swirl'd and sank and rose to the brim,
  Like the snawdrift on the lea,
And then in bells o' the rainbow's rim
  She sang away to the sea.

But the trees are fell'd, and the birds are gane,
  And the banks are lane and bare,
And wearily now she drags her lane
  With the heavy sough o' care ;
And fond lovers there shall meet nae mair,
  In the lang, lang simmer's e'en,
To pledge their vows 'neath the spreading boughs
  O' the birk and the beech sae green.

But I'll no gae back !   I'll no gae back !
  For my heart is sick and sair,
And I couldna' bide to see the wreck
  O' a place sae sweet and fair.
It wad wauken me, it wad wauken me
  Frae boyhood's blissfu' dream,
And ye ne'er could be sae dear to me,
  My ain beloved stream.

SCOTLAND REVISITED

WHEN mony a year had come and gane,
 And I'd grown auld and hoary;
And mony a hope had proven vain
 As mony a dream o' glory;
Then backward to my childhood's hame
 A weary langing sent me:
I found my native vale the same,
 But very few that kent me.

There were the hills my childhood saw—
 They look'd as if they knew me;
And well they might, when far awa',
 Oh, how they did pursue me!
And there amang the broomy braes
 I often paused and ponder'd
Upon the joys o' ither days,
 Then on again I wander'd.

At length our cot appear'd in view,—
 Oh, weel I kent the biggin'!
There was the same o'erhanging yew,
 And thack upon the riggin';
And there the winnock in the en',
 Wi' woodbine train'd sae trimly,
And up abune the cosie den
 Reek swirlin' frae the chimley.[7]

Oh, how my heart leap'd at the sight,
 Till I could hardly bear it!
I felt as if I would gang gyte,
 For I was maist deleerit.

And hurrying to that sacred spot,
    Ilk thump cam' quick and quicker.
I tried to pray, but in my throat
    The words grew thick and thicker.

To hide my tears I vainly strove,
    For nae ane came to meet me;
Nae mither wi' her look o' love,
    Nae sister, came to greet me.
For gane were they, both ane and a'—
    The dear hearts that I cherish'd—
Gane like the flow'rs o' spring awa',
    Or like a vision perish'd.

This was the spot o' a' maist dear,
    Where a' my dreams were centred;
And yet, wi' trembling and wi' fear,
    Beneath that roof I enter'd.
There was the place my faither sat
    Beside my mither, spinnin',
An' a' the bairns wi' merry chat
    In joy around her rinnin'.

There, in the cottage o' my birth,
    The same rooftree above me,
I stood a wand'rer on the earth,
    Wi' na ane left to love me.
Oh! I had often stood alone
    On mony a post o' danger,
And never wept till standing on
    My native hearth—a stranger.

I sought the auld kirkyard alane,
    Where a' the lov'd are sleeping,
And only the memorial stane
    Its watch abune them keeping.
It only said that they were dead,
    Once here, but now departed;
A' gane! a' gane! to their lang hame,
    The true, the gentle-hearted.

" Oh, life," I cried, " is all a woe,
    A journey lang and dreary,
If there's nae hame to which we go,
    Nae heart-hame for the weary ! "
I clear'd the weeds frae aff the stane,
    And lang I sat and ponder'd
Upon the days forever gane,
    Then weary on I wander'd.

RECOLLECTIONS OF CLYDESDALE

An Epistle to David Boyle, Esq., Toronto, Archæologist of
Ontario ; a native of Greenock

MY dear frien', Dawvit, hae ye time
    To hearken to a screed o' rime?
And tho' it mayna be sublime—
    A gem o' art—
It comes, as frae youth's joyous clime,
    Fresh frae the heart.

For e'en tho' I am auld and grey,
And frae the dear lan' far away,
The mem'ry o' youth's joyous May
    Still back doth bring
A touch o' blithe vitality
    Upon its wing.

Oh, what a worl' we liev'd in then !
O' cataract and brae and ben,
O' ruin'd keep in lonely glen,
    And castle hoar,
Faur frae the busy haunts of men,
    Brooding on yore.

A joyous youth was thine an' mine,
When Nature a' seem'd to combine
Aroon' oor path her floo'rs to twine,
      Wi' hope and joy—
The very memory divine
      Naught can destroy.

For then the earth seem'd fresh and new,
And bore such floo'rs o' glorious hue,
Fresh wi' the dawn and Eden dew
      Upon them a'—
Ah! then we dreamt not of, nor knew,
      Aught o' the Fa'.

Spring cam' in shoo'rs o' gowans white,
And hawthorn blossoms burst to sight,
And buttercups—what a delight!
      Wi' eglantine,
Still hingin' in the gowden light
      O' dear lang syne.

We kent whaur the " witch thummels " grew,
And bonnie bells in clusters blue,
Primroses—cells o' siller dew,
      Ha' blossoms white—
The sod wi' gowans peeping through
      In sheer delight!

And whaur the wee bit runnels leap,
And velvet mosses lo'e to creep,
And violets, wi' their dyes sae deep
      And modest mien,
That jouk, and jink, or bashfu' peep
      Frae nooks o' green.

I never hear a ballant rime,
But still, as in youth's joyous prime,
Despite o' distance, change and time,
      Wi' prood delight,
The Highlan' hills, tow'ring sublime,
      Stan' full in sight.

There, as o' auld, ance mair they stand,
The great auld hills—a giant band
And pride o' a' the mountain land—
    Benlomond hoar
Amid them tow'ring great and grand,
    King o' the core.

We've wander'd by the same clear rills,
Look'd on wi' awe the same auld hills,
We've music drank—the kind that fills
    The Scottish heart—
And oh, what patriotic thrills
    It did impart!

(Does not green Yarrow's vale belong
Unto the soul of past'ral song?
Affections—an undying throng—
    She gathers round,
And holds her court the groves among,
    Wi' lilies crown'd.

Is not the Scottish atmosphere
Laden wi' a' the heart holds dear?
Things that ne'er wither nor grow sear,
    Nor pass away,
But in oor hearts still re-appear,
    Free frae decay.)

Tho' we've baith wander'd faur and wide,
We ne'er forget the youthfu' pride
We cherish'd for our ain dear Clyde
    In boyhood's dream,
Ah, there it shall forever glide,
    Sole sovran stream!

Tho' frae Balclutha[8] faur away,
Yet frae the grand auld ruins grey
We still hear Ossian's mournfu' lay,
    'Mid grass sae tall,
And see the thistle 'mid decay
    Wave on the wall.
8

Tho' fortune holds me in despite,
I bless her first we saw the light
In a romantic land, made bright
 Wi' tale and sang,
O' heroes that focht for the right,
 Nor brook'd the wrang.

Land o' romance and mountain hoar,
Wi' sang and legend running o'er,
A land thy children a' adore !
 Tho' forced to part,
Still sacred art thou in the core
 O' ilka heart.

A land that tyranny did spurn,
The land o' Bruce and Bannockburn,
Oh ! let not Mammon e'er inurn
 Thy spirit free :
Still may the light o' freedom burn,
 Dear land, in thee.

———

P.S.—Juist here the muse got aff the track,
And as I canna ca' her back,
Nae langer noo my brains I'll rack,
 Sae let her gang,—
In hope we sune may hae a crack,
 I quat my sang.

AWAKENED MEMORIES OF SCOTIA

An Epistle to James L. Morrison, Esq., Toronto, on his
return from a visit to Scotland.

I SCARCE need say thou'rt welcome back
  Frae owre the lang and weary track.
Wi' you I lang to hae a crack
    'Bout Scotia dear,
And questions by the yard, in fac',
    I want to speer.

I only wish alang wi' thee
I could hae ventured owre the sea ;
For to oor ain green glens, ah, me !
    Glens o' the west,
Back like a bird I fain would flee
    To my young nest.

When winter shrouds this land in gloom,
And leafless trees talk o' the tomb,
Just speak o' Scotland's bonnie broom,
    And instantly
I'm wafted to youth's world o' bloom
    Ayont the sea.

What joy wi' thee to rove amang
Her hills and dales, renown'd in sang,
And battle-fields, where peasants sprang
    At freedom's ca',
And nobly dared against the wrang
    To stand or fa'.

There Freedom built her lofty dome,
And, issuing from her mountain home,
Defied the legions of old Rome
    Her to enslave—
No, not another step to come,
    Save o'er her grave.

To gaze upon the hills ance mair—
Auld monarchs on their thrones of air
Still tow'ring in their glory there
          As, when a boy,
I gazed on them wi' rapture rare—
          Oh, what a joy !

And let us wander where we may,
They never leave us by the way ;
At ev'ry hamely word or lay
          Hoo they will start,
Wrapt in their misty mantles grey,
          Up in the heart !

Oh, but to lie the broom amang,
And listen to the lav'rock's sang,
In notes, a perfect living thrang,
          A' rainin' doon ;
Back ev'ry foot I'd gladly gang
          To hear the soun'.

And then the wee grey lintie coy—
Ah, wasna he a living joy ?
While ev'ry wee enraptured boy,
          W' heart ahush,
Drank in the strains without alloy
          Frae tree or bush.

And wi' what joy ance mair to stray
By Crookston Castle's[9] ruins grey,
Where hapless Mary view'd the fray
          Upon Langside,[9]
Which doom'd her to a lot o' wae,
          Sair, sair to bide.

That ruin auld did ye explore ?
Still sitting in Glengarnock[10] hoar,
From which owre to Largs'[11] rugged shore,
          To face the Dane,
Hardyknute[10] in days of yore
          March'd not in vain.

Ah, weel I mind, 'mang youthfu' pranks,
I travel'd far wi' weary shanks
To gaze on Bothwell's bonnie banks,
        Still blooming fair,
And where the Covenanting ranks
        Were worsted sair.

Then a' the glories o' romance
Did ev'ry sight and sound enhance;
How grand upon her steeds to prance!
        Oh, why did truth
Awake us frae that glorious trance
        Wi' facts forsooth?

Dear early world! ere selfish sin,
Wi' a' her weary strife and din,
And wrath-wudhags, had enter'd in
        Wi' cursed greed,
To a' her heavenly glories blin'
        As bats, indeed.

Still looking back, wi' fond regret,
Youth's radiant world we ne'er forget:
The sun o' young Romance, tho' set,
        Still throws a haze
O' never dying glories yet
        Amang the braes.

But now I maun draw to an end,
In hopes to see you soon, my friend,
And ae haill day at least to spend,
        And hear o' a'
The things that roun' my heart still blend,
        Tho' far awa'.

AULD TOWSER

YE'RE turnin' auld, Towser, yer teeth nearly gane;
  Ye hae a sair fecht, noo, to hirple yer lane.
Ah, times are sair alter'd wi' baith you and me,
And the days we hae seen we can never mair see.

I'm wearin' doun wi' ye, for time, weel I ken,
Is no a bit partial to dugs or to men.
It canna be lang till we baith get the ca',
And gane and forgotten by ane and by a'.

But ye were aye faithfu', whatever befell;
I whiles wisht that I could say that o' mysel.
And after yer battles ye never kept spite—
Yer bark it was always far waur than yer bite.

And there was baith wisdom and wit in yer face;
Yer stature proclaim'd ye the lord o' yer race;
Baith big, black and gaucy, a great towsy tyke
As e'er chased a beggar, or lapt owre a dyke.

Ye never took up wi' the wild fechtin' dugs;
Yer freens were a' social, wi' lang-hingin' lugs;
And they wad fraise wi' ye, and beek in the sun,
Or start up a squirrel and chase it for fun.

Great was yer contempt for the wee barkin' dugs,
The things that hunt rattons wi' noses like pugs:
When they wad rush oot and bark up in yer face,
Ye seem'd to think shame they belang'd to yer race.

I whiles thocht ye had a bit spite at the pigs—
What fun ye had chasin' them doun the lea rigs!
Yer bark was mair wicked—it was na the same
That ye gied to the beggars or ocht aboot hame.

Ye never were beat whaur the fechtin' was fair
But that time ye tackled the big raucle bear :
Yon wrestlin' and huggin' was oot o' yer line,
But ye left him some tokens I'm thinkin' he'll min'.

And ye were a dour, an angry, big tyke,
That time ye attackit the bees in their byke :
They buzz'd oot upon ye like deils frae the pit,
And ye raged like a creature deprived o' its wit.

And vainly ye barkit, and vainly wad bite,
For still they stuck to ye like venom and spite ;
And still they came bummin' like legions o' deils,
So, like a wise dug, then ye took to yer heels.

Ye paid for yer knowledge (as I've often done),
And then had the wisdom sic comp'ny to shun ;
But I was not always made wiser by pain,
For I've sinn'd and I've suffer'd again and again.

When folk cam' for siller, and I'd nane to gie,
Ye kent them, auld Towser, as weel juist as me :
Ye show'd them yer tusks ; ye were ill, ill to please—
Oh, the limbs o' the law are faur waur than the bees !

How you and wee Charlie wad fondle and play,
And jink roun' the hay-rack the haill simmer day—
He lauchin', ye barkin', at fun o' yer ain,
Till I've wisht that I were a laddie again.

And when that he murmur'd, and sicken'd, and died,
No, naething could tempt ye to leave his bedside ;
Ye sat sad and silent, by nicht and by day,
And, oh, how ye moan'd when they bore him away !

Tho' some folk may ca' ye a useless auld brute,
Yet, Towser, as lang's ye can hirple aboot,
I'll share my bite wi' ye, and then when ye dee,
We'll bury ye under the auld apple tree.

And the bairns will greet for ye when they see ye laid,
All silent in death, 'neath its bonnie green shade ;
And aft by the ingle they'll ca' ye to min',
And dear thochts shall aye roun' yer memory twine.

———

THE OLD WAR HORSE

TIME'S writing his changes on a' things, we see,
    And sad anes his writing, auld War Horse, on thee.
How changed from the great steed that chafed at the rein,
With the fleet foot thy rider could hardly restrain !
Thy legs are sair shaughled ; thy hoof, once of fire,
Must drag Jamie's cart through the mud and the mire.
Ah, where's thy proud neck which could scarce brook the
    rein ?
Thy red " rolling eye," and thy great arching mane ?
Thy mane is a' tautit, and scrimpit's thy tail,
And the gall on thy shouther is no like to hale ;
Thy hide is a' runkled, scarce covering thy banes,
And ye dreadfully hobble amang the whun stanes.
My heart's wae to see ye lash'd hard when ye reest,
And hear ye ca'd nocht but an " auld stubborn beast."

And yet, my auld horse, thou hast lashed that same tail,
While dashing in madness amid the death-hail,
And neigh'd 'mid the thunder, the shout, and the smoke,
As ye swept like a thunderbolt to the death-shock.[18]

Thae feet, noo sae spavint, hae aft chased the flying,
And trampled to pieces the deid and the dying ;
And often I see ye ahobblin' come,
At the tout o' the town crier's auld crackit drum,
And cock up yer ears, and erect yer auld mane,
As if ye wad ae be a War Horse again.
This warrin' and fechtin', wi' a' its parade,
" Oh, the meal-pock's the end o't," as auld Eddie said ;

But lessons are lost baith on horses and men,
And why should I blame you when they winna men'?
Hear fallen Napoleon, in sorrow and woe,
Asking Marshal MacDonald, "Oh! where shall I go?"

And even 'mang horses there's great ups and downs,
As weel's amang monarchs wi' kingdoms and crowns.
Thy case is a hard ane, and I'm wae for thee,
Yet the auld sodger aften mair wretched we see.
Thy master is cruel, nor pities thy pains,
For he has a wife and some wee raggit weans :
To keep them in crowdie, and shed them frae snaw,
And buy him a drappy, taks a' ye can draw.

And yet my auld horse, tho' thou'rt sunk in distress,
I doutna ye whiles may hae glimpses o' bliss :
When Jamie's heart's ope'd wi' the blithe barley bree,
A great rip o' oats he will whiles fling to thee,
Saying, "Come up, *Auld Sodger*, and never say puir—
The auld cursin' Colonel ne'er offert ye mair.
Ye don't think I stole ye, man ! that ugly scar
Ye got at Corunna wad tell wha's ye were."

I doutna, auld horse, but ye try to explain
Your strange alter'd lot in some way o' your ain ;
And tho' ye had reason to guide ye, I fear
'Twad be but sma' comfort ye'd fin' with it here ;
For its puir consolation to man or to horse
To ken that there's thousands as bad, if no' worse ;
For mony proud humans, my auld horse, like thee,
Hae to come down the hill, and draw coals ere they dee.

THE LIFE OF MAN

IN youth our hearts are lighted up
   With hope's illusive beam,
And earth is an enchanted place,
   And life a joyous dream.
There's beauty underneath our feet,
   There's music in the air,
There's glory in the heav'ns above,
   And rapture ev'rywhere.

But time steals on with noiseless tread,
   And tho' the happy boy
May feel a change, 'tis still to him
   A change from joy to joy.
Then hopes of high achievements start,
   Of great things to be done,
Of undiscovered treasures vast,
   Of battles to be won.

The heroes of the present time
   Are paltry, poor, and small,—
He will go forth, and he shall be
   A hero worth them all.
An' then what dreams of happiness,
   What visions rich and rare,
What gorgeous tow'rs and palaces,
   What castles in the air !

Then love alights upon his heart,
   With all its joys and pains,
His pulse beats madly, and the blood
   Is leaping in his veins.
He sees but those love-beaming eyes,
   And all beside is dim,—
Oh, she is fair and beautiful !
   Worth all the world to him.

He drinks the strange, mysterious draught,
   The sweeter for its pain,
And reels delirious with a joy
   He'll never taste again ;
For time steals on, and oh, how soon
   His visions melt away,
And clouds are low'ring in the sky
   While yet 'tis noon of day.

And see, he sadly sits at last
   With children on his knee,
As he would fain forget his cares
   Amid their mirth and glee ;
But he must up, for he's the staff
   On which the helpless lean,
And he will make their lot in life
   More blest than his has been.

And there he sadly struggles on,
   A heavy-laden hack ;
And oh, how often in the midst
   He's tempted to look back !
But time must not be wasted thus
   In unavailing tears,
Or want will catch him in the vale,
   The gloomy vale of years.

Now, see him bending on his staff ;
   His locks are thin and grey,
And life, that was so bright before,
   Is all a winter's day ;
And this new generation's ways
   He cannot understand :
So changed is all, he feels himself
   A stranger in the land.

And o'er the happy days of youth
   He will, he must repine,
For oh, the world is nothing now
   To what it was lang syne ;

And mem'ry's lamp is waning fast,
　With faint and fitful gleam—
The living and the dead are mixed
　Like phantoms in a dream.

But childhood's streams are laughing yet,
　Its fields are fresh and fair,
And now, a little boy again,
　The old man wanders there ;
Then, feeble as a little child
　Upon its mother's breast,
Resignedly he leans his head
　And sinks into his rest.

THE SCOT

Inscribed to James Bain, Esq., of the Public Library, Toronto

A REAL enthusiast indeed,
　His heart is apt to tak' the lead,
And get the better o' his heid,
　E'en for a myth,
To ruin beyond a' remede
　Rins a' his pith.

Doure as a door-nail he's indeed ;
To change an item o' his creed
Is tearing hair oot o' his heid—
　He winna budge,
Nor will he either drive or lead,
　But juist cry, " Fudge ! "

And in his bonnet apt is he
To hae some great big bummin' bee,
Such as his Stuart loyalty,
　When hope is past ;
Despite their stupid tyranny,
　True to the last.

He's gi'en owre muckle to debating,
And theologic speculating :
On far-aff things he's contemplating,
 Lost in a trance ;
To be, as said, watching, waiting
 For the main chance.

If he'd but had the cunning gift,
And kent the way to dodge and shift,
And could tak' time to weigh and sift
 Ilk pile o' grain,
Nae ither nation 'neath the lift
 Could haud its ain.

A man o' passionate convictions,
A mixture queer o' contradictions,
Big, liberal, but wi' stern restrictions ;
 Yet, at the core,
To a' mankind wi' benedictions
 His heart rins o'er.

Instead o' cunning, deep and slee,
An open-hearted chiel is he ;
Excepting aye the barley bree,
 His fauts are few,
And they are such as, a' may see,
 Springs frae what's true.

And wheresoe'er ye find the Scot,
In stately ha' or humble cot,
Be sure the company he's got
 Are spirits rare—
Ye may depend that Burns and Scott
 Are always there.

A lover o' the minstrel's lays,
The very breath o' early days,
And young love's hived-up memories
 Nae hert can tine,
Are concentrated in his phrase
 O' auld lang syne.

Nae dearer thing the Muse has brought
Frae out the wondrous realms of thought,
Wi' a' the heart's young feelings fraught,
        Than that one line,
That to its heart the world has caught
        And ca'd divine.

'Twas by nae deep and double art,
Nae mere pretence or playing a part,
That ever could to being start
        That living line;
'Twas from a loving people's heart
        Leapt " auld lang syne ! "

————

WATCHERS ARE WEARY

THE watchers are weary, the Night's long and dreary,
        The stars of our boyhood are faded and dim ;
Our faith's sorely shaken, yet not all forsaken
        We sit 'mid the shadows all ghastly and grim.
History's pages are red with the ages
        Of crime and of madness they blush to reveal—
Ages of chivalry, darkness and devilry,
        E'en from ourselves we are fain to conceal.

With what avidity human stupidity,
        In its unreason, unconscious of shame,
Sent heroes 'mid laughter into the hereafter,
        From prisons and gibbets, on couches of flame.
But, 'mid our amazement at human debasement,
        What hosts of dead heroes start up to our view,
Who here did inherit the very Christ-spirit,
        And came our weak faith in frail man to renew.

For, sick of despising and mere theorizing,
        Men ask to be shown them the God-ordain'd way;
Few so love the evil that straight to the devil
        They run for the sake of his pitiful pay.

All good men are grieving o'er mutual deceiving,
  And long for the better way, could it be shown ;
Men lack not affection, they need but direction
  How ancient iniquities may be outgrown.

Aweary of warring, of hatred and jarring,
  Of mutual unhappiness, heart-break and strife,
Of old superstitions, and mutual suspicions,
  That poison the springs of the river of Life ;
While Nature each morning the earth is adorning,
  And spreading beneath us her carpet of green,
Despite the mad revels of gods, men, and devils,
  Some traces of Eden are still to be seen.

Despite degradations, still men's aspirations
  Are ever ascending to regions on high ;
Love's flow'rs are still growing, men's hearts still o'er-
    flowing
  With streams of affection that never run dry :
Still o'er the babe sleeping the mother is keeping
  Her watch, never weary the winter night long ;
Still fondly believing the tale Hope is weaving,
  She twines it in joy with her lullaby song.

Sisters and brothers, how prejudice smothers
  The love that is in you and keeps you apart !
This mutual concealing and all double-dealing
  By Love and by Knowledge uproot from the heart.
For, oh, in the darkness dense, big hearts in ignorance
  E'en with Love's yearning are often at strife :
O dear human kindness, how oft in mere blindness
  Thou add'st to the burdens and sorrows of life !

Tho' strong are temptations and false educations
  To lead e'en the upright from virtue astray,
Despite of all evil, we know that the devil
  Will surely be vanquish'd by Love in the fray.
For, sick of despising and mere theorizing,
  Men ask to be shown them the God-ordain'd way;
Few so love the evil that straight to the devil
  They run for the sake of his pitiful pay.

POESY

ALL hail! beloved Poesy,
　　For dearer thou hast been to me
Than light, and life, and liberty—
　　　Soul of each scene—
Yea, the very breath of life,
In the tumult and the strife,
　　　To me thou'st been.

In life's lowest vale thou found'st me,
Threw thy mystic spells around me,
And with cords of love thou bound'st me,
　　　As magic strains
Fill'd my soul with aspirations,
While thy mystic incantations
　　　Cours'd thro' my veins.

Currents of celestial fire
All my spirit did inspire ;
Ever mounting higher, higher,
　　　My spirit reeled.
Yet I stood, amid the hum,
Silent, stupefied, and dumb—
　　　My lips were sealed.

Dumb and baffled in the breach,
Vainly did I try to reach
After the celestial speech ;
　　　Thou took'st my hand,
Then thou led'st me to the mountains,
To the torrents and the fountains
　　　Of fatherland.

Then first I felt those awful thrills,
In presence of the soul that fills
The great old everlasting hills—
　　　That soul sublime,

Forever calmly looking through
The great o'erhanging arch of blue
    Down upon time.

Then ev'ry rock and mountain hoar
Were rooted in my bosom's core,
And ocean, moaning evermore,
    Gave me no rest.
Oh ! how those mighty waves did roll,
And heave, and struggle in my soul
    To be expressed.

And often, in thine awful moods,
We scaled those star-lit altitudes,
Where Wonder everlasting broods
    'Mong worlds sublime—
The planets in their mystic dance—
Astronomy, thou grand romance
    Of space and time !

On your wonders unexpounded,
On your magnitudes unbounded,
Gazing, till I grew confounded,
    I could only sigh ;
For my intellectual pride
Ruthlessly thou dash'd aside,
    For what was I ?

Upon that sea without a coast,
My own identity was lost,
All stagger'd by a powerful host,
    Baffled, amazed ;
And yet, tho' humbled by the view,
My spirit wide and wider grew
    The more I gazed.

Then Poesy, thou brought'st to view
Forms ever beautiful and new,
Fairer than aught that ever grew
    Upon this earth ;

9

Seen only by the inner eye,
Alighting from yon mystic sky,
          Their place of birth.

What draughts of glory then were mine !
All Nature was indeed divine,
I worshiped at no other shrine ;
          But yet I sought
After something that I wanted,
By a strange idea haunted,
          Hardly knowing what.

Then thou did'st touch thy sacred lyre,
And all my spirit didst inspire,
Even with a holy fire,
          Diviner strains—
And saidst, " Behold the true sublime ;
Look past the fleeting things of time
          To higher planes.

" Worship Nature as of yore ;
Love her in thy bosom's core ;
But believe there's something more
          To souls is given.
Be assur'd that Moral Duty
Is the highest form of beauty
          In earth or heaven."

PAISLEY ABBEY

ALL hail! ye ruins hoary,
   Still stately in decay,
Who rear'd your aisles and sacred piles,
   The michty in their day?
We boast of our achievement,
   We slight the ages mirk,
Nor seem to ken the michty men
   Wha built this " Haly Kirk."

And here the mitr'd abbots,
   In this their Abbey grey,
For ages reign'd, till glory waned,
   The sceptre passed away.
But still their spirits linger,
   And love to hover round
('Mid all the change that seems so strange)
   On consecrated ground.

The bell is toll'd by spectres;
   At hour o' midnicht deep,
Deid-lichts are seen the chinks between
   Where monks are lang asleep.
Just as the moon is waning,
   And waefu' east wind raves,
The abbots a' they heed the ca',
   And start frae lowly graves.

Their ruin'd altar they surround,
   In robes of white array,
For souls unblest, that canna rest,
   To kneel, to weep, and pray.
Still, as she hears the summons,
   'Mid depth of Gothic gloom,
The good old Queen,[12] with regal mien,
   Comes frae her altar tomb,

To plead for the hapless friar,
  Condemn'd thro' countless years
To weep and wail in the "Sounding Aisle,"
  And echo all he hears.
Then comes a kingly shadow[13]—
  The founder of this place—
And there he stands, with lifted hands
  Mute pleading for his race.

He looks to good Saint Mirin ;[14]
  The Saint can only say,
" They ne'er shall reign the land again,
  They've past like smoke away."
Then slowly there arises
  A dim, a shadowy train
Of souls that still have taint of ill,
  The mark of earthly stain.

And there are chiefs and barons—
  Each heads an ancient line—
With sword and dirk that did their work
  In bluidy days lang syne.
And these two wrathfu' spirits[15]
  Like dark clouds hover near,
Montgomery stern and proud Glencairn,
  Who kept the land in fear

With their Maxwells and Skermorlies,
  Wha did ilk other kill.
After a life of feud and strife
  They look defiance still ;
Or they avoid each other,
  With mutual hate and dread ;
Or meet and pass, as in a glass,
  But not a word is said.

And there's the great Lord Sempill,
  Wi' the bard of old Belltrees,[16]
And Ranter Rab and Piper Hab,
  Wi' buckles at their knees.

The twa auld droothie croonies,
    They canna yet forget
The song and tale—to beef and ale
    They look wi' lang regret.

There are the youthful gallants,
    The lords and ladies gay,
That still must moan in confines lone,
    Till sins are wash'd away.
A rueful band—there they stand,
    Yet scarcely seem to know
How licht o' love frae God above
    Should be their deadly foe.

They wha destroy'd the Abbeys,
    And heap'd the priests wi' scorn,
Ah, they've had time to rue their crime,
    They ne'er see licht o' morn.
And there comes Jenny Geddes,[17]
    And sits in lang deid sark
On creepie stool—the puir auld fool
    Sighs o'er that Sabbath's wark.

For a' wha grace resisted
    A waefu' weird maun dree;
They come to plead that Kirk may speed
    The hour that sets them free;
While a' wee bairns unchristen'd
    Come to the font to greet,—
The cock does craw, then one and a'
    Pass aff on noiseless feet.

MY MOTHER

THE clock in yonder old church tower
   Proclaims the midnight deep—
The time when spirits have the power
   To comfort those that weep.
Dear mother ! from thy realm above
   Canst thou my sorrow see ?
And still with all a mother's love
   Dost thou look down on me,
While here I'm sitting all alone,
   Recounting scenes of yore,
Till with thine ev'ry look and tone
   My heart is running o'er ?

No form is present to mine eye,
   No voice salutes mine ear,
And yet I feel, I know not why,
   Thy spirit's hov'ring near.
This world became a solitude
   The day we had to part,
For I've met none to whom I could
   Unbosom all my heart.
It seems to me that thou, of all
   On whom the sun did shine,
Hadst least of bitterness and gall,
   And most of the divine.

Nor have I felt such holy joy
   As when, beside thy knee,
A reverential little boy,
   I said my prayers to thee.
And, oh, how oft in doubt and dread,
   On life's tempestuous sea,
I've wish'd I could but lay my head
   Once more upon thy knee,

And tell thee, as of old, I ween,
  How life had gone with me,
And how the things that should have been
  Were destin'd not to be.

Oft as the length'ning shadows steal,
  At evening's holy hour,
Then, mother, as of old, I feel
  Thy presence and thy power.
I feel thee in the Sabbath calm,
  As if above me bending,
I hear thee in the simple psalm
  That's to the heav'ns ascending.
A voice that speaks, " Let troubles cease ! "
  Marshals the way before me ;
The very canopy of peace
  Seems always hanging o'er thee.

Tho' in this lower world of sense,
  By some mysterious law,
Thou seem'dst to live in realms immense
  Of wonder, love and awe,
It was a strange, mysterious thing,
  And not unmix'd with fear ;
Thy very presence seem'd to bring
  The spirit-world more near.
'Twas joy to watch how high the wave
  Of love and hope could rise,
By looking in thy solemn, grave,
  And meditative eyes.

The deeds that elevate our kind,
  Through strength of Love or Will,
They seem'd in passing through thy mind
  To grow more lovely still.
When some heroic deed was done,
  Despite the world's disgrace,
Some battle for the right was won
  Which honor'd all our race ;

The words which then fell from thy tongue
  Seem'd born of inspiration—
That with a veil of glory hung
  O'er visible creation—

And taught my op'ning soul to feel
  The power of moral beauty,
To walk erect, and never steal
  Along the line of duty.
How strange thou wert condemned by God
  To travel all alone,
Along a rough and weary road,
  For errors not thine own!
Ah! nature all grew dark and drear
  When death seal'd up thine eye,
And when I whispered in thine ear
  And thou gav'st no reply.

And as I knelt beside thy bier
  Sad were the tears I shed;
Something within distinct and clear
  Said, "*Mother is not dead!*"
Which roused me up, as from a sleep,
  From scales my vision freeing,
And gave my soul a wider sweep,
  And broaden'd out my being.
Oh, how my spirit did expand—
  Things never felt before,
And thoughts magnificent and grand,
  Rush'd in at every pore,

And gave to me a perfect faith,
  A blest assurance sweet,
That there's a region after death,
  Where we again shall meet;
That, when upon this earthly plain
  My weary race is run,
That we indeed shall meet again
  As mother and as son!

For 'twould not be a heav'n to thee,
   Nor yet to me, dear mother,
If there that we could never see
   And recognize each other.

Oh, tell me ! shall we have once more
   Those simple, homelike feelings
We cherish'd so in days of yore,
   With all their heart revealings ?
Oh, tell me ! are the dear ones there
   To whom love's tie has bound us ?
And are they still as dear and fair,
   And aye to be around us ?
Recounting over all the past,
   The bud, the bloom, the blight,
Together dwelling all at last
   By rivers of delight.

A VISION OF BOYHOOD

OH, MEM'RY, that ne'er lets the weary alane,
  Keeps aye looking back owre the lang dreary main,
    And, ere I'm aware,
    I'm a laddie aince mair,
Wi' a' my wee cronies aroon' me again ;
Aince mair in the land o' the bonnie green braes,
O' lovely May mornings, and lang simmer days,
    O' gowans in show'rs,
    O' lang gloamin' hours,
A land that's a' ringin' wi' legends and lays.

And oh, what a happy wee fairy-like train
As e'er ranged the woodland, the mountain, and plain !
    We're aff to the nooks
    Whaur the wee burnie jouks,
Mair happy than gin a' the earth were oor ain.

The cuckoo's proclaiming the presence o' spring,
The blackbird and mavis gar a' the woods ring,
    And green linties hover,
    And peesweep and plover,
And lav'rocks are singing aloft on the wing.

And there, in the sough o' the lane waterfa',
Among the fresh blooms o' the rowan and haw,
    The auld Castle hoary
    Is telling its story
O' lords and o' leddies a' deid an awa'.
We ken the wee wildings o' every hue
That glint 'mang the green grass a' wat wi' the dew ;
    The forms and the features
    O' a' the glad creatures
That, free and unfetter'd, range a' the wood through.

And oh ! wi' what joyous and wild beating breasts
We speel the old yews wi' the cusha-doos' nests,
    Or by the fauld dyke
    Hunt the foggy-bee's[6] byke,
And never a' day lang a moment at rest.
We follow the Spring as she scatters her flow'rs,
And oh, hoo we revel amang the green bow'rs !
    Nae care to pursue us,
    The pines nodding to us,
While Time joins the dance o' the loud laughing hours,

Till the shadows o' gloaming aroun' us deep fa',
And the corncraik's beginnin' to set up her ca',
    And the wee bleery mole
    Peepeth oot o' his hole,
And the bat on the wing comes to warn us awa'.
Then hameward we gang 'neath the licht o' the mune,
Wha sails in her ocean o' azure abune,
    Wi' sic love in her face
    As if earth were a place
Where there never could be ony sorrow or sin.[18]

Then we liv'd nearer heaven's great arching o' blue ;
Then surely the heart was mair tender and true,
For we crush down the heart
Wi' our science and art,
Till we lose a' the glory o' life's early dew.
But I wake frae my vision, and oh ! it seems vain,
For ah, tho' we crossed owre the wearifu' main,
Yet we couldna bring back
Our young herts owre the track,
Sae we'll never return to our Eden again.

Songs and Ballads

LOVE

WE'VE muckle to vex us, puir sons o' a day,
    As we journey along on life's wearisome way;
But what are the troubles with which we're opprest,
If Love makes our bosoms the hame o' her rest?

When Love lichts the hearthstane, there's joy in the ha',
And a sunshiny streak on ilk bosom doth fa';
The ingle blinks blither, affections increase,
And the cottage she turns to a palace o' peace.

Where'er she approaches, a' hearts grow sincere;
She hallows a' places, mak's ev'ry spot dear;
For wrang canna breathe in the sphere o' her grace,
And Hate flees awa' frae the licht o' her face.

Where'er she approaches, where'er she appears,
She cames aye to comfort, and wipe awa' tears,
To help on the weary and lichten their load,
And cheer them wi' sangs on their wearisome road.

And oh! her sweet smile mak's the fallen look up;
It's the ae blessed drap in their sorrowfu' cup!
Then oh, may this heart o' mine never grow sear!
Oh, let me, 'bune a' things, hold somebody dear!

Oh! leave me but Love—tho' my roof-tree should fa',
And the gear we hae gather'd tak' wings an' awa'—
For riches and grandeur, the things we haud dear,
Are a' but vain glories that die wi' us here;
But Love burns the brichter wi' our parting breath,
And lichts us at last thro' the valley o' Death.

CURLING SONG

WHEN winter comes to bridge the flood,
 And, wi' his icy nieve,
Tak's kings and cobblers by the beard,
 And never asks their leave;
Yet while sae bauld, wi' grip sae cauld,
 He fills their hearts wi' gloom,
He brings a joy without alloy
 To Brothers o' the Broom.

CHORUS:

While daidlin' bodies stay at hame,
 On ills o' life to think,
Be ours to join the merry game
 Upon the roaring rink.

Then loud or lowne may winter blaw!
 For in the jovial strife
Its sic a pleasure but to draw
 The very breath o' life:
When, like a flood, the bounding blood
 Through eve'ry vein doth pour;
And keen and tense is ev'ry sense
 Amid the wild uproar.

For in this strife the wave o' life
 Mounts to its heichest score,
And vim and nerve that never swerve
 A' mankind maun adore.
And there and then a' meet as men,
 To prove what each is worth,
And this the test that sets at rest
 The cant o' blood and birth.

For on the rink distinctions sink,
 An' caste aside is laid;
Whate'er ye be, the stane and tee
 Will test what stuff ye're made.

And this the school to teach the fool
 That only nerve and mind,
Acquirèd skill, and stubborn will,
 Are leaders o' mankind.

Not in the arm resides the charm—
 Your very weight o' brain,
Your ev'ry bit o' native grit,
 Maun a' gang wi' the stane :
Wha crowns the tee shall bear the gree,
 As in life's roaring game.

And, while contending for the prize,
 Tho' rous'd as by the fife,
Somehow we learn to humanize
 The battles o' oor life.
Sae time that's pass'd upon the rink,
 In this delightful strife,
I often think the happy blink,
 Worth a' the rest o' life.

————

MARY WHITE

D'YE mind o' the lang simmer days, Mary White?
 When we gaed to the auld Partick braes, Mary White?
When I pu'd the wild gowans, and wi' a delight
I hung them in strings roun' thy neck, Mary White?

D'ye mind o' the song ye wad raise, Mary White?
The song o' sweet "Ballenden Braes," Mary White?
It couldna be love, but a nameless delight,
That thrill'd through my bosom, my dear Mary White !

Oh, that was a sweet happy time, Mary White !
I've ne'er had sic moments since syne, Mary White,
When we look'd at ilk ither, and lauch'd wi' delight,
And hardly kent what for, my dear Mary White.

We were young, we were happy, indeed, Mary White ;
Noo care's strewn grey hairs on my heid, Mary White ;
My hopes hae a' wither'd, wi' sorrowfu' blight,
But still ye are green in my heart, Mary White !

And oh ! do ye e'er think on me, Mary White ?
Ah ! then does the tear blin' your e'e, Mary White ?
Or hae *ye* lang waked frae that spell o' delight,
And left *me* still dreaming, my dear Mary White ?

It's often I think upon thee, Mary White,
For still thou art dear unto me, Mary White ;
For a' that this heart has e'er kent o' delight
Was nocht to the moments wi' thee, Mary White !

Do ye 'mang the leevin' still bide, Mary White ?
Or hae ye cross'd owre the dark tide, Mary White ?
Oh ! how this auld heart wad yet loup wi' delight
Could I again see thee,[19] my dear Mary White !

SING ME THAT SANG AGAIN[20]

SING me that sang again !
Oh, how that lang refrain
Thrills thro' my heart till my bosom o'erflows,
And gars my ears tingle,
For those voices mingle
That lang hae been hush'd in a voiceless repose.
Sing me that sang again !
Oh, that beloved strain
Fills a' my heart and brain wi' a joy rare ;
Wafts me across the main,
By the burnside again,
Laps me in peace 'mang the gowans ance mair.

.   .   .   .   .   .

With heart still unwounded,
With faith still unbounded,
Entranced with the beauty o' earth and o' sky,
No dark clouds are brooding,
No dark doubts intruding,
That knock at the heart for an instant reply.
Sing me that sang again!
Blest be that magic strain!
One other draught o' its spirit divine
Pour into mem'ry's cup!
Oh, let me drain it up,
Yea, with the rapturous joy o' lang syne!

MY LOVE IS LIKE THE LILY FLOWER

MY love is like the lily flower
    That blooms upon the lea:
I wadna gie ae blink o' her
    For a' the maids I see.

Her voice is like the bonnie bird's,
    That warbles 'mang the bow'rs,
Her breath is like the hawthorn when
    It's wat wi' morning show'rs.

And frae the gowans o' the glen
    She's caught her modest grace,
And a' the blushes o' the rose
    Hae leapt into her face.

She bears aboot, I kenna hoo,
    The joy o' simmer days,
The voice o' streams, and happy dreams
    Amang the broomy braes.

And when the bonnie lassie smiles
   Sae sweetly upon me,
Nae human tongue can ever tell
   The heav'n that's in her e'e.

And a' the lee-lang simmer day
   I'm in a dream divine,
And aye I wauken but to wish,
   Oh, were the lassie mine !

WE'RE A' JOHN TAMSON'S BAIRNS[21]

OH, come and listen to my sang,
   Nae matter wha ye be,
For there's a human sympathy
   That sings to you and me ;
For, as some kindly soul has said,
   All underneath the starns,
Despite o' country, clime, or creed,
   Are a' John Tamson's bairns.

The higher that we clim' the tree,
   Mair sweert are we to fa',
And spite o' fortune's heights and houghs,
   Death equal-equals a' ;
And a' the great and mighty anes,
   Wha slumber 'neath the cairns,
They ne'er forgot, tho' e'er so great,
   We're a' John Tamson's bairns.

Earth's heroes spring frae high and low,
   There's beauty in ilk place,
There's nae monopoly o' worth
   Among the human race ;
And genius ne'er was o' a class,
   But, like the moon and starns,
She sheds her kindly smile alike
   On a' John Tamson's bairns.

10

There's nae monopoly o' pride—
  For a' wi' Adam fell—
I've seen a joskin sae transform'd
  He scarcely kent himsel';
The langer that the wise man lives,
  The mair he sees an' learns,
And aye the deeper care he takes
  Owre a' John Tamson's bairns.

There's some distinction, ne'er a doubt,
  'Tween Jock and Maister John,
And yet its maistly in the dress,
  When ev'rything is known ;
Where'er ye meet him, rich or poor,
  The man o' sense and harns,
By moral worth he measures a'
  Puir auld John Tamson's bairns.

There's ne'er been country yet, nor kin,
  But has some feeble flaw,
Yet he's the likest God abune[18]
  Wha loves them ane and a' ;
And after a' that's come and gane,
  What human heart but yearns
To meet at last in light and love
  Wi' a' John Tamson's bairns.

———

THE FLOWER OF THE SPEED

WHERE Speed rolls her waters
    Away to the lake,
Through quiet green pastures
  And tangled wood brake,
There lives a fair maiden
  A monarch might own—
Yea, pledge for her favor
  His kingdom and throne.

No cold marble beauty,
  No angel, is she,
But a sweet mortal maiden
  Who smiles upon me ;
A creature of feeling,
  Of hopes and of fears,
Of joys and of sorrows,
  Of smiles and of tears.

She's fair as the gowan
  On Scotia's green braes,
And dear as the mem'ry
  Of youth's happy days ;
Her ringlets are golden,
  Her eyes are of blue,
And the heart in her bosom
  Is tender and true.

That bosom's a fountain
  Of thoughts pure and fair,
And the streams of affection
  Are aye gushing there ;
And long by that fountain
  May peace spread her wing,
And joy love to linger,
  And hope love to sing.

And ne'er may she sigh
  O'er affection's decay,
O'er loves and o'er friendships
  All faded away ;
And faithful the lover
  Who's favor'd to lead
To love's holy altar
  The Flow'r of the Speed.

JEANIE'S LOCKS

OH, Jeanie's locks are like the gowd,
    Her bosom's like the snaw,
Her breath is sweet as ev'nin' winds
    That 'mang the vi'lets blaw.
Her e'e is o' the lift abune,
    A clear unclouded blue,
An' no' a streak o' sorrow yet
    Upon her bonnie broo.

Like blebs o' dew the blessèd words
    Aye frae her lips do fa';
She's artless as the little birds
    That warble in the shaw.
Oh, had I but an humble cot
    By Cartha's murm'rin' stream,
Hoo happy then wad be my lot
    Were she that cottage queen !

Her faither is a belted knight,
    An' I'm a widow's son ;
Was ever love in sic a plight,
    Or sic a leddy won ?
I daurna tell the love I feel,
    And ne'er a hope I've got ;
But tho' she never can be mine,
    Still happy be her lot.

An' oh, may sorrow never light
    Upon a thing sae fair,
An' never, never falsehood blight,
    Nor cloud her broo wi' care ;
But, like the little bird that sings
    The lee-lang simmer day,
With joyous dreams o' happy things
    May *her* life glide away.

JOHNNY KEEPS THE KEY O'T

MY heart is lock'd against the lads,
    'Tis little they can see o't :
They needna try its springs to pry,
    For Johnny keeps the key o't.

Auld Aunty says I scorn them a',
    And that I shouldna do it,
For lang ere I'm as auld as she
    I chance may sairly rue it.

She says I'm but a pridefu' queen,
    My heart, I've nane to gie o't ;
But little, little does she ken
    That Johnny keeps the key o't.

For scorn I'm surely no to blame,
    There's nane o' them will dee o't,
But oh, ma hert is no ma ain,
    For Johnny keeps the key o't !

CHARLOCH BAN *

THE simmer birds are gane,
    They're awa' across the main,
Yet I rove the woods alane,
    Charloch Ban, Charloch Ban.

You promis'd you'd be here
When the autumn leaf grew sear,
And ah ! noo its winter drear,
    Charloch Ban, Charloch Ban.

----

* Fair Charlie.

Oh, then you were my pride,
By the green Glengarry side,
When you said I'd be your bride,
  Charloch Ban, Charloch Ban.

You were a joy to see,
Wi' your tartans waving free,
And the garters at your knee,
  Charloch Ban, Charloch Ban.

Joy hung o'er wood and lake,
And the blackbird in the brake
Sang far sweeter for your sake,
  Charloch Ban, Charloch Ban.

Joy had a sweeter beam,
There was gladness in the stream,
Oh, the world was all a dream,
  Charloch Ban, Charloch Ban.

Now winds are howling loud
Through the weary winter's cloud,
And the world is all a shroud,
  Charloch Ban, Charloch Ban.

LOVELY ALICE

AWAKE, lovely Alice, the dawn's on the hill,
 The voice of the mavis is heard by the rill,
The blackbird is singing his song in the brake,
And the green woods are ringing—awake, love, awake !

The wild rose is blushing, the pea is in bloom,
The zephyr is brushing the long yellow broom ;
But thy voice is far sweeter than bird's on the tree,
And joy is far deeper, sweet Alice, with thee.

The voice of lone Locher comes mellow and sweet,
But sweeter to me were the fa' o' thy feet;
The hawthorn is hoary and rich with perfume,
But thou art the glory of nature in bloom.

Far deeper the joy, love, would nature impart
Were I but the lord of thine innocent heart;
And 'neath fortune's malice I ne'er would repine,
Wert thou, lovely Alice, oh, wert thou but mine!

————

WOMAN

THERE'S nothing that the world calls fame,
    There's no reward or prize,
That can be gain'd like what is rain'd
    From lovely woman's eyes.
The snob may cry, " Oh, fie! Oh, fie!"
    And threaten hard to stone us :
" A fig!" we cry, while Jeanie's eye
    Is raining blessings on us.

Ambition strong doth prompt man on,
    But woman's nobler far :
She's prompted on by Love alone,
    Her spirit's guiding star.
How oft our hearts would fail within,
    When hard the path of duty,
But 'mid the din we're roused to win
    The smiles of Love and Beauty.

Their smiles can make the weakest strong,
    The coward can inspire,
And even fill the poet's song
    With pure celestial fire ;

Oft we'd have struck to coward fear,
　Had ignorance o'erthrow us,
If there had been nae bonnie Jean
　To show'r her blessings on us.

Dear woman's still Misfortune's shield !
　The last one to forsake
The vanquish'd on the battle-field,
　The martyr at the stake.
Then let the mob of sneak and snob
　Still in its wrath disown us,
" A fig ! " we cry, while Jeanie's eye
　Is raining blessings on us.

———

LADY JANE

THERE'S no in bonnie Scotland's isle
　A mair enchanting scene
Than Castle Sempill's waving woods
　And lovely lawns o' green ;
And yet the heiress o' them a'
　Is pressed wi' grief and pain—
They canna get a smile ava
　Frae bonnie Lady Jane.

For they wad hae her wed a knicht,
　While ane o' laich degree
Is far, far dearer to her hert,
　The aipple o' her e'e.
And they wad hae her wed the knicht
　For titles and domain,—
They reckna tho' the hert they brak
　O' bonnie Lady Jane.

There's no an humble cottage maid
　But's blither far than she;
The lowest in their wide domain
　Has nae sic weird to dree.
As day fades o'er the Arran hills
　She wanders a' her lane
To sigh beside the murm'ring rills—
　Wae's me for Lady Jane!

Her bridal robes they hae prepared,
　And joy is in the ha',
But, like a startled midnicht ghaist,
　She glides frae 'mang them a'.
The rose is fading frae her cheek,
　Her lichtsome hert is gane;
They soon maun weave a winding-sheet
　For bonnie Lady Jane.

Nature Poems

PROLOGUE

NATURE always to my sight
    Was a passionate delight;
Even in my childhood, she
Was a wondrous mystery.
But I'd reach'd life's mountain-top,
Turn'd to take the downward slope,
Ere her secrets were reveal'd
And my inner eye unseal'd.
Then I first began to see,
E'en from flow'r and stone and tree,
Strange eyes looking out on me.
Next, with trembling joy and awe,
Mighty forms and shapes I saw—
Saw the Spirit of the Hills
Wand'ring by the mountain-rills;
Heard the Spirit of the Waves
Moaning in the sea-girt caves;
Heard the Maidens of the Deep
Rock the billows all to sleep,
With their songs, pure, undefiled,
As a mother rocks her child.
Still these anthems, moaning, roll
Through the caverns of my soul,
With the long-drawn heave and sweep
Of the great unfathom'd Deep.

Yes, Nature, for thy still retreats
How oft I left the busy streets!
And oh, how often from the jar
Of creeds I fled to thee afar!—

Starving for spiritual food
I sought the desert solitude :
When head and heart were all at strife,
I found therein the bread of life.
Thy temples all are unprofaned
By prejudice, nor passion-stain'd.
Yes, Nature, yes ! thine is the road
That leads directly up to God.[18]

Of those sweet Sabbaths of the heart
Should these, my lays, some taste impart
To parch'd souls, pent in cities vast,
To spirits weary and downcast,
I would rejoice, e'en with such joy
As when, a happy little boy,
On May-day morn, among the dew,
I welcom'd in the first cuckoo.

———

GOD

HAIL, Thou great mysterious Being !
   Thou, the unseen yet All-seeing,
      To Thee we call.
How can a mortal sing thy praise,
Or speak of all thy wondrous ways,
      God over all ?

God of the great old solemn woods,
God of the desert solitudes
      And trackless sea ;
God of the crowded city vast,
God of the present and the past,
      Can man know Thee ?

God of the blue vault overhead,
Of the green earth on which we tread,
      Of time and space ;

God of the worlds which Time conceals,
God of the worlds which Death reveals
    To all our race.

God of the glorious realms of thought,
From which some simple hearts have caught
    A ray divine ;
And the songs which rouse the nations,
And the terrible orations,
    Lord God, are thine.

All varied forms of beauty rare
That toiling genius molds with care—
    Yea, the sublime—
Those sculptured busts of joy and woe—
By Thee were fashion'd, long ago,
    In that far clime.

Far above earth, and space, and time,
Thou dwellest in Thy heights sublime ;
    Beneath Thy feet
The rolling worlds, the heavens, are spread ;
Glory infinite round Thee shed,
    Where angels meet.

From out Thy wrath the Earthquakes leap
To shake the world's foundations deep,
    Till Nature groans ;
In agony the Mountains call,
And Ocean bellows throughout all
    Her frighten'd zones.

But where Thy smile its glory sheds,
The lilies lift their lovely heads,
    And the primrose rare ;
And the daisy, deck'd with pearls
Richer than the proudest earls
    On their mantles wear.

These, thy preachers of the wild-wood,
Keep they not the heart of childhood
    Fresh within us still?
'Spite of all our life's sad story,
There are gleams of Thee and glory
    In the daffodil.

Nature's secret heart rejoices,
And the rivers lift their voices,
    And the sounding sea ;
And the mountains, old and hoary,
With their diadems of glory,
    Shout, Lord, to Thee !

Yet, tho' Thou art high and holy,
Thou dost love the poor and lowly
    With love divine.
Love infinite ! love supernal !
Love undying ! love eternal !
    Lord God, are thine !

———

FAR IN THE FOREST SHADE

FAR in the forest shade,
    Free as the deer to roam,
Where ne'er a fence was laid,
    I'll search me out a home.
I love not cities vast,
    Where want and wealth abide,
And all extremes are cast
    To jumble side by side.

Far in the leafy woods,
    Beside the lonely stream,
Where avarice ne'er intrudes
    Her snorting car of steam ;

Give me the cabin rude
  Of unhewn beechen-tree,
And one both fair and good,
  With heart that beats for me.

Away with pictured walls
  Of gaudy banquet-room !
Give me the great green halls,
  With wild-flow'rs all in bloom,
Where tow'rs the oak sublime ;
  Where, in the forest shade,
Man talk'd with infant Time
  Ere he had cities made.

Devotion's heart will rush
  To God in any scene ;
Hast heard that awful hush,
  In temples arch'd with green,
Where Tempest-Spirit speaks,
  Where ev'ry leaf's a tongue,
Where the pine's great bosom shrieks,
  While million arms are swung ?[22]

There's joy in cultured vales,
  In dewy dells of green ;
Peace like a spirit sails
  High in the blue serene ;
A spirit haunts the hills,
  A soul, the roaring sea ;
But awe the bosom fills,
  O great old woods, in thee.

THE HALL OF SHADOWS

THE sun is up, and through the woods
    His golden rays are streaming;
The dismal swamp and swale so damp
    With faces bright are beaming.
Down in the windfall by the creek
    We hear the partridge drumming,
And strange bright things on airy wings
    Are all around us humming.

The merry schoolboys in the woods
    The chipmunk are pursuing,
And, as he starts, with happy hearts
    They're after him hallooing.
The squirrel hears the urchins' cheers—
    They never catch him lagging—
And on the beech, beyond their reach,
    Hear how the fellow's bragging!

The red-bird pauses in his song,
    The face of man aye fearing,
And flashes like a flame along
    The border of the clearing.
The humming-bird above the flow'r
    Is like a halo bending,
Or like the gleams we catch in dreams,
    Of heav'nly things descending.

List to the humming of the bee
    Among the tufted clover!
This day, like thee, I'll wander free,
    My little wildwood rover!
Through groves of beech and maple green,
    And pines of lofty stature,
By this lone creek once more we'll seek
    The savage haunts of nature.

See ! there a noble troop of pines
  Has made a sudden sally,
And all, in straight unbroken lines,
  Are rushing up the valley;
Now round about that lonely spring
  They gather in a cluster,
Then off again, till on the plain
  The great battalions muster.

And there the little evergreens
  Are clust'ring in the hollows,
And hazels green with sumachs lean
  Among the weeping willows;
Or sit in pride the creek beside,
  Or through the valley ramble,
Or up the height in wild delight
  Among the rocks they scramble.

And here a gorge all reft and rent,
  With rocks in wild confusion,
As they were by the wood-gods sent
  To guard them from intrusion;
And gulfs all yawning wild and wide,
  As if by earthquakes shatter'd;
And rocks that stand, a grizzly band,
  By time and tempest batter'd.

Some great pines, blasted in their pride,
  Above the gorge are bending,
With rock elms from the other side
  Their mighty arms extending;
And midway down the dark descent
  One fearful hemlock's clinging—
His headlong fall he would prevent,
  And grapnels out is flinging.

One ash has ventured to the brink,
  And tremblingly looks over
That awful steep, where shadows sleep,
  And mists at noonday hover.

But farther in the woods we go,
  Through beech and maple alleys,
'Mid elms that stand like patriarchs grand
  In long dark leafy valleys.

Away! away from blue-eyed day,
  The sunshine and the meadows,
We find our way at noon of day
  Within the Hall of Shadows.
How like a great cathedral vast,
  With creeping vines roof'd over,
While shadows dim, with faces grim,
  Far in the distance hover

Among the old cathedral aisles,
  And gothic arches bending,
And ever, in the sacred piles,
  The twilight gloom's descending.
Yet, let me turn where'er I will,
  A step is aye pursuing ;
And there's an eye upon me still
  That's watching all I'm doing.

And in the centre there's a pool,
  And by that pool is sitting
A shape of Fear, with shadows drear,
  Forever round her flitting.
Why is her face so full of woe,
  So hopeless and dejected ?
Sees she but there, in her despair,
  Naught but herself reflected ?

Is it the gloom within my heart,
  Or ling'ring superstition,
Which draws me here three times a year
  To this weird apparition ?
I cannot tell what it may be :
  I only know that seeing
That shape of Fear draws me more near
  The secret Soul of Being.
    11

INFINITE

PART I

UNBAR the gates of eye and ear,
    Lo, what a wondrous world is here!
Marvels on marvels still appear—
        Infinite!

Great Mother, by whose breast we're fed,
With thy green mantle round thee spread,
The blue vault hanging o'er thy head—
        Infinite!

Why wert thou into being brought?
How were thy forms of beauty wrought?
Thou great upheaval of a thought—
        Infinite!

That scoop'd the vales where dew distils,
That led the courses of the rills,
And fix'd the everlasting hills—
        Infinite!

That call'd from darkness bright-eyed Day,
Baptized it with a heav'nly ray,
And sent it on its endless way—
        Infinite!

Ye waves that lash the hoary steep,
Ye mighty winds with boundless sweep,
Great courses of the trackless deep—
        Infinite!

And you, ye streamlets on your way,
Tho' laughing all the summer's day,
Ye only sing, ye only say—
        Infinite!

Sweet linnet singing on the lea,
Wild lark in heaven's wide azure sea,
The burden of your strain's to me
Infinite!

Lov'd violets 'neath my feet that lie,
Sweet hare-bells, can you tell me why
Your beauty only makes me sigh?—
Infinite!

Thou wild rose blooming on the tree,
Ye daisies laughing on the lea,
Sweet flow'rs, your message is to me,
Infinite!

'This dust's to spirit strangely wed,
'Tis haunted ground on which we tread,
The living stranger than the dead—
Infinite!

A Presence fills the earth and air,
Bends o'er us when we're not aware,
And eyes look on us ev'rywhere—
Infinite!

Earth, Ocean, Air, Heaven's azure sea,
Oh, ye have always been to me
A marvel and a mystery—
Infinite!

PART II

UNBAR the gates of eye and ear,
Lo, what a mystic world is here!
The heights of hope, the depths of fear—
Infinite!

Ye wise ones, can ye tell me nought
About this magic web of thought,
Or of the loom on which 'tis wrought?—
Infinite!

Ye strange, ye sacred human ties,
A mighty marvel in you lies,
A wondrous world of tears and sighs—
          Infinite !

This human love, so deep, so vast,
Ye sympathies which run so fast,
And bind the future with the past—
          Infinite !

Ye magic cords, where were ye spun ?
Ye strange affinities that run,
And warp the mystic web in one—
          Infinite !

Love's sacred fires, Grief's burning tears,
Faith's holy hope, and Doubt's dark fears,
Spring from a fount beyond the spheres—
          Infinite !

But who the secret clue can find
Of all the avenues which wind
Up to thy throne, immortal Mind ?—
          Infinite !

In the Soul's presence who are great ?
The wisest ones can but translate
Some passing look, some word of Fate—
          Infinite !

Who'll take the measure or the bound ?
No line of ours can ever sound
The fathomless, the great profound—
          Infinite !

Oh, were I but from self set free,
The Spirit then might speak through me
Of all this deep unfathom'd sea—
          Infinite !

AWFUL SPIRIT

GOD ! who can Thee comprehend?
    Without beginning, without end;
With no future, with no past;
Ever present, first and last;
In the great, as in the small,
Omnipresent, "All in All!"
Nature's ramparts—hill and rock—
Men's great cities—pass like smoke;
Time and Nature shrink away,
But Thou knowest no decay:
All shall perish 'neath the sun—
Thou art the Eternal One!
In thine everlasting now,
Awful Spirit!—What art Thou?

At Thy works, so great and vast,
Speculation stands aghast;
Ev'rywhere infinite might,
Height still tow'ring over height,
Far beyond mind's utmost sweep,
Deep still yawning under deep,
Heav'n above, earth rolling under,
All is wonder piled on wonder.
Wisdom! glory! power unbounded!
Until reason stands confounded.
What of Thee can mortals say?
Silence is for things of clay.
Still we ask the "whence and how"?
Awful Spirit!—What art Thou?

Artists ne'er can represent
Thy o'erhanging firmament,
Or the Morn, in robes of glory,
Walking on the mountains hoary;
When the shadows hear Thy voice,

And the awful hills rejoice,
With their peaks, in purple dyed,
In Thy smile all glorified.
Who can bring to soul or sight
Thy unfathom'd gulfs of Night?
Or the awful shadowy Pow'r,
Looking through the midnight hour,
When Repentance makes her vow?
Awful Spirit!—What art Thou?

How can poet catch the tune,
Rising from Thy groves at noon,
When each leaf and flow'ret sings
Of unutterable things?
Who can note the full-heart strains
Swelling from Thy forest-fanes,
Or the thunder and the leap
Of the torrents down the steep,
Or the laughter of the rills,
Or the silence of the hills,
Or divine the soul that broods
O'er Thine awful solitudes?
Or the calm on Ocean's brow?
Awful Spirit!—What art Thou?

Turn we wheresoe'er we will,
Thou, O God! art with us still:
We are never all alone,
There's a Presence in each stone;
All the air is full of eyes
Looking on us with surprise;
Sympathies run ev'rywhere;
Thoughts are hurrying through the air,
Bringing near related souls,
Tho' asunder as the poles;
Marvel upon marvel! still
Miracle on miracle!—
More than proud man will avow.
Awful Spirit!—What art Thou?

Yet Thine ancient bards have brought
Wonders from Thy realms of thought;
With their weird and wizard spells
They have wrought their miracles,
Started forms which make us start,
Things immortal as Thou art!
But those wondrous works divine,
Great Immaculate, are Thine!
Awful things the prophets saw
In their ecstasies of awe,
In the body laid asleep,
Sailing the eternal deep;
Faith the helm and Hope the prow—
Awful Spirit!—What art Thou?

Dreamer vain and Pantheist
May define Thee as they list;
As in childhood we would rather
Look up to Thee as " Our Father,"[21]
High in Heaven, Thy holy city,
Looking down in love and pity
On thy sons of fiery clay,
Fighting out life's tragedy.
We believe, " Almighty Father,"
Thou shalt all Thy children gather,
Where the light eternal flows,
And no wand'rer asks " Who knows? "
Seeing not as we see now—
Awful Spirit!—What art Thou?

THE PINES

I'M free at last from cities vast,
    And off to running brooks,
'Mong savage woods and roaring floods,
    And Nature's glorious nooks!
The branches spread above my head,
    Beneath the woodbine twines;
All hail, again, your blue domain,
    Great brotherhood of pines!

Untouch'd by time, ye tow'r sublime,
    Aloft in rocky steep;
Ye're seated there, like lords of air,
    In council-chambers deep.
On burnish'd breasts and gleaming crests
    A quiet halo shines,
While torrents sweep and roar and leap,
    Great brotherhood of pines!

When morn awakes from out the lakes,
    Ye pour your holy hymns,
And dying day in mantle grey
    With phantoms round you swims.
No harp can ring, no sounding string
    Such flood of song combines;
Old minstrels ye of the greenwoods be,
    Great brotherhood of pines![22]

When storms are high in midnight sky,
    And wild waves lash the shore,
Afar up there, with harps of air,
    Ye join in wild uproar.
With groaning woods and moaning floods
    Your awful voice combines—
The deep refrain of thunder's strain—
    Great brotherhood of pines!

By torrent's brim, on the rainbow's rim,
　I climb your magic hall,
To hear you join in song divine
　The thund'ring water-fall;
While through the screen of golden green
　A mystic spirit shines.
Hail one and all, in magic hall,
　Great brotherhood of pines!

———

AH, ME!

GO seek the shore to learn her lore,
　That great old mystic Sea:
With list'ning ear you'll surely hear
　The great waves sigh, "Ah, me!"

The great old wood holds a harper good:
　A mighty ode sings he;
While his harp sings in thousand strings,
　The burden is, "Ah, me!"

A glorious sight are the orbs of light
　In Heaven's wide azure sea;
Yet to our cry they but reply,
　With long deep sigh, "Ah, me!"

And Death and Time, in march sublime,
　Stay not to question'd be;
The hosts they bore to the dreamless shore
　Return no more—"Ah, me!"

MYSTERY [23]

MYSTERY! mystery! all is a mystery!
  Mountain and valley, and woodland and stream,
Man's troubled story, his shame and his glory,
  Are only a phase of the soul's troubled dream.

Mystery! mystery! all is a mystery!
  Heart-throbs of anguish, and joy's gentle dew
Fall from a fountain, beyond the great mountain,
  Whose summits forever are lost in the blue.

Mystery! mystery! all is a mystery!
  Sigh of the night-winds, the song of the waves,
Visions that borrow their brightness from sorrow,
  Tales which flow'rs tell us, the voices of graves.

Mystery! mystery! all is a mystery!
  Ah! there is nothing we wholly see through.
We are all weary, the night's long and dreary—
  Without hope of morning, oh! what would we do?

STARS

OH, tell me not of mighty wars!
  Shut out the world and all its jars;
Leave me with God and the silent stars.

Ah! there ye keep your courses bright,
Old revellers in the hall of Night,
Still looking on us with delight.

Ye in that mystic vault were hung
Ere mortals into being sprung—
Before Greece was, or Homer sung.

At God's command ye rose in space,
Bright beauteous orbs, to gem, to grace
The portals of His dwelling-place !

And priests and prophets, sages hoar,
Look'd up to worship and adore
In that old world which is no more.

Untouch'd by Time, or tempests' shocks,
As bright 's when David led his flocks
Among Judea's rugged rocks.

He gazed on you, as I do now,
With wond'ring heart and anxious brow,
And ask'd the unanswerable, " How ? "

We are the lords of but a day ;
Ye saw Great Alexander sway
An empire that has passed away.

Where is he ? Echo answers, " Where ? "
But still ye keep your courses there,
As bright, as beautiful, as fair.

Infinite temple, for no sect
Wert thou so wonderfully deck'd
By the Almighty Architect.

Tho' all those worlds shall cease to be ;
Yet, Father, thou hast given to me
The gift of immortality !

MAY

OH, sing and rejoice!
    Give to gladness a voice—
Shout a welcome to beautiful May!
    Rejoice with the flowers,
    And the birds 'mong the bowers,
And away to the green woods, away!
    As blithe as the fawn,
    Let us dance in the dawn
Of this life-giving, glorious day;
    'Tis bright as the first
    Over Eden that burst—
Then welcome, young joy-giving May!

    The cataract's horn
    Has awaken'd the morn—
Her tresses are dripping with dew;
    Oh, hush thee, and hark!
    'Tis her herald, the lark,
That's singing afar in the blue.
    Its happy heart's rushing
    In strains, wildly gushing,
That reach to the revelling earth,
    And sink through the deeps
    Of the soul, till it leaps
Into raptures far deeper than mirth.

    All Nature's in keeping!
    The live streams are leaping
And laughing in gladness along;
    The great hills are heaving,
    The dark clouds are leaving,
The valleys have burst into song.
    We'll range through the dells
    Of the bonnie bluebells,

And sing with the streams on their way;
   We'll lie in the shades
   Of the flow'r-cover'd glades,
And hear what the primroses say.

  So, crown me with flowers
 'Neath the green, spreading bowers,
With the gems and the jewels May brings;
   In the light of her eyes
   And the depth of her dyes
We'll smile at the purple of kings.
   We'll throw off our years,
   With their sorrows and tears,
And time will not number the hours
   We'll spend in the woods,
   Where no sorrow intrudes,
With the streams and the birds and the flowers.

AUTUMN

THE flowers of the summer have faded away,
   And Autumn is here with her mantle of grey;
The sear leaves are falling, the woodlands are mute,
And the sound of brooks wailing ascends like a lute;
The bow'r is forsaken, its beauty is gone—
One poor little robin is chirping alone—
And the winds wi' their soughing how sadly they say,
" All things that are lovely are passing away!"

The blackbird is silent beside the lone spring,
The lav'rock is folding her weary, wet wing;
Afar in the dell of the desolate yew
Is heard the deep wail of the lonely curlew;
The cuckoo is off and away with the spring,
And the heart vainly seeks for some beautiful thing,
 While the winds with their soughing, how sadly they say,
" All things that are lovely are passing away!"

So dark and unlovely's the Autumn of life,
For grey hair and mem'ry with joys are at strife ;
The bright past has perish'd, the future is black,
The heart's only pleasure's a long looking back—
A long looking back to life's early spring,
To hearts that have wither'd, to hopes taken wing ;
While forms of the lost ones come sadly and say,
" All things that are lovely are passing away ! "

And were they but shadows, false, fleeting, and vain ?
And shall I ne'er meet them in gladness again ?
Bright meteors that came but to dazzle the sight,
And then fade away in the bosom of night ?
Came they but to leave us in darkness and woe,
Aweary of all fleeting things here below ?
" They've gone and we'll follow," Hope sweetly doth say,
" Where nothing that's lovely shall e'er pass away."

———

DAY

NOW Morn is ascending from out the dark sea,
   A light crimson veil hanging o'er her ;
The lark leaves her nest on the bonnie green lea,
   And flutters aloft to adore her.
How gladly the living beams revel and leap,
   In purple and gold to enfold her !
And there the wild cataract, roused on the steep,
   Is shouting with joy to behold her !

The black steeds have vanish'd away from the view,
   That up from the dark Ocean bore her ;
How sweet and how tender the smile breaking through
   The golden gates op'ning before her !
Behold the great Mountains start up from the vale
   And rend their night-mantles, all hoary,
And join in their joy with the chorus, " All hail ! "
   To Day in her garments of glory.

SUNSET

THE glorious sun
His race has run,
And ere he sinks from sight,
Array'd in gold,
Fold upon fold,
He bids the world good-night;
And sea and sky
Commingled lie
In nameless colors dyed—
The molten mass
A sea of glass
In purple glorified.

And still, anon,
Temple and throne,
And tow'rs of amethyst,
And halls of blue
Heave into view
In islands of the blest.
A spirit fills
The great old hills—
The monarchs old and hoary:
They nearer draw
In joy and awe
To gaze upon the glory.

And now I stand
In Wonderland,
Imbibing at each pore
The soul's pure wine—
With joy divine
My spirit's running o'er;
But, oh, despite
The weary night

That on my heart hath lain,
    This glorious sight
    Of pure delight
Revives my soul again !

All trifles, all,
    The mean and small,
Are from my spirit fleeing ;
    Thoughts great and grand
    Lift and expand,
And broaden out my being ;
    While waves of song
    Tumultuous throng,
And through my spirit roll,
    Oh, could I shout
    The lyric out
That's surging in my soul !

MORNING

NOW Morn is awaking, her dark couch forsaking,
    Her herald's alighting afar on the hill ;
And, hark ! there's a humming announcing her coming
    To greenwood and valley, to river and rill.
And yonder lies Ocean, the type of commotion ;
    But to her own caverns her storms have withdrawn ;
With softest surrender she welcomes the tender,
    The trembling approaches and blushes of Dawn.

The firmament bendeth, the glory ascendeth,
    'Mid shadows receding in mantles of dun ;
'Mid phantom orbs reeling, still upwards she's wheeling,
    Till Earth, Air and Ocean are blended in one.
With azure eyes beaming, and golden locks streaming,
    She kindles the breast of the dark, heaving brine ;
Benlomond the hoary has caught up the glory,
    And round his scarr'd temples the purples entwine.

The glory's extending to this torrent, blending
  The foam of its fury with gold and with green,
While out of the splendor eyes saint-like and tender
  Look down on the tumult, all still and serene.
Alas ! we but mutter, attempting to utter
  The grandeur, the glory, these shadows put on—
These types of our being, sent by the All-seeing,
  These symbols of glories that circle His throne.

DAWN

OH, what a sight of pure delight !
    Night's curtain is withdrawn,
And like a boy I shout for joy :
    All hail, beloved Dawn !

Her herald streaks the mountain-peaks,
    The mists are put to flight ;
And how she shapes headlands and capes
    To halls of beauty bright !

Till sea and sky together lie
    In rainbow colors dight,
In an excess of loveliness—
    Hail, spirit of delight !

Earth is still as beautiful,
    With dews untarnish'd laden,
As when thou first in glory burst
    Among the bow'rs of Eden.

Great thoughts will sleep in spirits deep,
    Of which they little dream,
Till Beauty's spell or Music's swell
    Awakes them from their dream.

12

What glorious gleams of heav'nly dreams
  Around thee thou hast drawn !
What hymns of praise, what ecstasies !
  All hail, beloved Dawn !

————

THE SONG OF THE SUN

WHO'LL sing the song of the starry throng,
  The song of sun and sky ?
The angels bright on thrones of light,
  Not a mortal such as I.
How vast, how deep, how infinite,
  Are wonders spread abroad
On outward walls, on azure halls,
  The city of our God !

Men seldom look on the marv'lous book
  Which God writes on the sky ;
They cry for food as the only good,
  Like beasts which eat and die.
Awake ! and gaze on the glorious maze !
  For ev'ry day and night
God paints on air those pictures rare
  To thrill us with delight.

Oh, come with me, and let us flee
  Across the dewy lawn !
And see unroll'd in realms of gold
  The glories of the Dawn.
Behold, she streaks the mountain-peaks
  With faintest tinge of grey !
The glory hies, the mists arise,
  The shadows flee away.

The stars rush back from the conqu'ror's track,
　　The night away is driv'n,
The King of Day mounts on his way
　　Through the golden gates of heav'n.
His heralds fly athwart the sky
　　With radiant rainbow-hue,
Or hang around the deeps profound,
　　Th' unfathom'd gulfs of blue.

The great vault reels 'neath his chariot-wheels,
　　The thunder-clouds are riv'n,
Till they expire in crimson fire
　　On the burning floor of Heav'n.[18]
And then, oh, then! each hill and glen,
　　Each peak and mountain old,
With diadem of glory swims
　　In living seas of gold.

With gorgeous train, through the blue domain,
　　He rushes on and on,
Till with a round of glory crown'd
　　He mounts his noon-day throne;[18]
Then burning beams, with golden gleams,
　　He sheds in show'rs abroad.
We cannot gaze! oh, the glorious blaze!
　　The garments of the god.

Then from his throne, with azure zone,
　　The conqueror descends;
In robes of white through realms of light
　　His downward course he bends,
'Mid great white domes, like happy homes
　　Of ransom'd souls at rest,
Whose work is done, whose crowns are won,
　　Who dwell among the blest.

How calm, how still, how beautiful!
　　The very soul of Peace

Seems breathing there her secret pray'r
　That sin and strife may cease.
Then in the west he sinks to rest,
　Far down in Ocean's bed;
He disappears 'mid Ev'ning's tears,
　A halo on his head.

I cannot write the marv'lous sight,
　At his setting, last I saw;
I only feel, I only kneel,
　With trembling love and awe.
Who'll sing the song of the starry throng,
　The song of sun and sky?
The angels bright on thrones of light,
　Not a mortal such as I.

―――――

THE EARLY BLUEBIRD

YE'VE come far too early,
　My bonnie bluebird;
There's no sign of green leaves,
　Of summer no word.
What tempted you here from
　The green sunny bow'rs
Of the sweet smiling South and
　The region of flow'rs?

Thou'rt chasing a phantom!
　Some folly, I fear,
Has urged thee, my bluebird,
　To venture forth here.
Thou type of the herald,
　Who comes to proclaim
The advent of peace in
　Strife's weary domain.

The Bard, who still hopes for,
  'Mid sorrow and pain,
The "good time that's coming,"
  Love's long-looked-for reign,
Has come far too early,
  My poor bird, like thee;
The good times ye sing of
  Ye'll no likely see.

Cold days are to come yet,
  And deep drifts of snow,
And storms from the bleak north,
  Ere winter shall go.
There are tempests for thee, bird,
  Ere spring comes with peace,
And tears, toil, and trouble,
  Ere man's sorrows cease.

Like thee, my poor bird, I
  Was tempted to roam,
By the distant, the future,
  The lovely unknown:
Like thine, my bright visions
  Were all overcast—
Like thee, I must bend 'neath
  The cold wintry blast.

Thou'rt right, my poor bluebird,
  With prospects so bare,
Still, still cling to Hope, nor
  Give up to Despair:
In the deepest, the darkest,
  Its beams brightest shine—
Without them this heart would
  Have broken lang syne.

INDIAN SUMMER

WELCOME! welcome, Indian summer!
Welcome, thou the latest comer
　　To the wood and chase!
Thee we hail with deeper gladness
Even for the tinge of sadness
　　That is in thy face.
Young October's reign was splendid;
Old and sear, her glory's ended,
　　And, to gild her fall,
Thou descend'st on Nature hoary,
With a spiritual glory
　　That surpasseth all—
A glory that no other land
Has ever seen, howe'er so grand
　　Its lakes or woods may be—
A glory even bards of old
Were not permitted to behold
　　In climes beyond the sea.

Down from the blue the sun has driv'n,
And stands between the earth and heav'n
　　In robes of smould'ring flame;
A smoking cloud before him hung,
A mystic veil, for which no tongue
　　Of earth can find a name.
And o'er him bends the vault of blue,
With shadowy faces looking through
　　The azure deep profound:
The stillness of eternity,
A glory and a mystery,
　　Encompass him around.
The air is thick with golden haze,
The woods are in a dreamy maze,
　　The earth enchanted seems—

Have we not left the realms of care,
And enter'd in the regions fair
  We see in blissful dreams?

Oh, what a sacred stillness broods
Above the awful solitudes!
  Peace hangs with dove-like mien:
She's on the earth, she's in the air,
Oh, she is brooding everywhere—
  Sole spirit of the scene!
And yonder youths and maidens seem
As moving in a heav'nly dream,
  Through regions rich and rare—
Have not their very garments caught
A tone of spiritual thought,
  A still, a Sabbath air?
Yon cabins by the forest side
Are all transform'd and glorified!
  Oh, surely, grief and care
Or poverty, with strife and din,
Or anything like vulgar sin,
  Can never enter there!

The ox, let loose to roam at will,
Is lying by the water still;
  And on yon spot of green
The very herd forget to graze,
And look in wonder and amaze
  Upon the mystic scene.
See! yonder Lake Ontario lies,
As if a wonder and surprise
  Had hush'd her heaving breast—
Calm lies she there with awful eye
Fix'd on the quiet of the sky,
  Like passion sooth'd to rest.
Yon very maple feels the hush,
That trance of wonder, that doth rush
  Through Nature ev'rywhere;

And meek and saint-like there she stands
With upturn'd eye and folded hands,
    As if in silent prayer.

O Indian Summer, there's in thee
A stillness, a serenity—
    A spirit pure and holy—
Which makes October's gorgeous train
Seem but a pageant light and vain,
    Untouch'd by melancholy.
But who can paint the deep serene—
The holy stillness of thy mien,
    The calm that's in thy face,
Which makes us feel, despite of strife,
And all the turmoil of our life,
    Earth is a holy place.
Here, in the woods, we'll talk with thee ;
Here, in thy forest sanctuary,
    We'll learn thy simple lore ;
And neither poverty nor pain,
The strife of tongues, the thirst of gain,
    Shall ever vex us more.

———

BOBOLINK [24]

MERRY mad-cap on the tree !
    Who so happy is as thee ?
Is there aught so full of fun,
Half so happy, 'neath the sun ?
With thy merry whiskodink—
    Bobolink !   Bobolink !

With thy mates such merry meetings,
Such queer jokes and funny greetings ;
Oh, such running and such chasing !

Oh, such banter and grimacing !
Thou'rt a wag, of wags the pink—
     Bobolink ! Bobolink !

How thou tumblest 'mong the hay,
Romping all the summer's day !
Now upon the wing all over,
In and out among the clover—
Far too happy e'en to think—
     Bobolink ! Bobolink !

Now thou'rt on the apple tree,
Crying " Listen unto me ! "
Now upon the mossy banks,
Where thou cuttest up such pranks,
One would swear thou wert in drink—
     Bobolink ! Bobolink !

Nothing canst thou know of sorrow—
As to-day shall be to-morrow ;
Never dost thou dream of sadness—
All thy life a merry gladness ;
Never may thy spirits sink—
     Bobolink ! Bobolink !

————

TO A HUMMING-BIRD

HUSH thee ! hush thee !—not a word !—
    'Tis the lovely humming-bird !
Like a spirit of the air
Coming from—we know not where !
Bursting on our raptured sight,
Like a vision of delight.
Circled in a radiant ring,
Oh, thou glory on the wing !
Thou'rt no thing of mortal birth—
Far too beautiful for earth—

But a thing of happy dreams,
Rainbow glories, heav'nly gleams;
Something fall'n from out the sky
To delight man's heart and eye
In this weary world of ours—
Wand'ring spirit of the flow'rs!

Thou'rt a wonder and a joy
To that happy little boy,
As in ecstasy he stands,
Gazing with uplifted hands.
In a rapture of surprise,
He devours thee with his eyes.
Thou shalt haunt him many a day,
Even when his locks are grey;
Thou'lt be a remember'd joy—
Happy, happy little boy!

Yonder old man's face the while
Brightens with a welcome smile—
Toiling at his daily duty,
He is startled by thy beauty;
Out of all his toils and cares
Thou hast ta'en him unawares—
Ta'en him in a moment back
O'er a long and weary track.
Once again the mountains grey
In that dear land far away,
And his father's humble cot,
Round him in a vision float—
And, despite of age and pain,
He's a little boy again.

Welcome! welcome, happy sprite!
Welcome, spirit of delight!
Deeper than the joy of wine
Or the ancient songs divine;
For my spirit thou dost carry
Back into the realms of Fairy.

Round my heart thou com'st to weave
Things we hope for and believe,
Things we've long'd for since our birth,
Things we've never found on earth ;
Oh, how weary we would be
Save for visitants like thee !

But, like pleasure, lovely thing,
Thou art ever on the wing ;
Like the things we wish to stay,
Thou'rt the first to pass away—
Flying like our hopes the fleetest,
Passing like the joy that's sweetest ;
Even now, like music's tone,
Thou'rt a glory come and gone.

OCTOBER

NOT in russet, sad and sober,
  Com'st thou here, belov'd October,
  As in Europe old ;
Not with aspect wan and hoary,
But array'd in robes of glory,
  Purple, green, and gold.
Over continent and sea,
To hold the full year's jubilee,
  Thou again hast come—
Borne on thine own fairy pinion
To our dear belov'd Dominion,
  Our green forest home !

O ye, who live in cities vast,
Aside your weary ledgers cast,
  Tho' 'twere but for an hour.
Oh, come and see this magic sight—
This revel of all colors bright,
  This gold and purple shower !

Oh, come and see the great arcades,
And catch the glory ere it fades.
    Come through no sense of duty ;
But see, with open heart and eye,
This glory underneath the sky, .
    This miracle of beauty !

See how the great old forest vies
With all the glory of the skies,
    In streaks without a name ;
And leagues on leagues of scarlet spires,
And temples lit with crimson fires,
    And palaces of flame !
And domes on domes that gleam afar
Through many a gold and crimson bar,
    With azure overhead ;
While forts with tow'rs on tow'rs arise,
As if they meant to scale the skies
    With banners bloody red.

Here, orange groves that seem asleep ;
There, stately avenues that sweep
    To where the land declines ;
There, starting up in proud array—
With helmets flashing to the day—
    Troop upon troop of pines.
Here, evergreens that have withdrawn,
And hang around the open lawn,
    With shadows creeping back ;
While yonder girdled hemlocks run,
Like fiery serpents to the sun,
    Upon their gleaming track.

And in the distance, far apart,
As if to shame man's proudest art,
    Cathedral arches spread ;
While yonder ancient elm has caught
A glory past the reach of thought
    Upon his hoary head.

But ev'ry object, far and wide,
The very air, is glorified—
   A perfect dream of bliss.
Earth's greatest painters never could—
Nor poet in inspirèd mood—
   Imagine aught like this.

Oh ! what are all ambition's gains—
What matters it who rules or reigns—
   While I have, standing here,
Gleams of unutterable things,
The work of the great King of Kings,
   God of the full-crown'd year?
October ! thou'rt a marvelous sight,
And with a rapture of delight
   We hail thy gorgeous pinion ;
To elevate our hearts thou'rt here,
To bind us with a tie more dear
   To our belov'd Dominion.

MAY MORNING

THERE'S joy in the greenwood with Morn's early note,
   O'er mountain and valley her song is afloat ;
A joy as of Eden, a gladness, a bloom,
As if earth contain'd not a tear, not a tomb.

On hills and in valleys the lambs are at play ;
The cuckoo is calling in woods far away ;
The streams are rejoicing to wander with spring—
With the song of their revel the green valleys ring.

The spirit of Beauty is ranging abroad,
And show'ring her daisies to deck the green sod ;
She's over the mountain and thro' the deep dell,
And hangs by the fountain her pretty bluebell.

She clothes with her ivy the old ruin'd wall,
And leans o'er the cliff and the steep waterfall ;
And where she has tarried beside the clear stream
The primrose bank hangs like a beautiful dream.

Her footsteps we trace where the violet grows,
And the joy of her face in the laughing wild rose.
A mighty emotion, old Ocean, thou art,
But the song of the syren has hush'd thy great heart.

The wild bee is humming, the lark is on wing,
The cushat is cooing beside the lone spring ;
The poet is coming to join the glad throng,
Impell'd by Love's spirit, the soul of his song.

WHIP-POOR-WILL [25]

THERE is a lonely spirit
    That wanders through the wood,
And tells its mournful story
    In ev'ry solitude.
It comes abroad at eventide,
    And hangs beside the rill,
And murmurs to the passer-by,
    " Whip-poor-will !   Whip-poor-will ! "

Oh ! 'tis a hapless spirit,
    In likeness of a bird—
A grief that cannot utter
    Another woful word—
A soul that seeks for sympathy—
    A woe that won't be still—
A wand'ring sorrow murmuring,
    " Whip-poor-will !   Whip-poor-will ! "

THE SPIRIT OF DEVOTION

OH! what art thou, mysterious power,
   That lov'st to sit and brood,
At dawn of day and ev'ning grey,
   In ev'ry solitude?
That wand'rest through the valleys lone,
   And forests old and hoar,
Where ev'ry leaf and mossy stone
   With worship's running o'er.

I've seen thee hanging o'er the steep
   Which topples by the sea,
And heaving with the heaving deep
   Thy bosom seem'd to be—
Till there did start from out thy heart
   A sigh—oh, how profound!
While tree and stream, as in a dream,
   Were list'ning all around.

And ever at the dawn of day,
   Beside the mountain-rills,
Thou wand'rest like a hermit grey,
   Communing with the hills;
Or far away in moorlands lone—
   Waste places of Creation—
Thou sittest on some old grey stone,
   And talk'st with Desolation.

And I have felt in deserts wild,
   E'en at the noontide hour,
Among the rocks all rudely piled,
   Thy presence and thy power;
And I have stood with mute surprise,
   Yea, with a thrill of awe,
For watching me through stony eyes,
   Thine awful face I saw.

Or seated on a crag sublime,
　　Beside yon mountain river,
I've heard thee questioning old Time,
　　That rusheth on forever.
I've seen thee look from yonder tower
　　Through loop-holes of decay,
Commenting upon human power
　　And glory pass'd away.

And I have listen'd to thee then
　　As if a spell had bound me,
For shadows of the mail-clad men
　　Were hov'ring all around me ;
And in yon deep secluded glen,
　　Where Pity sits and raves,
I've seen thee bend as to a friend
　　Above the Martyrs' graves.

Or hanging by the water-fall,
　　'Mong shadows lengthening dim,
Or on the hills, I've heard thee call
　　To join thy evening hymn ;
And on the Sabbath evening oft,
　　While stillness fill'd the air,
With upturn'd eyes, hands raised aloft,
　　Lo ! thou wast kneeling there.

Or, seated in thy robes of white,
　　With an imperial crown,
From great Benlomond's tow'ring height
　　I've seen thee looking down,
As if in wonder, at our strife,
　　Our hurry, fret, and fume—
Ignoring love, the sun of life,
　　To stumble in the gloom.

When to yon mountain cavern hoar,
　　From earth's distractions fleeing,
There I have found thee pond'ring o'er
　　The mystery of being.

But whether in thy temples green,
  Or caverns by the sea,
Great spirit, thou hast ever been
  A mystery to me.

Thy presence ever came unsought,
  At morn or midnight hour ;
And unto me thou'st ever brought
  A great uplifting power.
O spirit of majestic mien !
  Amid the darkness dense,
Art thou interpreter between
  The world of soul and sense ?

Art thou the soul that link'st in one
  This visible creation
With yonder spiritual sun
  Of vast imagination ?
I only know where thou art not,
  That we are grov'lers low,
But where thou art there in the heart
  Celestial virtues grow.

———

SIGHS IN THE CITY

WEARILY my days are past,
    For my heavy lot is cast
In the crowded city vast.

How my spirit longs to be
From this dreary prison free—
Oh, the laughing meads for me !

Oh ! to follow the cuckoo,
While the glades are drap'd wi' dew
And the lark is in the blue !

13

Oh ! to tread the flow'ry sod
Free from all this heavy load—
One with Nature and with God !

Spring is forth with joyous air,
Strewing gems so rich and rare,
Show'ring gowans ev'rywhere.

I will go where'er she goes,
Pausing often where she throws
The violet and the red, red rose.

And we'll seek the glades of green
Where the honeysuckles lean
And the blewarts ope their een ;

Where the auld witch-hazels hing,
And the woodbines creep and cling
Round about the lonely spring ;

Where the birds are blithe abune,
And the laughing runnels rin
Onward in their merry din ;

Treading paths the wild bee knows,
Where the grass the greenest grows,
In the haunts of the primrose ;

Where the foxglove fair and tall
Leans against the rocky wall,
List'ning to the water-fall ;

Where the bonnie hawthorn hings,
And the wee grey lintie sings
Of unutterable things ;

And, half hidden by the weeds,
Bonnie bluebells hing their heids,
Draped wi' dew like siller beads ;

And the lily, meek and mild,
Blooming in the lonely wild—
Nature's dear adopted child!

Little wildings, pure and bright,
Still, as to my childhood's sight,
Ye're a rapture of delight!

Far from those who buy and sell
I will seek the quiet dell—
Lonely ones, with you to dwell!

Where no worldling soils the sod
I'll live in your green abode—
One with Nature and with God.

Canadian Idyls

THE GENIUS OF CANADA

WHEN the Genius of Canada came
 From o'er the eastern wave,
  'Neath southern skies
  She heard the cries
 Of ev'ry weeping slave.[26]

"I'll seek the northern woods," she cried,
 "Tho' bleak the skies may be;
  The maple dells,
  Where Freedom dwells,
 Have special charms for me;

"For moral worth and manhood there
 Have found a fav'ring clime.
  I'll rear a race
  For long to grace
 The mighty page of Time.

"The arts shall flourish 'neath their care,
 The palm of Peace shall wave
  O'er homes of rest
  For the opprest,
 A refuge for the slave."[27]

Away to northern woods she flew,
 A lovely home she found,
  Where still she dwells
  In quiet dells,
 Her giant brood around.

" Behold ! " she cries, "the hearts we mold
   In land of lakes and pines,
     Where Shamrock blows,
     And English Rose
With Scottish Thistle twines."

SPARKING[28]

GIVE me the night with moonshine bright !
   The stars come forth to meet her,
The very snow is all aglow,
   The dismal swamp looks sweeter ;
When cows are fed, old folks in bed,
   And young lads go a-larking,
And no one by with prying eye,
   Oh, that's the time for sparking !

When all the " chores " are done out-doors,
   The hearth is swept up trimly,
And the backlog bright, like jovial wight,
   Is roaring up the chimley.[7]
I listen oft his signal soft,
   Till Tray sets up his barking—
For dogs as well as folks must tell
   When anybody's sparking.

I've sat with him till the log burn'd dim,
   And the owls were all too-whooing ;
(For don't they spark, too, in the dark ?
   Ain't that their way of wooing ?)
I ne'er could bear love anywhere,
   Where folks were all remarking—
You act a part, but, bless your heart,
   That's not what I call sparking.

At public halls, picnics and balls,
  The lads will try to please you ;
But it takes the bliss all from a kiss
  If anybody sees you.
My old aunt says, in her young days,
  Folks never woo'd the dark in ;
It may be so, but oh, dear, oh !
  They little knew of sparkin'.

———

THE PICNIC

NOW morning fair with golden hair
    Is through the pine woods streaming,
And of a day of mirth and play
  The youngsters all are dreaming ;
No sound of ax salutes the ear,
  The ox is freed from logging,
And neighbors all, both great and small,
  Are to the picnic jogging.

The girls and boys, how they rejoice !
  So merrily they're driving,
And far and wide from ev'ry side
  In happy pairs arriving.
Bill's mounted on his idol there—
  With boughs he has array'd her—
And boasts the virtues of that mare
  To Dick, the great horse-trader.

Dick stumps him just to try a heat :
  " Come, bring your scarecrow hither,"
And in such loving converse sweet
  They trot along together ;
They pass beside the ridge of beech,
  And by the hemlocks hoary,
And leave the noble clump of pines
  All tow'ring in their glory.

They reach the groves of maple green,
  Beside the winding river—
Still at the song it sung so long
  To Red Men gone forever ;
And it will leap and laugh along,
  As gay and happy-hearted,
And it will sing this very song
  When we, too, have departed.

A table's spread beneath the trees—
  Some busily partaking,
While others swing or romp and sing,
  All bent on merry-making.
The old folks talk about the crops,
  The little boys are larking,
With damsels fair and sweet and young
  The lads are busy sparking.

They form a circle round the spring,
  The sparkling waters quaffing,
All poking fun—and ne'er a one
  Of all can keep from laughing
At am'rous John, still sparking on—
  At sixty-two a " wanter "—
Or roaring at the great exploits
  Of Bill, the mighty hunter—

His treeing coons 'neath autumn moons,
  His fishings and his forays,
His great affairs with angry bears,
  His terrible wolf stories.
When Fred comes with his violin,
  By young and old invited,
With shouts of joy the bashful boy
  They circle round delighted.

Tho' he is but a backwoods lad,
  A native-born musician,
What strains he brings from those mere strings—
  Oh, he's a real magician !

He plays a quick and merry tune—
　With joy each eye is glancing—
Now he appeals to all their heels,
　And sets them all a-dancing.

That mother with her joyous air,
　Her baby how she dandles !
While Bill and Dick are dancing quick,
　And shouting out like vandals.
The chipmunk peeps from out the logs,
　And wonders at the flurry ;
And, all amazed, with tail upraised,
　Makes tracks in quite a hurry.

The grey owl opens up his eyes,
　And looks in stupid wonder,
While through the wood the partridge brood
　Are rolling off like thunder.
The old coon's in the elm above,
　Pretending that he's sleeping,
But with one eye the old boy sly
　A wond'ring watch is keeping.

Fred's mood has changed, and in the midst
　Of all our merry madness
He makes us drink, ere we can think,
　The deeper joy of sadness.
The youths and maidens hush to hear—
　Tho' 'tis no tale of glory—
And drink in with a greedy ear
　That simple backwoods story.

His voice he flings among the strings—
　They seem with sorrow laden—
Oh ! hear the sighs and wailing cries
　Of the poor hapless maiden :
" Ah ! thou art laid in thy death-bed,
　Beneath the grassy cover ;
Why did the tree not fall on me
　Which fell on thee, my lover ? "

That wail of woe, so long and low,
    Is in the distance dying,
And there the rude sons of the wood
    Are all around him sighing ;
Yes, there they stand, the rude, rough band,
    Untutor'd by the Graces,
As spell-bound there by that wild air,
    Tears streaming down their faces.

And while their hearts within them leap—
    Those hearts unused to weeping—
Oh, what a silence still and deep
    The maple trees are keeping !
The grove is all a magic hall,
    And he the necromancer—
The master of the wizard-spells
    To which our spirits answer.

Time steals along with tale and song,
    Until the warning shadow
Is stretching seen from maples green,
    And creeping o'er the meadow.
Old folk begin to think 'tis time
    That they are homeward going,
And so they sing a parting hymn
    With hearts all overflowing.

The boys must see the girls all home ;
    So they hitch up for starting,
And merrily they drive along
    To have a kiss at parting.
As Dick trots home, that little song
    He can't keep from repeating,
While Bill declares, " Those backwoods airs
    Are good as go-to-meeting ! "

THE GIPSY BLOOD

THE spring is here, with voice of cheer,
    For winter winds are gone;
And with the birds and antler'd herds[29]
    My roving fit comes on.
I long to be in the forest, free
    From civilization's chains;
For there's a flood of gipsy blood
    Still running in my veins.

My soul is sick of smoke and brick,
    I long for breath that's free—
The desert air, the hunter's fare,
    The woods, the woods, for me!
Where things unbroke by curb or yoke
    Bound through the green domains;
For there's a flood of gipsy blood
    Still running in my veins.

I'm sick of trade, its ways have made
    These artificial men;
I long to be both wild and free
    In trackless savage glen.
All, all my life has been a strife
    With bridles, curbs, and chains;
For there's a flood of gipsy blood
    Still running in my veins.

Why should I moil and strain and toil
    For lifeless things of art,
While greenwood bow'rs and wildwood flow'rs
    Are springing in my heart?
Yes, deep at heart, devoid of art,
    A savage spot remains;
For there's a flood of gipsy blood
    Still running in my veins.

Let who may dwell to buy and sell,
  I'm off with the roving clan !
What are your gains but curbs and chains
  To the free-born soul of man ?
I'm off ! away with joyous May
  To Freedom's glorious fanes !
For there's a flood of gipsy blood
  Still running in my veins.

ACRES OF HIS OWN

HERE'S the road to independence !
  Who would bow and dance attendance ?
Who, with e'er a spark of pride,
While the bush is wild and wide,
Would be but a hanger on,
Begging favors from a throne,
While beneath yon smiling sun
Farms by labor can be won ?
Up, be stirring, be alive !
Get upon a farm and thrive !
He's a king upon a throne
Who has acres of his own !

Tho' the cabin's walls are bare,
What of that, if love is there ?
What altho' thy back is bent,
There is none to hound for rent ;
What tho' thou must chop and plow,
None dare ask, " What doest thou ? "
What tho' homespun be thy coat,
Kings might envy thee thy lot.
Up, be stirring, be alive !
Get upon a farm and thrive !
He's a king upon a throne
Who has acres of his own !

Honest labor thou would'st shirk?
Thou art far too good for work?
Such gentility's a fudge—
True men all must toil and drudge.
Nature's true nobility
Scorns such mock gentility!
Fools but talk of blood and birth—
Ev'ry man must prove his worth.
Up, be stirring, be alive!
Get upon a farm and thrive!
He's a king upon a throne
Who has acres of his own!

————

NEIGHBOR JOHN

THERE'S neighbor John, dull as a stone,
    An earthly man is he;
In Nature's face no single trace
    Of beauty can he see.
He's wrought with her for sixty years—
    Believes he's done his duty—
Yet all that time seen naught sublime,
    Nor drank one draught of beauty.

His only joy since when a boy
    Has been to plod and moil,
Until his very soul itself
    Has grown into the soil.
He has no visions, hears no voice
    To make his spirit start;
The glory and the mystery
    Ne'er settled on his heart.

The great vault's hanging o'er his head,
    The earth is rolling under,
On which he's borne from night till morn,
    With not one look of wonder.

Talk not to him of yonder clouds,
  In glory mass'd together,
John but beholds in all their folds
  Some index of the weather.

Talk not of old cathedral woods
  Their Gothic arches throwing,
John only sees in all those trees
  So many saw-logs growing.
For in the woods no spirit broods,
  The grove's no longer haunted,
The gods have gone to realms unknown,
  And earth is disenchanted.

In day, with all its bright array,
  And black night still returning,
He never saw one gleam of awe,
  Tho' all their lamps were burning.
The seasons in their mystic round
  Their magic work are doing ;
Spring comes and goes, the wild-flow'r blows,
  And Winter's storms are brewing ;

And Indian summer steps between,
  In robes of purple gleaming,
Or in a maze of golden haze
  The live-long day is dreaming :
John stands with dull, insensate look,
  His very soul grown hoary,
And sees in all but sear leaves fall,
  And not one gleam of glory.

For beauty and sublimity
  Are but a useless blunder ;
And naught can start awe in his heart—
  Save loudest peals of thunder !
He knows the world's a solid world,
  And that a spade's a spade,
But thinks for food and raiment all
  The heav'ns and earth were made.

THE MAN WHO ROSE FROM NOTHING

AROUND the world the fame is blown
  Of fighting heroes, dead and gone;
But we've a hero of our own—
    The man who rose from nothing.

He's a magician great and grand:
The forests flee at his command;
And here he says, "Let cities stand!"—
    The man who rose from nothing.

And in our legislative hall
He tow'ring stands alone; like Saul,
A head and shoulders over all—
    The man who rose from nothing.

His efforts he will ne'er relax,
Nor faith in figures and in facts;[21]
He always calls an ax an ax—
    The man who rose from nothing.

This gentleman in word and deed
Is short and simple in his creed:
"Fear God and help the soul in need"—
    The man who rose from nothing.

In other lands he's hardly known,
For he's a product of our own,
Could grace a shanty or a throne—
    This man who rose from nothing.

Here's to the land of lakes and pines,
On which the sun of Freedom shines,
Because we meet on all our lines
    The man who rose from nothing.

THE MEN OF THE DOMINION

HEROES there are that tower sublime,
Of ev'ry creed, in ev'ry clime,
Of high or humble birth,
With heads to think and hearts to feel,
And labor for the common weal—
True leaders on this earth.
Such men to fashion never bow—
Like Cincinnatus at the plow,
They feel no degradation ;
They're always placing moral worth
The highest rank attain'd on earth,
In any rank or station.

The man of downright common-sense
Scorns make-believe and all pretence,
Puts intrigue far apart,
Despising double-dealing work,
And ev'ry little dodge and quirk,
With all his head and heart.
With freeman written on his brow—
His ancient badge the spade and plow—
A true-born son of Adam—
A brother of humanity,
He shows the same urbanity
To plowman and to madam.

Such men are here to do and dare,
The burdens of the weak to share,
So heavy in our day.
No true man asks their blood or birth,
For homage to all moral worth
Instinctively they pay.
These men are to themselves a law,
And never need to stand in awe
Of party or opinion.

They do the work they find to do,
And stand up for the just and true,
  In this our dear Dominion.

Who stand erect in their own shoes
Are just the men that snobs abuse,
  With hatred in excess ;
For they despise gentility
That's purchas'd by servility
  And want of manliness ;
And they proclaim such snobs a curse,
Whose tamp'ring with the public purse
  Will make, in their opinion,
A common byword, for the mirth
Of all the nations on the earth,
  Of this our dear Dominion.

Of Gladstone's high, heroic cast,
They nail their colors to the mast,
  Inspired by love of right ;
They cannot, will not be downcast,
Are always sure to stand at last
  Triumphant in the fight.
Then let us ever hope and pray,
In this our own progressive day,
  May freedom spread her pinion
O'er heads that think and hearts that feel,
And labor for the common weal
  In this our dear Dominion.

YOUNG CANADA

I LOVE this land of forest grand,
   The land where labor's free ;
Let others roam away from home,
   Be this the land for me !
Where no one moils and strains and toils
   That snobs may thrive the faster,
But all are free as men should be,
   And Jack's as good's his master !

Where none are slaves that lordly knaves
   May idle all the year ;
For rank and caste are of the past—
   They'll never flourish here !
And Jew or Turk, if he'll but work,
   Need never fear disaster ;
He reaps the crop he sowed in hope,
   For Jack's as good's his master.

Our aristocracy of toil
   Have made us what you see,
The nobles of the forge and soil,
   With ne'er a pedigree.
It makes one feel himself a man,
   His very blood leaps faster,
Where wit or worth's preferr'd to birth,
   And Jack's as good's his master.

Here's to the land of forests grand,
   The land where labor's free ;
Let others roam away from home,
   Be this the land for me !
   14

For here 'tis plain the heart and brain,
    The very soul, grow vaster,
Where men are free as they should be,
    And Jack's as good's his master.

HURRAH FOR THE NEW DOMINION

L ET others raise the song of praise
    To lands renowned in story;
The land give me of the maple tree,
    The pine in all his glory !

Hurrah for the grand old forest land,
    Where freedom spreads her pinion !
Hurrah with me for the maple tree !
    Hurrah for the New Dominion !

Be hers the light and hers the might
    Which liberty engenders ;
Sons of the free, come join with me—
    Hurrah for her defenders !

And be their fame, in loud acclaim,
    In grateful strains ascending—
The fame of those who met her foes,
    And died, her soil defending.

Hurrah for the grand old forest land,
    Where freedom spreads her pinion !
Hurrah with me for the maple tree !
    Hurrah for the New Dominion !

𝔍𝔡𝔶𝔩𝔰 of the 𝔓ioneers

THE EMIGRANT

ARGUMENT

Introduction : The poet apostrophizes Canada as a land where Nature's operations are on a large scale, and which, though without extended national history, yet supplies a theme for the poet in the struggles of the pioneer settlers.

LEAVING HOME

I. He asks his companion to sit down with him while he recounts the story of his journey from the fatherland.
II. He moralizes on the changes of fifty years.
III. He recalls the friends who met to bid him farewell.
IV. It was a morning in spring when all nature, though beautiful, seemed to have an air of sympathetic sadness.
V. His grandfather comes to give him his blessing.
VI. The grandfather's parting counsel.

THE JOURNEY

I. He describes the motley company on the ship.
II. The teacher, the preacher, the mechanic, the politician, etc.
III. When the sea is calm they tell each other their story.
IV. Tom's song : " Old England is eaten by knaves."
V. Mac's song : " Farewell ! Caledonia."

THE ARRIVAL

I. The journey through the woods ; camping at night.
II. They sing in praise of rural life : " The Greenwood Shade."
III. After rest on bare ground they struggle through a swamp.
IV. In a forest of maples and beeches they find birds of beauteous hue, but devoid of song.
V. Bill from Kent shoots a deer.
VI. The dead hind.
VII. They reach the promised land. The poet pauses to reflect on his departed companions, all gone but himself.

Cutting the First Tree

    I. The tent raised on a point of land jutting into the lake.
   II. A duck, a crane, a stag, take alarm and flee.
 III. The first attempt to fell an elm.
 IV. Lazy Bill despairs of success.
    V. The fall of the tree.
  VI. Their rejoicing.
 VII. The orator's exulting speech.
VIII. Doubting John prepares to speak.
 IX. He tells a parable in favor of co-operation.

The Log Cabin

The poet describes its solitary situation and surroundings.

    I. The Summer's work.
   II. Autumn and Indian Summer.
 III. Visits of wolves.
 IV. Amusements of Winter.
    V. Little Mac's song: "I ask not for Fortune."
  VI. The applause of the listeners.
 VII. The hunter's song: "The Indian Maid."
VIII. Tales told by the old.
 IX. Ballad: "The Gipsy King."

The Indian Battle

    I. Lazy Bill announces the onset of the Mohawks.
   II. Commotion among the settlers.
 III. Muster of the fighting men.
 IV. March to a little height where the attack is awaited. Sounds of a struggle in the woods. Then silence. A scout announces that two tribes are fighting.
    V. The chiefs agree to settle the quarrel by single combat.
  VI. Description of "Eagle."
 VII. Description of "Hemlock."
VIII. The combat. Victory of "Eagle" and scalping of "Hemlock."
 IX. The Hurons carry off their dead chief.

Donald Ban

    I. The Highland hunter with the spirit of an ancient bard, who loves to commune with Nature and peer into her mysteries.
   II. Destruction of the old home of his race, and banishment from his native land.
 III. Solace in playing the pipes.
 IV. Song of the exile: "Why Left I my Country."

INTRODUCTION : APOSTROPHE TO CANADA

LAND of mighty lake and forest !
    Where stern Winter's locks are hoarest ;
Where warm Summer's leaf is greenest,
And old Winter's bite the keenest ;
Where mild Autumn's leaf is searest,
And her parting smile the dearest ;
Where the Tempest rushes forth
From his caverns of the north,
With the lightnings of his wrath
Sweeping forests from his path ;
Where the Cataract stupendous
Lifteth up her voice tremendous ;
Where uncultivated Nature
Rears her pines of giant stature—
Sows her jagged hemlocks o'er,
Thick as bristles on the boar—
Plants the stately elm and oak
Firmly in the iron rock ;
Where the crane her course is steering,
And the eagle is careering ;
Where the gentle deer are bounding,
And the woodman's ax resounding,—
Land of mighty lake and river,
To our hearts thou'rt dear forever !

Thou art not a land of story ;
Thou art not a land of glory ;

No traditions, tales, nor song
To thine ancient woods belong ;
No long line of bards and sages
Looking on us down the ages ;
No old heroes sweeping by
In their war-like panoply.
Yet heroic deeds are done
Where no battle's lost or won ;
In the cottage in the woods,
In the desert solitudes,
Pledges of affection given
That will be redeem'd in heaven.
Why seek in a foreign land
For the theme that's close at hand ?
Human nature can be seen
Here within the forest green ;
Let us wander where we will,
There's a world of good and ill.
Poetry is ev'rywhere—
In the common earth and air,
In the pen and in the stall,
In the hyssop on the wall,
In the wand'ring Arab's tent,
In the backwoods settlement.
Have we but the hearing ear,
It is always whisp'ring near ;
Have we but the heart to feel it,
Mother Nature will reveal it.

LEAVING HOME

I

Let us sit upon this stone,
With its grey moss overgrown,
While we talk about the past,—
For I'm left the very last
Of that simple, hardy race
Who first settled in this place ;

At whose stroke the forest fell,
And the sound of Sabbath bell
Startled Desolation's brood
In the trackless solitude.

II

Half a century has roll'd,
With its burdens manifold,
Since I left my home so dear,
Came, a young adventurer, here.
Many faces Fortune wears
In the space of fifty years ;
Strange mutations, smiles and frowns,
Unexpected ups and downs.
Oh, what crowds have crost the path
To the rendezvous of death !
Men, so mighty in their day,
Gone to nothingness away !
What great teachers and their schools !
Prophets time has proven fools !
Transcendental meteors high,
That have faded from the sky—
Tho' the fashion of a day,
Gone like shadows all away !

III

Fifty years have pass'd away,
Fifty years this very day,
Since I left, at Fortune's call,
Friends and Fatherland and all.
I was then a happy boy ;
Earth, a scene of hope and joy.
I have now grown old and grey,
Yet it seems but yesterday.
Ev'ry circumstance comes back
O'er that long and weary track :

Friends, the loving and true-hearted,
Who have long in death departed,
Crowd around me in the dell,
Where I bade them all farewell.

IV

It was a lovely morn in spring;
The lark was high upon the wing,
The bonnie bells in clusters blue,
The gowan with its drop of dew,
The cowslip and the primrose pale,
Were forth in Cartha's lovely vale.[5]
Ah! there they were, so chaste and meek,
Not silent, tho' they did not speak—
It seem'd to me as if they knew
I'd come to bid them all adieu;
For we had been companions dear,
And could not part without a tear.
And Cartha had a mournful voice—
She did not, as of old, rejoice;
And vale and mountain, flower and tree,
Were looking sadly upon me;
For, oh! there is a nameless tie—
A strange, mysterious sympathy—
Between us and material things,
Which into close communion brings
Our spirits with the unseen pow'r
Which looks from ev'ry tree and flow'r.
There was the bonnie bush of broom,
Just op'ning into golden bloom,
Beneath whose tassels, many a day,
I listen'd to the blackbird's lay;
Yonder the mountains looming through,
Benlomond tow'ring in the blue—
How kingly! tho' his forehead wears
The furrows of six thousand years.
Oh! how I lov'd those mountains grey,
Which pass not, like man's work, away,

But are forever seated there,
Old monarchs on their thrones of air.
And were they not the first to draw
From out my soul the sigh of awe,
Till down the mighty shadows came,
And lifted me aloft to them?
High seated with the monarchs there,
Above this little world of care,
My spirit burst the bonds of time,
And revel'd in the realms sublime;
And now it seem'd they closer drew,
As if to bid me sad adieu.

v

Things there are in mem'ry set,
Things we never can forget.
Still I see the very spot,
Close beside our lowly cot,
Where my grandsire, old and grey
(Blessèd be his memory),
While upon his staff he bent,
Thus did bless me ere I went:

vi

A Grandfather's Blessing

Your journey's but beginning now,
 While mine is nearly ending—
You're starting up the hill of life,
 I to the grave descending;
With you 'tis bright and buoyant spring,
 With me 'tis dark December,
And my injunctions, oh, my son!
 I'd have you to remember.

I've seen, in threescore years and ten,
 So many strange mutations,
So many sides of Fortune's face
 To families and nations;

I've learn'd to know she can't be caught
    By whip, by spur, or bridle;
She is not caught by running fast,
    Nor yet by standing idle.

While she within your hopeful heart
    Her wondrous tale rehearses,
In noting all, be sure and leave
    A margin for reverses.
Should you be rich, trust not in wealth,
    From you it may be taken,
But if you put your trust in God,
    You'll never be forsaken.

Men toil to reach the earthly heights,
    From which by death they're hurled,
Be your ambition what you'd not
    Exchange for all the world.
Should you be poor, sit not and sigh,
    Nor deem yourself neglected;
The kindest lift that e'er I got
    Was when I least expected.

Grieve not at the decrees of fate,
    Tho' they may be distressing—
A blessing's mixt with ev'ry woe,
    A woe with ev'ry blessing;
The hollow's close beside the height;
    Whenever much is given,
Something or other is withheld
    To bring the balance even.

Look Fate and Fortune in the face,
    In that there's worth and merit;
The greatest poverty on earth
    Is poverty of spirit.[18]
Have aye some object in your view,
    And steadily pursue it,
Nor grow faint-hearted, come what may,
    But like a man stick to it.

Hope not to find a good on earth
    But what you'll have to pay for;
The fruit that drops into the mouth
    Is aye devoid of flavor.

If you will lean on any man,
    All Nature will upbraid you :
Then trust but to your own right arm,
    And to the God that made you.

Strive manfully in ev'ry strait,
    And after you have striven,
With hands unstain'd, with heart upright,
    Leave the result to heaven.[18]
Profess to be but what you are,
    Avoid all affectation ;
If you are truth's, you sit upon
    A rock of deep foundation.

Be guided by your sense of right
    Where Scripture may not aid you,
For that's the ray from heav'n direct,
    The light from Him who made you.
Philosophers are all afloat
    Upon a sea of troubles ;
They dash like waves against the rocks,
    And give birth but to bubbles.

They cannot tell us whence we came,
    Or why we were sent hither,
But leave us hopeless, in the end,
    To go we know not whither.
Trust not in knowledge—small indeed
    Is all that we can gather—
But always ask the guidance of
    The universal Father.

There's much which we must teach ourselves,
    That is not taught at college ;
Without a sympathetic soul,
    How vain is all our knowledge !
Be charitable when you speak
    Of man and human nature ;
Who finds no worth in human hearts
    Must be a worthless creature.

If you would have your brother's love,
    Then you must love your brother ;
Heart leaps to heart o'er all the world,
    Affections draw each other.

Then cherish still within your breast
    Affection's sacred blossom ;
Strive to be rich enough to keep
    A heart within your bosom.

Farewell ! my son, we meet no more ;
    The angel death, which gathers
The green and ripe, must shortly come
    To take me to my fathers.
Farewell ! may heaven be the height,
    To which you would aspire,
And think at times, when far away,
    Upon your old grandsire.

THE JOURNEY

I

In the good ship *Edward Thorn*
O'er the billows we were borne.
A motley company were we,
Sailing o'er that dreary sea.
Many from their homes had fled,
For they had denied them bread ;
Some from sorrow and distress,
Others from mere restlessness ;
Some because they long'd to see
The promis'd land of liberty ;
Some because their hopes were high,
Others for—they knew not why.

II

There was doubting John, the teacher,
Spouting Tom, nicknamed "the preacher,"
Gen'ral John, the mechanician,
Lean, lank Tom, the politician,
Lazy Bill, the bad news bringer,
Little Mac, the jocund singer ;
And there was Aleck, the divine,

As bristly as the porcupine ;
And there was fighting Bill from Kent,
Who always was on mischief bent ;
With wives and children, three or four,
With youths and maidens, half a score ;
And lastly, tall orator* John,
Always thoughtful and alone—
A motley crew as ever went
To form a backwoods settlement.

III

When the winds were all asleep,
Hush'd their wild and restless sweep,
Not a breath the sails to fill,
And the vessel lay as still
On the bosom of the deep
" As a sea-god fast asleep ; "
Some would stroll around the deck,
Telling tales of storm and wreck ;
Others, through the smile and tear,
Mourn'd the land they lov'd so dear,
Told that tale of dire distress,
Hungry, hopeless wretchedness,
Made them ocean's dangers brave,
Seeking homes beyond the wave.
Then a-singing Tom would start,
As he said, to ease his heart ;
In a rude and boist'rous vein
He would thunder out this strain :

IV

Old England is Eaten by Knaves

Old England is eaten by knaves,
    Yet her heart is all right at the core ;
May she ne'er be the mother of slaves,
    May no foreign foe land on her shore.

---

* In Scotland *orator* is often pronounced to rime with *debater*.

I love my own country and race,
  Nor lightly I fled from them both ;
Yet who would remain in a place
  With too many spoons for the broth ?

The Squire is preserving his game—
  He says that God gave it to him—
And he'll banish the poor, without shame,
  For touching a feather or limb.

The Justice, he feels very big,
  And boasts what the law can secure ;
With two different laws in "his wig,"
  Which he keeps for the rich and the poor.

The Bishop he preaches and prays,
  And talks of a heavenly birth ;
But somehow, for all that he says,
  He grabs a good share of the earth.

Old England is eaten by knaves,
  Yet her heart is all right at the core ;
May she ne'er be the mother of slaves,
  May no foreign foe land on her shore.

v

Then little Mac would sing the lays
Of Scotia's bonnie woods and braes :
Of hoary hill, of dashing stream,
Of lonely rock where eagles scream,
Of primrose bank, and gowany glen,
Of broomy knowe, and hawthorn den,
Of burnside where the linnet's lay
Is heard the lee lang summer's day—
The scenes which many a simple song
Still peoples with an airy throng.
And still I hear them tell their tale
In ev'ry strath and stream and vale,
In swells of love, in gusts of woe,
Which thrill'd our hearts so long ago.

As mournful groups around him hung
The sigh from many a breast was wrung,
For eyes grew dim, and hearts did swell,
While thus he sang his last farewell :

Farewell, Caledonia !

Farewell, Caledonia, my country, farewell !
Adieu ev'ry scarr'd cliff and lone rocky fell.
Your dark peaks are fading away from my view—
I ne'er thought I lov'd you so dearly till noo ;
For fortune hath chased me across the wild main,
And the blue hills of Scotland I'll ne'er see again.

Farewell, lovely Leven ! dear vale of my heart,
'Twas hard frae the hame o' my childhood to part :
Our lowly thatch'd cottage, which stands by the mill,
The green where we gambol'd, the church on the hill.
I lov'd you, sweet valley, in sunshine and rain ;
But oh ! I shall never behold you again.

How bright were my mornings, my evenings how calm !
I rose wi' the lav'rock, lay down wi' the lamb ;
Was blithe as the lintie that sings on the tree,
And licht as the goudspink that lilts on the lea ;
But tears, sighs, and sorrows are foolish and vain,
For the light heart of childhood returns not again.

Oh, sad was the morning when I cam' awa',
And big were the tears frae my e'en that did fa' !
My mother was weepin', my father was wae,
And " Farewell, my laddie," was all they could say ;
While the tears o'er their haffets were fa'in' like rain,
For they thocht that they never would see me again.

Awa' frae our cottage I tried then to steal,
But frien's gather'd round me to bid me fareweel ;
E'en Towser cam' forth wi a sorrowful whine,
And the auld women said 'twas an ominous sign :
It spak' o' disaster, o' sorrow and pain,
That the blue hills o' Scotland I'd ne'er see again.

And then when I tarried, and mournfully took
Of all the lov'd scenes my last sorrowful look,
The hills gather'd round me, as if to embrace,
And the bonnie wee gowans look'd up in my face,
While the birds 'mang the branches in sorrowful strain [18]
Sang " Oh, no ! ye will never see Scotland again."

THE ARRIVAL

I

The weary world of waters pass'd,
In Canada arrived at last—
Pioneers of civilization,
Founders of a mighty nation—
Soon we entered in the woods,
O'er the trackless solitudes,
Where the spruce and cedar made
An interminable shade ;
And we pick'd our way along,
Sometimes right, and sometimes wrong.
For a long and weary day
Thus we journey'd on our way ;
Pick'd a path through swale and swamp,
And at ev'ning fix'd our camp
Where a cool, refreshing spring
Murmur'd like a living thing—
Like sweet Charity, I ween,
Tracking all its path with green.
Underneath a birchen tree
Down we sat right cheerfully,
Then of boughs a fire we made.
Gipsies in the greenwood shade,
Hunters in the forest free,
Never camp'd more gleefully ;
And the woods with echoes rang,
While in concert thus we sang :

II

The Greenwood Shade

Oh, seek the greenwood shade,
   Away from the city din,
From heartless strife of trade,
   From fumes of beer and gin;
Where Commerce spreads her fleets,
   Where bloated Luxury lies,
Where lean Want prowls the streets,
   And stares with wolfish eyes.

Flee from the city's sin,
   Its many-color'd code,
Its palaces raised to sin,
   Its temples rear'd to God;[18]
Its cellars dark and dank,
   Where ne'er a sunbeam falls,
'Mid faces lean and lank
   As the hungry-looking walls;

Its fest'ring pits of woe,
   Its teeming earthly hells,
Whose surges ever flow
   In sound of Sabbath bells.
O God! I'd rather be
   An Indian in the wood,
To range through forest free
   In search of daily food.

Oh! rather I'd pursue
   The wolf and grizzly bear,
Than toil for the thankless few
   In seething pits of care.
Here Winter's breath is rude,
   His fingers cold and wan;
But what's his wildest mood
   To the tyranny of man?

To trackless forest wild,
   To loneliest abode,
The heart is reconciled
   That's felt Oppression's load.
The desert place is bright,
   The wilderness is fair,
If Hope but shed her light—
   If Freedom be but there.

15

III

Singing thus we circl'd round.
All beyond was gloom profound,
And the flame upon us threw
Something of a spectral hue—
Such a scene, so wild and quaint,
Rosa[30] would have lov'd to paint.
But, ere long, with sleep opprest,
There we laid us down to rest,
With the cold earth for our bed,
And the green boughs overhead ;
And again, at break of day,
Started on our weary way,
Through morasses, over bogs,
Wading rivers, walking logs,
Scrambling over fallen trees,
Wading pond-holes to the knees ;
Sometimes wand'ring from the track,
Then, to find it, turning back ;
Scorning ills that would betide us,
Stout of heart, the sun to guide us.

IV

Then there came a change of scene—
Groves of beech and maples green,
Streams that murmur'd through the glade,
Little flowers that lov'd the shade.
Lovely birds of gorgeous dye
Flitted 'mong the branches high,
Color'd like the setting sun,
But were songless, ev'ry one : [31]
No one like the linnet grey
In our home so far away ;
No one singing like the thrush
To his mate within the brush ;
No one like the gentle lark,

Singing 'tween the light and dark,
Soaring from the dewy sod,
Like a herald, up to God.
Some had lovely amber wings—
Round their necks were golden rings—
Some were purple, others blue,
All were lovely, strange and new ;
But, altho' surpassing fair,
Still the song was wanting there.
Then we heard the rush of pigeons,
Flocking to those lonely regions ;
And anon, when all was still,
Paus'd to hear the whip-poor-will ; [25]
And we thought of the cuckoo,
But this stranger no one knew.

V

Circling round a little lake,
Where the deer their thirst would slake,
Suddenly a lovely hind
Started up and snuff'd the wind.
Instantly bold Bill from Kent
Through its brain a bullet sent.
Desperate did the creature leap,
With a cry so wild and deep ;
Tried to make another bound,
Reel'd, and sank upon the ground.
And the sound the rifle made
Woke the herd within the shade :
We could plainly hear them rush
Through the leaves and underbrush.
Fled afar the startled quail ;
Partridge, with their fan-like tail,
Whirring past, with all their broods,
Sought the deeper solitudes.

VI

There the gentle thing lay dead,
With a deep gash in its head,
And its face and nostrils o'er
Spatter'd with the reeking gore ;
There she lay, the lovely hind,
She who could outstrip the wind,
She, the beauty of the wood,
Slaughter'd thus to be our food.

VII

Then we journey'd on our way,
And, with the declining day,
Hail'd with joy the promis'd lot,
Sat down on this very spot ;
Saw Ontario wind her way
'Round yon still, secluded bay.
Then it was a lonely scene,
Where man's foot had never been ;
Now it is a busy mart,
Fill'd with many a thing of art.
Here I love to sit and trace
Changes that have taken place :
Not a landmark when we came,
Not a feature, seems the same.
My companions, where are they ?
One by one they dropt away,
So of all I'm left the last, •
Thus to chronicle the past.

CUTTING THE FIRST TREE

I

Then to work we blithely went,
And we soon got up a tent,
On a point 'round which the lake
Wound like an enormous snake,
As 'twould bind it hard and fast.
Then it stretch'd away at last,
Till in the horizon lost,
Swallow'd in its cloud-built coast.

II

There our humble tent was spread,
With the green boughs overhead,
Such as wand'ring Arabs rear
In their deserts lone and drear.
'Twas a temporary thing,
Yet it made our hearts to sing;
And the wild duck, floating by,
Paus'd, and, with a startl'd cry,
Call'd her scatter'd brood to save—
Soon she dived beneath the wave.
And the crane that would alight
Scream'd at the unlook'd-for sight,
Then, like a bewilder'd thing,
Lakeward bent her heavy wing;
And the stag that came to drink,
Downward to the water's brink,
Show'd his branching head, and then
Bounded to the woods again.[18]

III

One sturdy elm I mind right well—
It was the first we tried to fell—
I think I could point out to you
The very spot on which it grew.

Together soon we at it went—
'Twas a kind of sacrament,
Like to laying the foundation
Of a city or a nation ;
But the sturdy giant stood,
Let us strike him as we would ;
Not a limb nor branch did quiver—
There he stood, as straight as ever.

IV

While we labor'd, lazy Bill
On a rotten log sat still.
There he sat, and shook his head,
And in doleful accents said : [18]
" Oh ! this chopping's horrid work,
Even for a barbarous Turk !
Many a doleful day of gloom
Have I groan'd upon the loom,—
Oh, that was a weary curse,
But this chopping's worse and worse !
Sleep will heal the wretch's woes,
Longest days draw to a close,
Time and tide will hurry past,
Look'd-for-long will come at last ;
Whigs may wear a cheerful face,
Even when they're out of place ;
Tories cease to rule the roast,
Britain learn to count the cost ;
Radicals may yet have pow'r,
Britain perish in an hour ;
Yankees cease their boasting, too,—
Who can tell what time may do ?
That a miracle would be,
Yet might happen possibly ;
There is even room to hope
For the Devil and the Pope.
Changes strange we all may see,
But we'll never fell that tree."

V

He had just repeated *never*,
When the limbs began to quiver,[21]
And a rent, which made us start,
Seem'd to split the giant's heart ;
And the branches, one and all,
Seem'd preparing for the fall—
Sway'd a moment to and fro,
As in doubt which way to go—
Then his head he gently bent,
All at once away he went—
Down he came, as loud as thunder,
Crushing limbs and brushwood under.

VI

Then we gazed upon the sight
With the consciousness of might,
And we cheer'd, as when a foe
Or a tyrant is laid low.
Soon, the orator, elated,
On the stump got elevated,
And, without premeditation,
Thus began a long oration :

VII

" Invaders of the ancient woods,
Dark primeval solitudes,
Where the prowling wolf and bear,
Time unknown, have made their lair,
We are God-commission'd here,
This rough wilderness to clear,
Till with joy it overflows,
Blooms and blossoms like the rose.
Trees, of which the poet sings,
May be very pretty things,
And these green-arch'd solitudes,

Where no traveller intrudes,
May be fine, I do not doubt,
Just to sit and sing about.
Sentiment's for those at ease,
But I fear they fell no trees ;
Not the sentimental tear,
But strong arms are needed here—
Stout hearts and determin'd will—
Don't give up like Brother Bill.

" Not by wringing of the hands
Shall we win the fertile lands,
But by honest, manly toil
Lords we shall be of the soil.
He who would in aught be great,
He must toil, and he must wait.
Favors drop not from the skies—
Perseverance gains the prize.
Hear ye what the sages say :
' Rome was not built in a day.'
With the giants bending o'er us,
We have work enough before us ;
Let us tramp on doubt and fear,
Work must be the watchword here.

" 'Tis too soon to count the winning,
Yet we've made a good beginning ;
And, you know, the half is done
When a job is well begun.
Triumph crowns the persevering—
By and by we'll have a clearing.
There's one giant overcast ;
Stubborn, but he fell at last.
There he lies, like Cæsar, slain,
And he'll never rise again.
Cæsar's mantle could not show
Half as many stabs, I trow,
When stern Brutus o'er him stood
With the dagger dripping blood.

I'm no seer, yet I can see
From the felling of a tree
Greater consequences rise
E'en than when a Cæsar dies.
Who would be a patriot now,
Sweat, not blood, must bathe his brow.
Like a patriotic band
Let us all join heart and hand ;
Let us use but common sense,
Industry and temperance ;
And God's blessing on our task
Let us now with reverence ask ;
For, with these, we'll hardly miss
Health and wealth and happiness."

VIII

When the speech drew to a close
Slowly doubting John arose,
Gave a quiet cough, and then
Said he, " Listen, fellow-men ;
Pay attention, and I will
Speak to you a parable.

IX

" In the days, long, long ago,
Ere the world was fill'd with woe,
In a lone, retirèd place
Liv'd a simple, honest race.
They were ignorant of art,
Yet they had far more of heart
Than the people nowadays,
With their dark and crooked ways.
They gave pow'r and place to no man
And had ev'rything in common ;
No one said, ' This is mine own '—
Money was a thing unknown ;
No lawgiver, and no pelf,

Each a law was to himself.
They had neither high nor low,
Rich nor poor—they did not know
Such distinctions e'er could be,
Such was their simplicity.
Yea, they were a happy band,
Cutivating their own land ;
Herds and flocks did fast increase,
And they ate their bread in peace.
Now, my inference is plain,
What has been may be again.
Just compare their simple ways
With the doings in our days :
Ev'ry man is for himself,
Hunting after pow'r and pelf ;
Not a moment can he rest,
Grasping like a thing possest ;
Running, racing, here and there,
Up and down and ev'rywhere,
Hunting for the root of evil,
Restless as the very devil—
He'll do aught to gain his end,
Kiss a foe, or stab a friend ;
He'll be either rude or civil,
Play the saint, or play the devil.
Neither scrupulous nor nice,
Follow Skinflint's last advice—
It is short and soon repeated,
Simply ' *Cheat or ye'll be cheated.*
A' moral creeds are strings o' blethers ;
The world's a goose, pluck ye her feathers ;
Nae matter how ye rax and draw,
If ye aye keep within the law ;
And ye may lie, and dodge, and wheel,
A' 's fair as lang 's ye dinna steal ;
And be ye either saint or sinner,
A' 's richt as lang as ye're the winner ;
So get cash, if ye can come at it
By fair means, but be sure and get it.'

" Now, my friends, 'tis clear as day,
  If we choose the proper way,
  Like the tree we've now laid low,
  We shall conquer vice and woe.
  I can see no reason why
  We might not unite and try,
  Like those simple men of old,
  To redeem the world from gold.
  Each for all and all for each
  Is the doctrine that I preach.
  Mind the fable of the wands
  ('Tis a truth that always stands) :
  Singly, we are poor and weak,
  But united, who can break ? "

THE LOG CABIN

The little log cabin is far in the woods,
  And the foot of the wayfarer seldom comes there.
Around it are stretching the great solitudes,
    Where the deer loves to roam, and the wolf makes
      his lair,
And the Red Man crawls on the surly bear,
  And the dead tree falls with a heavy crash ;
And the jagged hemlock and pine are there,
    And the dismal swamp and the dreary ash,
    And the eagle sits waiting the moment to dash.

And the roving son of the wilderness,
  While tracking the steps of the gentle deer,
The little log cabin will seldom miss,
  For the ringing sound of the ax he'll hear.
As he comes to taste of the welcome cheer,
  The children, who first had gazed in affright
When they saw his shaggy wolf-dog appear,
    Now run out to meet him with wild delight—
    And the heart of the savage is tamed at the sight.

The little log cabin is all alone ;
  Its windows are rude, and its walls are bare,
And the wind without has a weary moan.
  Yet Peace, like an angel, is nestling there ;
And Hope, with her rapt, uplifted air,
  Beholds in the distance the eglantine,
And the corn with its silver tassel,[32] where
  The hemlock is anchor'd beside the tall pine,
  And the creeping weed hangs with its long fringing
    vine.

And close by the cabin, tho' hid in the wood,
  Ontario lies, like a mirror of blue,
Where the children hunt the wild-duck's brood,
  And scare the tall crane and the lonely mew.
The eldest has fashion'd a light canoe,
  And with noisy glee they paddle along,
Or dash for the cliff where the eagle flew,
  Or sing in their gladness the fisherman's song,
  Till they waken the echoes the green woods among.

I

All was speed and bustle now,
Hurry sat on ev'ry brow ;
Naught was heard upon the breeze
But the sound of falling trees ;
Rough logs over streams were laid,
Cabins built, and pathways made ;
Little openings here and there,
Patches to the sun laid bare,
Growing larger ev'ry day ;
Time sped merrily away.
Troubles had we not a few,
For the work was strange and new ;
Mishaps neither few nor small,
Yet we rose above them all.

II

Then a change came o'er the scene :
Forests doff'd their garb of green
For a tawny brown attire,
Streak'd with grey, and gold, and fire.
Moan'd the wind like thing bereft,
As the little bluebird left,
And the wild-fowl of the lake
Sought the shelter of the brake ;
The humming-bird was seen no more,
And the pigeon southward bore ;
Soon the robin and the jay
With the flow'rs had pass'd away ;
Of a change all Nature spoke,
And the heav'ns were swathed in smoke ;
The sun a hazy circle drew,
And his bloody eye look'd through.
Thus the Indian summer ended,
And the sleety showers descended.
All the trees were stript, at last,
And the snow fell thick and fast,
While the lake with sullen roar
Dash'd her foam upon the shore,
And the wind in angry mood
Swept the leafless solitude.

III

Then the wolves their visits paid us,
Nightly came to serenade us.
In the middle of the night
I have started with affright,
For there were around my dwelling
More than fifty demons yelling—
I could plainly hear them tramp
Round the border of the swamp.
I have look'd into the dark,
Tried to make old Towser bark.
He would only fawn and whine,

While the terror-stricken swine
Ran around like things insane,
And the sheep, in fear and pain,
Huddled all within a nook—
How they trembled and they shook !
And the frighten'd cattle bore
Close and closer to the door—
I could see the savage ire
Flashing from their eyes like fire.
Then I'd hear a long-drawn howl,
Then a little snappish growl,
Then a silence deep as death,
Till the furies drew their breath ;
Then, with voices yelling o'er us,
Fifty demons joined in chorus.
Thus they'd howl till dawn of day,
Then they'd scamper all away.

IV

Tho' winter's cold was long and dreary,
We were hopeful, we were cheery ;
We had many merry meetings,
Social gath'rings, kindly greetings ;
To the wall the log was laid,
And a roaring fire was made.
Tho' the storm might rave without,
We were blithe with song about ;
With the maidens' laugh for chorus,
Then the youths would tell their stories
Of the hunting of the coon,
All beneath the autumn moon—
Of the logging in the fall—
Of oxen terrible to haul—
Of the mighty chopping match,
Gain'd by but a single natch.
Thus the time would steal along,
With the tale and with the song ;
Little Mac would sit and sing
Till the very roof would ring :

V

I Ask Not for Fortune

I ask not for fortune,
    I ask not for wealth,
But give me the cabin,
    With freedom and health ;
With some one to love me—
    Joy's roses to wreathe—
With no one above me,
    And no one beneath.

Let tools be officious
    And flatter the great,
Let knaves be ambitious
    To rule in the state ;
Give alms to the needy,
    Give fame to the fool,
Give gold to the greedy,
    Let Bonaparte rule,

But give me the cabin,
    Tho' far, far apart ;
I'll make it love's dwelling,
    The home of the heart ;
With some one to love me—
    Joy's roses to wreathe—
With no one above me,
    And no one beneath.

VI

Then we'd cheer him loud and long
For the jolly hunter's song,
Who, while roving in the shade,
Woo'd and won the Indian maid :

VII

The Indian Maid

Oh, come, my love ! Oh, come with me
    To my sweet home afar ;
This arm will guard—no guide need we
    Save yonder ev'ning star.

I am not of thy clime or creed,
    Yet be not thence afraid ;
Love makes these accidents, indeed,
    My pretty Indian Maid !

Thine eyebrow is the vault of night,
    Thy cheek the dusk of dawn,
Thy dark eye is a world of light,
    My pretty, bounding fawn !
I'll deck thy hair with jewels rare,
    Thy neck with rich brocade,
And in my heart of hearts I'll wear
    My pretty Indian Maid !

Then come, my love ! Oh, come with me !
    And ere the braves awake
Our bark will speed like arrow free
    Across the mighty lake ;
Where faces pale will welcome thee,
    Sweet flow'ret of the shade,
And of my bow'r thou'lt lady be,
    My lovely Indian Maid !

VIII

Then the elder ones would tell
Of the great things that befell ;
Of the feats unsaid, unsung,
In the days when they were young ;
Of the worth existing then—
Maidens fair and mighty men ;
Or they'd sing the ballad rimes,
Histories of other times,
Of the manners past away,
Living in the minstrel's lay :
Gil Morice, the Earl's brave son ;
Chevy Chase, so dearly won.
It may be that I'm growing old,
Or that my heart is turning cold,
Or that my ear is falsely strung,
Or wedded to my native tongue ;
Yet those strains, so void of art,
Those old gushings of the heart,

Heaving, swelling, like the sea,
With the soul of poetry,
They must live within the breast,
Till this weary heart's at rest.
Then our tears would fall like rain,
List'ning to old Aunty Jane,
While in mournful tones she'd sing
The ballad of the Gipsy King :

IX

The Gipsy King

Lord Sempill's mounted on his steed,
  And to the greenwood gane ;
The Gipsy steals to the wicket gate,
  And whispers Lady Jane.
The lark is high in heav'n above,
  But his lay she does not hear,
For her heaving heart is rack'd with love,
  With hope, with doubt, and fear.

" Thy father's halls are fair and wide,
  The Sempill woods are green ;
But love can smile, oh ! sweeter far,
  In Gipsy tent, I ween.
The crawflow'r hangs by Cartha's side,[5]
  The rose by Elderslie,
The primrose by the bank of Clyde,
  The heather bell on Dee ;

" But I've built our bow'r beside the Gryffe,
  Where hangs the hinny pear ;
For I've seen no spot in my roving life
  To match the vale of Weir."
The sweet flow'rs drink the crystal dew,
  The bonnie wee birds sing ;
But she hears them not, as off she flies,
  Away with the Gipsy King.

But the false page hurries to my Lord,
  And the tale to him doth bear ;
He swears an oath, as he dashes off
  And away to the vale of Weir.

16

The day fades o'er the Lomond's green,
  But gloamin's hour is long,[33]
He lights him at the Gipsy's tent
  And mars the bridal song.

" Thou'st stolen the pride of my house and heart,
  With thy spells and magic ring ;
Thy head goes out at my saddle bow,
  Wert thou thrice a Gipsy King.'
" I used no spell but the spell of love—
  And love knows no degree ;
I ne'er turned back on friend or foe,
  But I will not fight with thee."

The Gipsy reels on the bloody sod,
  And the lady flies between ;
But the blow that redd'ns her raven locks
  Was meant for the Gipsy King.
" Oh, what have I done?" Lord Sempill cries,
  And his sword away doth fling ;
" Arise, my daughter, oh ! arise,
  And wed with your Gipsy King ! "

He lifts her gently in his arms,
  And holds her drooping head ;
But the tears are vain that fall like rain,
  For Lady Jane is dead.
They laid her where the alder waves,
  With many a sigh and tear ;
And the grey cairn still points out her grave,
  Adown the vale of Weir.

And the maid of the hamlet seeks out the spot,
  And loves the tale to tell ;
The " Place of Grief" is the name it bears
  Adown the dreary dell.

THE INDIAN BATTLE

I

This happen'd (I forget the year)
Shortly after we came here.
All upon a summer day
Was I busy with the hay.
While I paus'd to wipe my face,
I could see, with hurried pace,
Someone coming down the hill—
What! can that be Lazy Bill?
Sure there's something in the blast
When poor Billy runs so fast!
Up he came, and down he sat,
Puffed, and laid aside his hat;
Wiped the sweat from off his face:
"Oh, my vitals, what a race!
Go! oh, go, and get your gun,
Or we're murdered, every one!

"All the Mohawks are upon us—
May the Lord have mercy on us!
They are thick as pigeons—Hush!
Hear them yelling in the brush!
Death in any shape is horrid,
But 'tis awful to be worried!
Oh! to think that I came here
To be roasted like a deer!
Little did I think, oh, Dee,
That would be the end of me.
Had I but a gun and sword
I would dash among the horde;
On the cannibals I'd set—
I'd do something desperate!"

II

Home we went, where all were arming,
For the thing look'd quite alarming :
Children, with imploring looks,
Running into secret nooks ;
Women seeking hiding-places,
With their terror-stricken faces ;
Men were running here and there,
Hunting weapons everywhere—
Anything that could be found,
Aught that would inflict a wound ;[18]
For we all resolv'd we should
Sell our lives as dear's we could.

III

There was fighting Bill from Kent
(Bill was in his element),
Stalking, like a soldier born,
With his gun and powder-horn ;
Then there was old soldier Hugh,
With his sword, and musket, too :
Like a gen'ral there he stood,
In his old commanding mood.
Soon we muster'd fifty men,
But of muskets only ten ;
Seven pitchforks and a dirk,
They would help us do the work ;
Each man had an ax, at least,
And a will to do his best.
Soldier Hugh assumed command,
And the line of battle plann'd,
Sent his scouts, that he might know
The manœuvres of the foe.
" Muskets to the front ! " cried he ;
" Keep your ranks, and follow me ! "

IV

Then, with pulses beating high,
On we marched to do or die.
When we reach'd yon little height,
Then we halted for the fight ;
Where we all in silence stood,
Looking down upon the wood.
Then there rose a fearful yell,
As of fiends let loose from hell ;
We could hear the arrows whirring,
And the very leaves seem'd stirring.
" Now, my lads, be firm and steady ;
When order's giv'n, be ye ready.
Pikemen, you protect the rear ;
Presently we'll have them here."
Not a whisper, not a breath,
In a silence deep as death,
With grim faces, there we stood
Looking down upon the wood.
Minute after minute pass'd,
And suspense grew great at last ;
We would have giv'n much to know
The motions of our hidden foe ;
But at last a scout came in,
Saying, with a laughing grin,
We might safely all disarm,
For 'twas but a false alarm—
'Twas two tribes in war array
That had fought since break of day,
And their chieftains, fierce and cruel,
Were preparing for a duel.
This was welcome news indeed !
From the fear of danger freed,
Off we started with delight
To behold the coming fight.

V

In the bosom of the wood,
With his tribe each chieftain stood.
An old windfall's level green
Form'd an open space between,
And the silence was unbroken,
Not a single word was spoken.
Yet anxiety and hope
In each bosom seem'd to cope.
Hate, the horrid heritage
Handed down from age to age,
In the swarthy faces shone
As the chiefs came slowly on.

VI

Eagle, tall and straight and daring,
Stept out with a lordly bearing ;
Ease and grace were in his tread,
An eagle's feather on his head.
Agile as the stag was he,
Brave and beautiful to see,
Courage in his very walk ;
In one hand a tomahawk,
And the other grasp'd a knife—
Thus he stalk'd on to the strife.

VII

Hemlock seem'd much less in height,
Broader and of greater might ;
Shoulders of herculean strength,
Arms of an enormous length ;
Muscular and firmly set,
Strength and cunning in him met ;
On his head a raven's plume,
In his eye a savage gloom.
Many a war-path he had walk'd,
Many a foe had tomahawk'd—

A model savage, dark and dun,
Devil, if there e'er was one,
He approach'd with stealthy pace,
And the cunning of his race.

VIII

Each stood still to eye his foe
Ere he'd make the fatal throw.
Hemlock seem'd about to fling,
Eagle gave a whoop and spring,
Seem'd as if he taller grew ;
Both upon the instant threw.
Eagle wheel'd, the weapon pass'd,
Or that whoop had been his last ;
Hemlock, sinking on the plain,
Quick was on his feet again ;
Down his face a stream of red,
Deep the gash upon his head.
There a moment he did stand,
Grasp'd the long knife in his hand,
Then he bounded on apace ;
Eagle met him in the race.
Closing with a fearful yell,
Grappling, they together fell.
O'er each other there they roll'd,
Clasping each in deadly hold ;
And, anon, with seeming ease,
Hemlock rises to his knees
(Still his foe is in his grasp,
Lock'd within his deadly clasp) ;
On his haunches, like a bear,
Holds him for a moment there.
In his eyes the blood is streaming ;
I could see the long knife gleaming.
Ere the blow could fall amain
He is rolling on the plain.
Sudden as the panther fleet,
Eagle springs upon his feet ;

Like the serpent in the brake,
Or the deadly rattlesnake,
With a quick, unerring dart,
Strikes his victim to the heart;
On him leaps with deadly glare,
Twines his fingers in his hair,
And, before his kindred's eyes,
There he scalps him ere he dies.

IX

There the rival nations stood,
Umpires of the deadly feud ;
Silent, yet with wild delight,
Watch'd the fortunes of the fight ;
But the Hurons, one and all,
When they saw their chieftain fall,
Tho' they seem'd a moment crush'd,
Like a tempest on they rush'd ;
When Eagle, with triumphant cry,
Waved their chieftain's scalp on high ;
Then he bounded like a deer
To the Mohawks, hast'ning near.
Then the Hurons stood at bay,
Bore their slaughter'd chief away ;
Far into the woods they bore,
And were seen and heard no more.

DONALD BAN *

I

'Twas here, upon this very spot,
    Where weeds so wildly grow,
Old Donald's log-built cabin stood
    Full thirty years ago.
Erect he was, and tall and fair,
    The perfect type of man,
And Highland bards had sung of him
    As stalwart Donald Ban.

---

* Fair Donald.

He was a hunter in his youth,
  Had travel'd far and wide,
And knew each hill and vale and stream
  From John o' Groat's to Clyde.
And well he lov'd to sit and tell,
  As well I lov'd to hear,
Of feats of strength and daring while
  He tracked the fallow deer.

The spirit of the mighty hills
  Within his breast he bore,
And how he loved to sit and sing
  Their ballads o'er and o'er ;
For he had treasur'd in his heart
  The legends and the lays,
The loves, the joys, the smiles, the tears,
  The voice of other days.

The fields where heroes fought and fell,
  The graves wherein they sleep,
And many a mountain-robber's hold
  Where captives used to weep ;
The mossy cairns by strath and stream,
  Renown'd in Highland lay—
A strange old world of shade and seer
  Has pass'd with him away.

And he had gazed on Nature's face,
  Until his spirit caught
Some strange mysterious whispers from
  The inner world of thought.
He lov'd the things far deepest which
  He could not understand,
And had a strange, wild worship of
  The gloomy and the grand.

Each mountain had a heart and soul,
  A language of its own—
A grand old monarch seated there
  Upon his cloud-built throne.

The wailing of the winter winds,
 The whispers of the glen,
Were living and immortal things
 A-watching mortal men.

And how the old man griev'd to think
 That he should hear no more
The earthquake wrestling with the hills,
 Or Corrybrechtan's[3] roar.

II

Ah! poor Donald, who can tell
The heart-break of your last farewell?
When Oppression's iron hand
Drove you from that mountain land,
Forced you from the strath and fell,
From the hills you loved so well;
When you took your last adieu
Of Benlomond in the blue,
Looked upon Ben Nevis hoar,
Never to behold him more;
Last the old roof-tree did view,
That so long had sheltered you—
You and all your stalwart race—
Set in flames before your face;
And beheld the lofty pine,
Emblem of the honor'd line,
Fell'd without remorse or shame—
Fell'd to feed the wasting flame
That consumed your humble dwelling;
Who can blame your heart for swelling?
Who condemn the blows you gave
To the tyrant and his slave?
Who condemn the curse that sprung
Ever ready from your tongue,
Or the imprecations deep
That from out your heart would leap

When you thought upon that day
And the blue hills far away,
Or the tears that would o'erflow
When you told that tale of woe?

III

Often at the close of eve
He would sit him down and grieve,
Then he'd take his pipes and play
Till his heart was far away ;
On the spirit of the strain,
Wafted to the hills again ;
Or, while tears his eyelids wet,
Sing this sweet song of regret :

IV

Why Left I My Country

"Why left I my country, why did I forsake
The land of the hill for the land of the lake?
These plains are rich laden as summer's rich sky,
But give me the bare cliffs that tow'r to the sky ;
Where the thunderer sits in the halls of the storm,
And the eagles are screaming on mighty Cairngorm !
Benledi ! Benlomond ! Benawe ! Benvenue !
Old monarchs forever enthroned in the blue ;
Ben Nevis ! Benavin !—the brotherhood hoar
That shout through the midnight to mighty Ben More !
Tho' lovely this land of the lake and the tree,
Yet the land of the scarr'd cliff and mountain for me !
Each cairn has its story, each river its song,
And the burnies are wimpling to music along ;
But here no old ballads the young bosom thrills,
No song has made sacred the forest and rills ;
And often I croon o'er some old Scottish strain,
Till I'm roaming the hills of my country again.
And oh ! may she ever be upright and brave,
And ne'er let her furrows be turn'd by a slave ;
And ne'er may dishonor the blue bonnet stain,
Altho' I should ne'er wear the bonnet again."

V

Hard was poor old Donald's fate :
In a strange land, desolate,
Scarcely had he crost the sea
When his son, the last of three,
He, the beautiful and brave,
Found an exile's nameless grave.
Then his wife, who was his pride,
At Point Saint Charles too early died,
And he made for her a grave
By the lone Saint Lawrence wave ;
And at last, when all were gone,
Heartsick, homeless, wander'd on.
Still one comforter he found
In poor Fleetfoot, his staghound.
They had climbed the hills of heather
They had chased the deer together,
And together they would mourn[18]
Over days ne'er to return.

VI

After wand'ring far and near,
Built he last a cabin here ;
'Twas at least a kind of home,
From which he would never roam ;
Hoped afflictions all would cease,
And he'd end his days in peace.
Ah ! poor Donald ! 'twas God's will
There was one affliction still
That was wanting to fill up
To the brim your bitter cup ;
And it came in loss of sight,
Leaving you in endless night,
Helpless on a foreign shore,
Ne'er to see " Lochaber more."

VII

For a little while he pined,
But, becoming more resign'd,
Then he wander'd far and wide,
With poor Fleetfoot for his guide.
In the Highland garb array'd,
On the Highland pipes he play'd.
Ever at the welcome sound
Youths and maidens gathered round—
More than fifty I have seen
Dancing barefoot on the green,
Tripping it so light and gay
To the merry tunes he'd play.
While he blew with might and main,
Looking almost young again,
Playing up the old strathspeys
With the heart of early days,
Then to see him, who could know
He had ever tasted woe?

VIII

Thus for many years he went
Round each backwoods settlement ;
But, wherever he might roam,
Here was still his house and home.

Always, as the Autumn ended,
Ere the sleety show'rs descended,
When the leaves were red and sear
And the bitter days were near,
When the winds began to sigh,
And the birds away to fly,
And the frost came to the ground,
Donald's steps were homeward bound.
Long before he would appear,
Loud his pipe's note we could hear.
At the glad, the welcome sound,

All the neighbors gather'd round ;
Many a young heart leap'd with joy,
Many a happy little boy
Bounded onward, glad to meet
Old companion, faithful Fleet.
Then would Donald sit and tell
Of the strange things that befell
At the places where he play'd,
Of the friends his music made,
Of the hearts touch'd by his strains,
Of his triumphs and his gains,
Always ending with this song,
In the woods remember'd long :

IX

The Old Highland Piper

Afar from the land of the mountain and heather,
    An old Highland piper look'd sad o'er the sea,
And sigh'd o'er the time when the sound of his chanter
    Was known from the Isles to the bank of the Dee.

And oft, as the shades of the night would foregather,
    And day was forsaking the weary pine plains,
He sang of the hills of the dark purple heather,
    The hills that so often re-echo'd his strains.

Oh ! sad was the heart of the old Highland piper,
    When forced from the hills of Lochaber away,
No more to behold the gigantic Benlomond,
    Nor wander again on the banks of the Tay.

But still, as sleep comes to my lone, weary pillow,
    I hear Corrybrechtan again in my dreams,
I see the blue peaks of the lone cliffs of Jura,
    And wander again by her wild, dashing streams.

What tho' I must roam in the land of the stranger,
    My heart's 'mong the hills of Lochaber the while ;
Tho' welcom'd, ah ! 'tis in the tongue of the Sassenach,
    'Tis not the heart-welcome they give in Argyle.

They know not the heart of the old Highland piper,
　And little they think that it bleeds to the core,
When, weary with mirth and the dance, they invite me
　To play them the wail of " Lochaber no more."

How little they know of the weight of affection
　The scattered descendants of mighty Lochiel
Still bear in their bosom to aught that reminds them
　Of the dark purple heather and land of the Gael.

They ne'er saw the tempest in Glen Avin gather,
　Nor heard the storm shrieking round Colonsay's shore,
Nor felt the cliffs quake 'neath the tramp of the thunder,
　Nor heard the hills join in the mighty uproar.

And little they know of the tie that still binds us—
　A tie which the stranger, no, never can feel—
The love which we bear to the land left behind us,
　The wounds of our parting which never can heal.

And still, as day fades o'er the placid Pacific,
　To brighten the hills that look'd lovely of yore,
I seek the lone sea-beach, and play till the waters
　And pine forests ring with " Lochaber no more."

X

Thus the years with Donald sped
Till his health and strength were fled.
Time had changed his flowing hair,
Furrow'd deep his forehead fair ;
But tho' old and blind and maim,
Yet his heart was still the same.
But 'twas plainer ev'ry day
He was wearing fast away—
All his wand'rings and his woes
Drawing swiftly to a close.
Well I mind of all that pass'd
When I went to see him last.
On his bed I found him lying,
And the poor old man was dying ;
No one near to soothe or guide him,

Not a living soul beside him :
Only Fleetfoot—faithful hound—
Met me with a welcome bound,
Lick'd my hand and led the way
Where his dying master lay ;
Placed his paws upon the bed,
With a loving kind of dread ;
Looked the rev'rence of his race
In his dying master's face ;
Ask'd me with his anxious eye,
"Will he live, or will he die ? "
When he saw me shake my head,
Down he lay beside the bed,
Whining there so long and low
That mine eyes did overflow.

"Down, Fleet, down ! " the old man said,[18]
"Let us walk with noiseless tread ;
Yonder herd of fallow deer
Know not that the hunter's near ! "

Soon his brain was wandering fast
From the present to the past ;
Now he talk'd of other times,
Singing snatches of old rimes.
In a quick and hurried tone,
This disjointed talk went on :

"Hush ! the hills are calling on me,
Their Great Spirit is upon me ;
Listen ! that is old Ben More ;
Hush ! that's Corrybrechtan's roar ;
See ! a gleam of light is shed
Afar upon Ben Nevis' head ;
There ! 'tis on Benlomond now,
The glory's resting on his brow ;
From his locks the gold is streaming,
And his purple mantle's gleaming ;
The crimson and the amber rest

On the deep folds of his vest,
And still anon some isle of blue
Is for a moment heaving through.
The clouds are rolling fast away,
The dark is dappling into day;
Come, my love, we are aweary
Of these woods so lone and dreary;
We have tarried far too long
From the land of love and song.
Ah! they told me thou wert dead,
By the lone Saint Lawrence laid;
And our children, sons and daughters,
Gone like music on the waters.
Bring my staff! let us away
To the land of mountains grey,
Never, never more to roam
From our native ' Highland home.'"

XI

He seem'd as if about to rise,
When suddenly he closed his eyes,
And his spirit pass'd away
From its weary house of clay.

XII

After all your toil and cumber,
Sweetly, Donald, may you slumber.
Your life's little tragedy
Shall not wholly pass away,
For there were, indeed, in thee
Gleams of a divinity,
Longings, aspirations high,
After things which cannot die.
And your soul was like your land,
Stern and gloomy, great and grand.
Yet each yawning gulf between
Had its nooks of sweetest green;
17

Little flow'rs, surpassing fair—
Flow'rs that bloom no other where—
Little natives of the rock,
Smiling 'midst the thunder-shock ;
Had its rainbow-gleams of glory,
Hanging from the chasms hoary,
Dearer for each savage sound,
And the desolation round.

XIII

Much remains still to be told
Of these men and times of old—
Of the changes in our days
From their simple honest ways—
Of the quacks, on spoil intent,
That flock'd into our settlement—
Of the swarms of public robbers,
Speculators, and land jobbers—
Of the sorry set of teachers,
Of the bogus tribe of preachers,
Of the host of herb physicians,
And of cunning politicians.
But the sun has hid his face,
And the night draws on apace ;
Shadows gather in the west,
Beast and bird are gone to rest.
With to-morrow we'll not fail
To resume our humble tale.

COMPANIONSHIP IN BOOKS

THIS generation ne'er can know
　　The toil we had to undergo
While laying the great forest low.

For many a weary year I wrought,
With poverty and hardship fought,
And hardly had I time for thought.

In ev'ry stroke, in ev'ry blow,
In ev'ry tow'ring pine laid low,
I felt a triumph o'er a foe.

Each knotty hemlock, old and brown,
Each elm in thunder hurling down,
A jewel added to my crown.

If e'er my heart within me died,
Then up would start my stubborn pride,
And dash the coward thoughts aside !

Hope ever singing in my ear,
" Be brave, for what hast thou to fear ?
The heav'ns are watching o'er thee here ! "

But, fighting with those stubborn facts,[18]
My spirit paid a heavy tax—
My soul grew callous as my ax.

But still some wand'ring sympathy,
Some song, learn'd at my mother's knee,
Came as the bread of life to me.

Save for those raindrops from on high—
Those fountains opened in the sky—
My life-streams would have all gone dry.

Until that time, I little knew
What books for lonely hearts can do,
Till spirits round my heart they drew.

My cabin seem'd a whole world wide ;
Kings enter'd in without their pride,
And warriors laid their swords aside.

There came the Saxon, there the Celt,
And all had knelt where I had knelt,
For all had felt what I had felt.

I saw, from clime and creed apart,
Still heaving 'neath their robes of art,
The universal human heart.

And Homer and Sir Walter Scott—
They enter'd in my humble cot,
And cheer'd with tales my lowly lot.

And Burns came singing songs divine,
His heart and soul in ev'ry line—
A glorious company was mine !

I was a brother to the great—
Shakspeare himself on me did wait,
With leaves torn from the book of fate.

They ask'd me not of rank or creed,
And yet supplied my spirit's need—
Oh, they were comforters, indeed !—

And show'd me by their magic art
Those awful things at which we start,
That hover round the human heart ;

Fate ever watching with her shears,
And mixing all our hopes with fears,
And drenching all our joys in tears.

They show'd how contradictions throng,
How by our weakness we are strong,
And how we're righted by the wrong ;

Unveil'd new regions to my sight,
And made the weary winter's night
A perfect revel of delight.

THE SETTLER'S FIRST SABBATH DAY

WOULDST thou know the soul of silence?
    Go to the untrodden woods ;
Lift thy voice aloud, and listen
    To the answering solitudes.
Wouldst thou have deep confirmation
    That a God indeed doth reign—
Feel the awful, unseen Presence?
    Go, and never doubt again.

Far in a Canadian forest,
    Underneath a spreading oak,
Ere the solitude had echo'd
    To the woodman's cheerful stroke ;
Ere the branching elm had fallen,
    And the cedar and the pine,
Ever since Time's birth, had blossom'd
    Undisturbed by man's design ;

Here some power-expatriated
    Sons of Scotia, sad, forlorn,
Met, their father's God to worship,
    On a quiet Sabbath morn.
Poverty, perchance oppression,
    Drove them to the woods to dwell,
Leaving half their hearts behind them
    'Mong the hills they loved so well.

Want, the mother of affliction,
   Had been their familiar long ;
Yet to battle with the forest
   Hearts they brought both stout and strong.
Some, the soldiers of affection,
   Soldiers of the noblest kind,
Came to seek a home for parents,
   Left in poverty behind.

Some, from wives and children parted,
   Hope allaying their distress,
For she whisper'd she would find them
   Freedom in the wilderness.
Some were creatures of misfortune ;
   Of tyranny and wrong were some ;
Yet their hearts were griev'd within them,
   Parting from their childhood's home.

'Mid this group of humble beings
   There was one old grey-haired man
Who was loved, yea, as a father—
   Round him all the children ran.
He had look'd upon the world,
   Yea, for three-score years and ten,
Had still in his heart unbounded
   Love for all his fellow-men.

Things for which the world is struggling,
   Honor, riches, power, and pelf,
Were to him but moping shadows
   Groping in the cell of Self.
Love had lent him strength to wrestle
   Even with the storms of fate ;
In his heart he bore no hatred,
   Only to the soul of Hate.

Yea, he would have been a poet
   Had not penury, the while,
And a sense of duty, doom'd him
   To a life of ceaseless toil.

Yet by times the God within him
   Would lift up His awful voice,
And the melodies imprison'd
   Burst their fetters and rejoice.

And his pent-up human feelings
   Ever and anon would start
Into words which found an entrance
   Even to the roughest heart.
Surely 'twas the God of Jacob
   Honor'd this old man to raise,
Here in Nature's green cathedral,
   To His name the song of praise.

In that awful leafy temple
   Not a sound the silence broke,
Save his voice in prayer ascending
   From the shadow of the oak.
Their full souls to his responded,
   As to some old prophet seer ;
Anxiously they circled round him,
   Hush'd their very hearts to hear.

The Address

" We are met, belov'd friends, in this temple of green,
   A fit place to worship the awful Unseen,
Who guided us safely across the great deep,
And hushed the wild waves and their billows to sleep.
In the city and mart man may not recollect
To ask the Great Father to guide and protect :
Too often we've seen him bent under a load—
A burden of guilt—as he travel'd life's road ;
But here in the forest, with danger beset,
Ah ! dead must the heart be that e'er can forget.

" We have left a loved land where we suffer'd sore wrong,
   But in these wild forests we'll sing a new song.

Our wrongs we'll forget ; let it now be our care
To cherish the virtue which still blossoms there.
Our hearts to affection can only give way
When we think of our homes and the hills far away.
Ah ! yes, I had hoped to be laid down at last,
When life, with its toils and its troubles, had pass'd,
Beside the old church where the lone willows weep,
Where our friends and our kindred all silently sleep.
My time must be short, and I well could have borne
By injustice and wrong that my heart should be torn,
But oh ! it has been the long wish of my life
To help man to shake off deception and strife.
I'm sick and I'm weary of havoc and hate,
Let love be the genius, the soul of this state !
In peace let us found a community here ;
We'll govern by love, not by hatred and fear.
I thank you, my children, for that deep Amen,
And I'll die with the hope that you'll all be true men.

" Then on ! on ! ye brave, to the battle of peace !
And hasten the time when men's sorrows shall cease.
The ax is your weapon, the forest your foe,
And joy, peace and plenty come forth at each blow.
Ah, poor is the triumph the warrior feels !
Humanity weeps while his work she reveals.
How long shall the demons of ruin and wrath
With bleeding hearts cover the war-wasted path ?
How long shall Oppression her bloody lash wave,
And the poor tool of Mammon a brother enslave ?

" I see in the future a sweet smiling plain,
With green pastures waving, and rich golden grain.
What will they avail you, if folly and sin,
Or greed, blight the flow'rs of affection within ?
What will it avail, tho' your herds may increase,
If still ye are strangers to virtue and peace ?
For virtue alone is the soul of a state—
Without it we vainly are wealthy and great.
Ah ! yes, there is treasure more precious than gold,

Not found in the markets—a treasure untold.
The heart longs for something on which to rely,
A something the wealth of the world cannot buy;
A something which beauty, which virtue foreshows,
Which genius announces, but cannot disclose;
A something above the dark regions of sense,
Akin to the spirit which beckons it hence.
And mind, my lov'd children, that, go where we will,
There danger and death surely follow us still;
There are shafts in the quiver of fortune and fate,
That, say what we will, we can ne'er feel elate.
Be we rich, be we poor, there's a death hanging o'er us,
An awful eternity stretching before us;
We're hurriedly wafted on this wave of time
To the great mighty ocean that's stretching sublime;
And if the rude tempest and storms overtake us,
Aye mind there is One that will never forsake us!
There's only one Pilot can bid the storm cease,
And bring us at last to the haven of peace;
Sublime was the sorrow His human heart bore,
That headaches and heartaches might know us no more.

"Then oh! let us live so that at the great day
When the framework of Nature shall burst and give way,
When 'midst the great ruin the Judge will descend,
Eternity with Him, and time at an end;
Oh! then we may enter and taste of the joy
Which time, death and sorrow can never destroy;
Oh! then may we look back from that happy sphere
With joy to the Sabbath we first worshipt here,
Communing with angels, with Christ for a Friend,
And a Sabbath of glory which never shall end."

And many years have pass'd away—
    The forest all is torn,
Save the old oak, in memory left
    Of that sweet Sabbath morn.
And some are with the living still,
    And some are with the dead,

Who treasured up within their hearts
　　The words the old man said.

His work still lives, tho' he is laid
　　Within the quiet grave ;
The old oak is the monument
　　Which over him doth wave.
Some one has graven on its trunk,
　　Who holds his memory dear :
"Stranger, this is a sacred spot ;
　　A Christian slumbers here."

————

THE BACKWOODS PHILOSOPHER

WELL, as I said, I'm forest bred,
　　A rough uncultured critter,
Yet in my way I've read per day
　　Some page of forest natur'.
Among the first things I obsarv'd—
　　My mates it didn't strike—
What ar we do, we'll nar get two
　　That see a tree alike.

Folks may be honest and sincere,
　　And may ha' eyes to see through,
And hold a principle as dear,
　　Tho' they don't see as we do.
Now that's a very leetle fact,
　　It seems as plain as prattle ;
Would folks but see 't, 'twould save much heat,
　　An' many an' many a battle.

Another thing which took my eye
　　Was Natur's moral statur',
For Natur' will not tell a lie,
　　Nor won't have lies, will Natur'.

A tree will fall the way she's cut,
    No words aside can win her,
And smash you splay, if in her way,
    Let you be saint or sinner.

And when you go to square her up,
    Nar heed what fools may say;
Cut to the chalk—aye, that's the talk—
    Let chips strike who they may.
He who would talk you off the straight,
    You tell him that he drivels;
The right is right ! 'twill stand the light,
    Be 't God's law or the devil's.

And he's no better than a fool,
    A little silly critter,
Who thinks by cunnin' to out-pull
    Or cheat old Mother Natur'.
Another thing which did me strike,
    While through the forest goin'—
Your timber's always somethin' like
    The soil on which it's growin'.

The elm will root him firm, I ween,
    'Mong rocks, and he will thrive
Upon the spot where maples green
    Could hardly keep alive.
And he will thrive and flourish thar,
    And to the winds he'll call,
And talk wi' spirits o' the air
    Beside the waterfall.

Yon oak's exposed to wind and rain,
    To ev'ry storm that swells,
So ev'ry fibre, leaf and grain
    His long life-battle tells.
He gathers strength from ev'ry shock,
    And tougher still he grows,
And looks defiance from the rock
    To ev'ry storm that blows.

While far within the shelterin' vale
　　The lady-maple leans,
And tells her quiet, peaceful tale
　　To gentle evergreens.
Close by, a brother all-misplaced,
　　In an unfriendly soil,
He fights and frets until he gets
　　Demoralized the while.

Then sad and lone and woe-begone,
　　To ev'ry wind he sighs,
Resigns the strife for light and life,
　　And sullenly he dies.
So, like the tree, what we would be
　　Depends not on our skill;
And wrong or right are we, despite
　　Our wishes or our will.

———

DR. BURNS *

Preaching in the Scotch Block.

GENTLE, dove-like Peace is brooding
　　O'er the woods this Sabbath morn;
Save the ox-bell's distant tinkle
　　No sound on the air is borne—
Not a breath the leaves to rustle,
　　Not a breath to stir the waves,
Oh! how deep the quiet hanging
　　O'er these green, forgotten graves!

There the church in her grey glory—
　　Deeper is the holy shade
Round the sacred spot where all the
　　Ancient foresters are laid.

---

* Dr. Robert Burns, Minister of Knox Church, Toronto, 1845-56, afterwards
Professor in and Principal of Knox College, Toronto.

Hush! there's something 'mong the willows,
  Whisp'ring to the silent dead ;
Yea, the heart hears their communing—
  Hears, tho' not a word is said.

Surely 'tis not idle fancy
  That still whispers in my breast,
Spirits of the dead are with us
  On the hallow'd morn of rest.
Hark ! the bell's deep hollow summons,
  Calling Scotia's sons to pray'r—
See ! from wood and field they're coming,
  With a deep devotional air.

Mountaineers, with deep mark'd features,
  Tartans showing clannish pride ;
Shepherds from the Vale of Ettrick,
  Peasants from the Strath of Clyde.
There old Donald Bane, from Badenoch—
  Whose grandsire at Preston fell—
Of the hapless house of Stuart,
  Weeping, still the tale he'll tell.

These are kindred of Rob Ruadh,
  From Loch Lomond's sounding shore ;
Still they wear their hero's tartan,
  Tho' his hills they'll see no more.
Old John, from the Braes of Yarrow,
  In his shepherd's plaid appears ;
Its warm folds around his bosom
  Wake the thoughts of other years,

Till he hears the lark in heaven,
  Sees the sheep among the hills,
Hears the Yarrow, till his dim eye
  With the tear of mem'ry fills.
And tho' his clear'd fields have cost him
  Years of labor and of pain,
He would give them all to be but
  A poor shepherd boy again.

In the rudely-fashion'd pulpit
Now a little man appears,
Resolute in soul, tho' bending
'Neath the weight of eighty years.
He had fought beside great Chalmers
'Gainst the tyranny of state,
Left the Church—yea, of his fathers—
More in sorrow than in hate.

Rude in voice, and rough in feature,
Nothing gentle is within;
On his brow is plainly written:
" There's no quarter here for sin."
Nothing flow'ry in his language—
Yea, it is sublimely bare—
Rude as are his country's mountains,
Yet a naked grandeur's there!

He tells of the unbelieving
Spirit of the present time,
Which would rob us weary mortals
Even of the hope sublime.
He denounces Mammon's worship,
Yea, the god of this vain age;
How the veins start in his forehead
As he points to history's page!

To the covenanting heroes,
To the mighty men of old—
Listen! for he speaks of peasants
Who could not be bought or sold.
" Sons of sires who did a tyrant
With his myrmidons withstand,
Let the faith of your great fathers
Guide you in this forest land.

" Sons of sires who did a bigot
Even on his throne rebuke,
Cling ye to their faith, which torture
Never for a moment shook.

'Mid the Church's desolation,
   Still they put in God their trust ;
Rallied they round Zion's banner,
   Torn and trampled in the dust.

" For amid the lonely moorlands,
   In the deep, sequestered glen,
God has heard the pray'r at midnight
   Of these persecuted men.
Heavy is the tyrant's burden,
   Cruel is oppression's rod,
Yet these humble peasants dreaded
   Nothing save the wrath of God.

" Why should they the passing mandate
   Of a dying king obey ?
Had they not a higher edict,
   Which shall never pass away ?
Why should they dread men's death-warrant ?
   Is not death the common road
Either to the nether regions
   Or the city of our God ?

" Had they not a higher mandate,
   Which knows neither change nor time,
Issued amid smoke and thunder
   On the trembling Mount sublime ?
They were men of earnest natures,
   Looking to the soul of things ;
What cared they for crowns and sceptres ?
   What cared they for earthly kings ?

" What cared they for passing splendor ?
   They had gleams of the divine !
What to them were stars and garters,
   Evil as the sparkling wine ?
Were they not the heirs of glory
   Earthly kings might never see ?
Were they not the priests and prophets
   Of a higher dynasty ?

" Crowns depart and princes perish,
     Empires crumble and decay ;
But the Truth endures forever,
     And shall never pass away.
Still the cairn among the mountains
     Marks the spot whereon they fell ;
Still with swelling heart the shepherds
     Love upon their deeds to dwell.

" May their mem'ry never perish,
     May their graves be ever green ;
They were peasants, and such peasants
     As the world has rarely seen.
Go ! and may their God go with you—
     Yea, the God of the opprest.
Plant their faith, the Faith of Freedom,
     'Mong these forests of the West."

———

THE SETTLER'S PRAYER

WELCOME to the weary worn,
     Welcome to the heart forlorn,
Welcome, sacred Sabbath morn !

Peace from yonder cloud's descending,
Heav'n and earth again are blending,
And the woods in worship bending.

Yonder distant hill-pines lie
On the bosom of the sky,
Musing on things deep and high.

Yea, the very swamp has caught
Something like a holy thought,
And its face with love is fraught;

While yon ancient elms extend
Their great arms, and arch and blend
Into cloisters without end,

Forming many a still retreat
Where the noon-tide shadows meet,
Ever on their noiseless feet.

Blessèd morn ! thou'rt welcome here
To the backwoods pioneer,
Far from all his heart holds dear.

He has wander'd far away
From the land of mountains grey
Where his children are at play.

Urged by independence on,
Far into these wilds unknown
He has ventured all alone.

Freedom whisper'd in his breast
He would find a home of rest
In the forests of the West ;

But he found it hard to part
From the partner of his heart,
In that cottage by the Cart,[5]

And his little children three,
Crowding all around his knee,
Whom he never more might see.

In his log-built cabin rude,
In the forest solitude,
There he sits in thoughtful mood.

" Who," he asks, " at God's behest,
Will lead forth His poor opprest
To this refuge in the West ?
18

" While these wilds cry out for toil
To produce their corn and oil,
Men starve on their native soil.

"Willing hearts are left to wither ;
Bring, oh, bring the workers hither!
Bring the lands and hands together."

From such thoughts he turns away,
For on this, God's holy day,
He would hear what prophets say.

Even Burns he puts aside—
Burns, his week-day joy and pride !
Burns, so human, wild, and wide !

And he brings from out its nook
That great Book of books—the Book !
On its sacred page to look.

Now some song of Israel's King
Comes, as on an angel's wing,
Through his very soul to sing

Songs that bring a joy untold,
Songs more precious far than gold,
Songs that never can grow old ;

Sung by martyrs in the glen,
That in sorrow's darkest den
Cheered the souls of weary men.

Now he reads the tragic story
How the world, in sin grown hoary,
Crucified the Son of Glory :

He—the Hope of every clime,
He—the sole bright Star in time,
Solitary soul sublime !

Then his knee to heav'n he bends ;
For his children and his friends
All his soul in prayer ascends.

May God guide them o'er the deep,
As a shepherd guides his sheep,
Watching kindly o'er their sleep.

Now he prays for all in pain,
For the wretched and insane,
While the teardrops fall like rain ;

Pleading for the sons of crime,
The despised, the dross, the slime—
Wretched, Lord, in ev'ry clime—

For the outcast in his lair,
All that need a brother's care,
Houseless vagrants ev'rywhere ;

Prays that mists may cease to blind
Fellow-workmen left behind,—
" May they, Lord, have strength of mind

" To resist the drunken feast,
Scorning all that has increas'd
Their relation to the beast.

" Let their worth appear in deeds,
Not in whining of their needs,
Or in mouthing of the creeds.

" Let them try to fill the ditch
That divides the poor and rich
Like a seething lake of pitch ;

" Ever doing what they can,
Working out each noble plan,
Calling forth the God in man !

"Break, O Lord ! the spell of birth ;
  Haste the time when moral worth
  Shall take highest rank on earth.

"Break the chains of creed and caste,
  Heal the wounds of all the past,
  Bring the reign of Love at last."

'Til the evening shadows grey
  Clothe the woods in dark array,
  Thus he keeps the Sabbath day.

————

FIRE IN THE WOODS

WHEN first I settled in the woods
      There were no neighbors nigh,
And scarce a living thing, save wolves,
  And Molly dear, and I.
We had our troubles, ne'er a doubt,
  In those wild woods alone ;
But then, sir, I was bound to have
  A homestead of my own.

This was my chosen field of strife,
  The forest was my foe,
And here I fought, I plann'd, I wrought,
  To lay the giants low.
I toil'd in hope, got in a crop,
  And Molly watch'd the cattle ;
To keep those "breachy" steers away
  She'd many a weary battle.

The "devil's dears" were those two steers !
  Ah ! they were born fence-breakers,
That sneak'd all day and watched their prey,
  Like any salt-sea wreckers.

And gradually, as day by day
   The grain grew golden yellow,
My heart and hope grew with that crop,
   I was a happy fellow.

That crop would set me on my feet,
   And I'd have done with care;
I built away the live-long day
   Such "castles in the air."
I'd beaten poverty at last,
   And, like a little boy
When he has got his first new coat,
   I fairly leapt for joy.

I blush to think upon it yet
   That I was such a fool,
But young folks must learn wisdom, sir,
   In old Misfortune's school.
One fatal night I thought the wind
   Gave some unwonted sighs;
Down through the swamp I heard a tramp,
   Which took me by surprise.

Is this an earthquake drawing near?
   The forest moans and shivers;
And then I thought that I could hear
   The rushing of great rivers.
And while I look'd and listen'd there,
   A herd of deer swept by—
As from a close pursuing foe
   They madly seem'd to fly.

But still those sounds, in long, deep bounds,
   Like warning heralds came,
And then I saw, with fear and awe,
   The heav'ns were all aflame.
I knew the woods must be on fire—
   I trembl'd for my crop
As I stood there in mute despair—
   It seem'd the death of hope.

On, on it came, a sea of flame,
　　In long, deep rolls of thunder,
And drawing near, it seem'd to tear
　　The heav'ns and earth asunder.
How those waves snored, and raged, and roared,
　　And reared in wild commotion !
On, on they came, like steeds of flame
　　Upon a burning ocean.

How they did snort in fiendish sport
　　As at the great elms dashing !
And how they tore 'mong hemlocks hoar,
　　And through the pines went crashing !
While serpents wound the trunks around,
　　Their eyes like demons' gleaming,
And wrapt like thongs around the prongs,
　　And to the crests went screaming.

Ah ! how they swept, and madly leapt
　　From shrieking spire to spire,
'Mid hissing hail, and in their trail
　　A roaring lake of fire !
Anon some whirlwind all aflame
　　Growl'd in the ocean under,
Then up would reel a fiery wheel,
　　And belch forth smoke and thunder.

And it was all that we could do
　　To save ourselves by flight,
As from its track we madly flew—
　　Oh, 'twas an awful night !
When all was past, I stood aghast,
　　My crop and shanty gone,
And blacken'd trunks, 'mid smouldering chunks,
　　Like spectres looking on.

A host of skeletons they seem'd
　　Amid the twilight dim,
All standing there in black despair,
　　With faces gaunt and grim.

And I stood there, a spectre, too ;
   A ruin'd man was I,
With nothing left—what could I do
   But sit me down and cry?

A heavy heart indeed was mine,
   For I was ruin'd wholly ;
And I gave way that crushing day
   To moping melancholy.
I'd lost my all in field and stall,
   And nevermore would thrive ;
All, save those steers—the " devil's dears "
   Had saved themselves alive !

Nor would I have a farm to-day
   Had it not been for Molly ;
She cheer'd me up, and charm'd away
   My wretched melancholy.
She schemed and plann'd to keep the land,
   And cultivate it, too,
So on I moil'd, and strain'd, and toil'd,
   And fought the battle through.

Yes, Molly play'd her part full well ;
   She's plucky, every inch, sir ;
It seem'd to me the Deil himsel'
   Could not make Molly flinch, sir.
We wrought and fought, until our star
   Got into the ascendant :
At troubles past we smile at last,
   And now we're independent.

A BACKWOODS HERO

Canada is prolific in heroes of her own ; men who venture out into the wilderness, perhaps with little save an ax and a determined will, and hew their way to independence. Almost every locality can point to some hero of this kind, who overcame difficulties and dangers with a determination which, in a wider sphere, would have commanded the admiration of the world. They were energetic, inventive, sleepless souls, who fought with wild nature, cleared seed-fields in the forest, built mills, schools and churches, where, but a few years before, naught was heard save the howl of the wolf and the whoop of the Indian. Such gathered, perhaps, a little community of hardy pioneers around them, to whom they were carpenter, blacksmith, architect, miller, doctor, lawyer, judge—all in one.

The following is a real portrait of such a one, a brother-in-law of the poet, Daniel McMillan by name, looked on as founder of Erin village, Wellington county, long called " McMillan's village."

WHERE yonder ancient willow weeps,
The father of the village sleeps ;
And, tho' of humble birth,
As rare a specimen was he
Of Nature's true nobility
As ever trod the earth.
The busy head and hands are still ;
Quench'd the unconquerable will,
Which fought and triumph'd here ;
And tho' he's all unknown to fame,
Yet grateful hearts still bless his name,
And hold his me'mry dear.

He hither came in days when this
Was all a howling wilderness,
With little save his ax ;
And cut and slash'd and hew'd his way,
And scarce a moment, night or day,
His efforts did relax.
For at it with a will he went,
And all his energies he bent,
Determin'd to get through ;

To him all labor seem'd but sport,
The summer day was far too short
  For all he had to do.

He chopp'd, he logg'd, he clear'd his lot,
And into many a darken'd spot
  He let the light of day ;
And through the long and dismal swamp,
So dark, so dreary and so damp,
  He made a turnpike way.
The church, the school-house, and the mill,
The store, the forge, the vat, the kiln,
  Were triumphs of his hand ;
And many a lovely spot of green
Which peeps out there, the woods between,
  Came forth at his command.

What was it that he would not face ?
He bridged the stream, he cut the race,
  Led water to the mill ;
And plann'd and plodded, night and day,
Till ev'ry obstacle gave way
  To his unconquer'd will.
And he was always at our call,
Was doctor, lawyer, judge and all ;
  And this throughout the section.
Oh ! there was nothing could be done,
No field from out the forest won,
  Save under his direction.

He drew up deeds, he measured land,
For all the people thought and plann'd,
  Did aught to help a neighbor ;
He always had so much to do,
I wonder'd how he e'er got through
  With such a load of labor.
But something in his face said " Work "—
The very dullest could not shirk,
  The deafest had to mind him ;

And if he only look'd, or spoke,
Or only said a word in joke,
　　He left his mark behind him.

All prosper'd where he had a hand—
The houses that he built would stand,
　　The seed he sow'd would grow ;
And for his bait the fishes fought,
The deer seem'd willing to be caught—
　　'Twas strange, but it was so.
His plan of things was aye the best,
Success from failure he would wrest,
　　He had such art about him,
And truly nothing could go on,—
Wer't but the rolling of a stone,
　　It roll'd not right without him.

Yet he would never follow rules ;
Systems of colleges and schools
　　To him were all unknown ;
And in mechanics and in trade
His calculations all were made
　　By systems of his own.
Few were his words, yet what he said
Had aye the ring of " go-ahead "—
　　Improvement was his passion ;
Tho' into order much he brought,
You always found him in a coat
　　An age behind the fashion.

A feeling heart was in his breast,
And cruelty to man or beast
　　Found him a foe unsparing ;
The two things which he could not bear,
Which to condemn he did not spare,
　　Were gossip and tale-bearing.
Newcomers, should their crops e'er fail,
Would come and tell their mournful tale,
　　And he would fill a sack ;

It always seem'd to do him good
To give a hungry mortal food,
 And send him smiling back.

If roughs assembled at a " bee,"
And, steaming with the " Barley Bree,"
 They raged and roar'd and swagger'd,
As soon as e'er his face they saw
It held in reverential awe
 The most regardless blackguard !
He had his enemies, no doubt—
Such men as he are ne'er without
 A brood of spiteful lies ;
Tho' styled by some "The Autocrat,"
He paid as small regard to that
 As to the summer flies.

He sought not fame, nor did he e'er
Find fault with his too narrow sphere,
 Tho' many a person said
He was the man who should be sent
To rule our rabble Parliament—
 It wanted such a head.
And here he rul'd, and here he reign'd,
And no man lost by what he gain'd ;
 And here he lies at rest !
Yet may his mem'ry never fade,
And may the turf upon him laid
 Lie lightly on his breast !

[EDITOR'S NOTE.—In 1900, mementos of McMillan still remain
in and around Erin village. " The race " still carries water to the
mill, a new one erected on the site of the original. " The church "
and " the school " have been superseded by new structures. His house
is still in use, as a hotel, we believe. " The turnpike way " still serves.
McMillan injured a finger while working in his mill ; blood-poisoning
ensued, resulting in his death, on the 17th December, 1849, at the early
age of thirty-eight.]

OLD HOSS

YOU educated folk, no doubt,
    At spinning yarns are bosses ;
Well, for some trade each man is made,
    I'm number one at hosses.
I'm known o'er all the township, sir,
    By hired hand and boss ;
As I go by the children cry,
    " There goes the great Old Hoss ! "

I often wonder—and to know
    I'm really at a loss—
What kind o' soul a man can have
    That doesn't love a hoss.
I love the critters ev'ry one,
    And that's the way, you see,
That ev'ry critter 'neath the sun
    A likin' has for me.

If ever I gets badly riled,
    If ever I gets cross,
'Tis when I see brutality
    Inflicted on a hoss.
They knows it, too, as well as you ;
    And ev'ry hoss I meet,
Lor' bless your heart ! it nods to me
    As I goes down the street.

A hoss, sir, has ideas, sir !
    And if you truly love him,
And educate him as you ought,
    You'll make a Christian of him.
A hoss, sir, will be good or bad—
    Its all in how you break him—
He'll be a Christian or a brute,
    Just as you've sense to make him.

For, be we either man or hoss,
  We've all some inborn sin ;
And what is Christianity
  But just a breakin' in?
Now, I gives all my hosses, sir,
  A Christian edication ;
And nar a one but has some sense
  Of moral obligation.

He knows a man that is a man,
  And feels that he's his master ;
Detects a knave or coward slave—
  No woman does it faster !
He hates them blusterin' bullies, sir,
  Them fellers that are gross ;
Be good yourself, if you would be
  Respected by a hoss !

No doubt, at times, as 'mong ourselves,
  You'll come across a fool ;
He'll try your temper fearfully,
  But you must just keep cool.
I've had some heart-breaks in my time—
  Some awful stupid asses !
To make them moral animals
  All human skill surpasses.

For you may treat them as you may,
  They're crooked as a fence.
In man or hoss, the want of wants
  Is want of common-sense !
But really in a common way
  I'm very seldom beat ;
And, as I say, I'm thank'd each day,
  When walking down the street.

Scottish Portraits

Ye whom in youth I knew so well,
The story of your life I'd tell;
Yea, how ye toil'd and thought,
In joy or sorrow, love or strife,
As on the magic loom of life
The tangled web ye wrought.

HALLOWE'EN

EV'RYBODY kens that spirits
   Walk abroad on Hallowe'en,
And the little playful fairies
   Hold their revels on the green;
Ev'rybody kens they're partial
   To auld Scotland's bonnie glens—
No' a lintie o' the valley
   Ilka green nook better kens.

Mony a shepherd at the gloamin'
   Scarcely can believe his e'en,
Coming unawares upon them
   Dancing in their doublets green;
Singing sangs, and drinking dew-drops
   Out o' cowslip cups sae pale,
Or a' riding on the moonbeams
   Doun the dingle and the dale.

Mony a chuffy-cheekit laddie
  They hae wiled by birken-shaw,
Mony an' mony a bonnie bairnie
  On that nicht they've charm'd awa';
Weel it's kent they watch o'er lovers,
  A' their hearts to them are seen,
A' their quarrels and their matches
  They mak' up on Hallowe'en.

Weel it's kent they're faithfu' ever
  To the genius o' oor laun',
And in a' her cares and troubles
  Send her aye a helping haun';
They it is, should Donald waver
  'Mid the battle's loudest din,
That keep yelling thro' the bagpipes
  Till he gars the foeman rin.

'Tis frae them the Scottish minstrels
  Learn sae weel their melting art,
Get the magic words that open
  A' the fountains o' the heart.
Nane can dance oor "Gillie Callum,"
  Sing oor Scottish sangs, I ween,
Saving them wha've tippl't wi' them
  On the dews o' Hallowe'en.

On that nicht, there's nae denyin't,
  Mony a Scot, as weel's mysel',
Hae had munelicht dealings wi' them,
  Gin the truth they like to tell.
Weel, ae Hallowe'en at gloaming,
  Drowsy sleep bow'd doun mine e'e,
And to my surprise I wauken'd
  Daundering on the midnicht lea.

There the big horn'd mune was glow'ring
  Doun upon me frae the sky,
And the wee bit stars a' trembling
  Like the tears in Beauty's eye.

Suddenly I heard a rustle
   Doun beside the lonely spring ;
Gliff't was I nae doubt to see there
   Elves and fairies in a ring.

There they were a' sitting singing
   Blithely on the velvet green,
And the owrecome o' the sang was
   " Hey, for Scotland's Hallowe'en ! "
Frae their lips ilk word was fa'ing
   Sweet as ony dewy gem—
Kennedy himsel' ne'er warbled
   Scotia's ballads like to them.

In the midst a hoary matron
   Wi' auld Scotland's spinning-wheel—
" Scotland's auld, respected Mither,"
   Oh, I kent her face fu' weel !
Gazing on her rugged features
   What unutterable things
Stirr'd my spirit, while above me
   Flapt innumerable wings.

Shades o' ancient Scottish worthies,
   Heroes wi' the laurel crown'd,
Martyrs, patriots, and prophets,
   Saints and sages, hover'd round ;
A' the preachers and the poets,
   A' the spirits great indeed,
Wha hae twin'd a wreath immortal
   Round oor puir auld Mither's heid.

A' the stalwart chiels wha perish'd—
   Perish'd ! no, they never dee !—
Scotland, 'neath thy bluidy banner
   Wha lay down their lives for thee.
Lovingly she gazed upon them,
   Proudly claimed them for her sons ;
And wi' a' a mither's fondness
   Ca'd them " her immortal ones."

Then she turned, as to her children
  Exiled far across the sea,
Saying, "Lads and bonnie lasses
  That I nurs'd upon my knee,
Tho' the ocean rolls between us
  Distance canna hearts divide ;
Still in spirit ye are with me
  By the Forth, the Tweed, the Clyde.

"Tho' amid Canadian forests
  Or on Ganges' banks ye be,
Or in Afric's wilds, ye ever
  Turn wi' longing hearts to me ;
Tho' in distant lands ye triumph,
  Still for Scotia's hills ye pine—
Ever thinking o' oor ingles,
  And the Hallowe'ens lang syne ;

"And the quiet o' oor Sabbaths,
  And oor psalm-tunes' solemn tones,
And oor altars, old and hoary,
  'Mid the grey memorial stones.
Weel I ken my early lessons
  Deep in a' your hearts are set—
Ah ! the Bible and the ballads,
  No, ye never can forget !

"Ne'er be Fenian fules amang ye ;
  Stick to country, kirk, and Queen,
And wherever ye may wander,
  Aye keep up auld Hallowe'en !"
Even while she spoke, the grey cock
  Clapt aloud his wings and crew,
And, or e'er I wist, the pageant
  Past awa' like morning dew.

19

THE WEE LADDIE'S SUMMER DAY

A T the ca' of the blithe cuckoo,
    In the leafy lanes o' June,
Wee barefooted laddies, I trou,
    We scampert awa' frae the toun ;
To speel up the High Craig rock,
    The haunt o' the hinny-bee,
Like a troop o' wee fairy folk,
    Wi' oor happy herts gaed we.

And never was king upon his throne
    Sae free frae ev'ry care,
For the licht o' oor herts on nature shone,
    Making sunshine ev'rywhere.
We ranged the dells and the forest free—
    To oor joy the valleys rang—
Or sat us down on the gowany lea
    To drink in the wild-bird's sang.

We kent the place whaur the blue-waups bide,
    An' the howff o' the hoodie craw,
An' the holes where the wee moss-cheepers hide—
    We kent them ane an' a'.
And oh ! a mair joyous band than we
    Was never aneath the sun,
While we howkit for the hinny-bee
    In his bike aneath the grun'.

Oh, then what a feast o' the hinny blabs,
    As wee laddies only ken ;
Sic nectar never cross'd the gabs
    O' the very greatest men !
We caredna for sic sma' affairs
    As their kingdoms and their crouns,
Or the busy world wi' a' its cares,
    An' its weary ups an' douns.

We thocht that oor joy wad never fade,
　That the world was made for play,
An' 'twas nonsense a' what the auld folks said
　O' the sorrows on oor way.
Sae we rumple-tumpl'd down the brae,
　Wi' oor herts sae fu' o' glee,
Or swung the lee-lang simmer's day
　On the auld witch-hazel tree ;

Or follow'd the burn, wi' its twists an' crooks,
　As it jink'd roun' the spunky knowe,
Or sat us doun in the fairy nooks,
　Whar a' the wee violets grow.
And oh, what joy was the wild-rose tree,
　Awa' in the lonely glens,
And the glint o' the bonnie gowan's e'e,
　Frae her ain wee cosie dens.

Oor herts had the glow o' the violets rare,
　And the freshness o' the dew,
And the lilt o' the sang that filled the air
　Frae the speck in the bonnie blue.
And naething cam' oor joy to mar,
　Till the sun sank in the west,
And the laverock drapt frae the e'ening star,
　And the cusha socht her nest.

And gloamin' doun upon bank and scaur
　In her mantle grey wad lie,
And the great auld Highland hills afar
　Were leaning against the sky.
And the craik cam' oot frae amang the braes,
　Awa' by the " Peeseweep Inn,"
And hame we gaed 'neath the gleaming rays
　O' the red, red rising mune.[18]

Ah, happy hearts ! we can meet nae mair !
　There's been mony a change since then.
If in life ye be, ye're changed, like me,
　Into auld, world-weary men.

But the hived up memory o' thae days
    Your hearts they can never tine,
And aft wi' me 'mang the braes ye'll be
    As in happy days lang syne.

———

WHEN WE WERE BOYS THEGITHER

Inscribed to my old companion, Alexander B. Barr, Duart, Ont.

WE'RE auld and frail, and hirplin through
    The valley o' regret,
For, oh, the days when life was new
    We never can forget !
For Nature then was in her prime,
    Then a' was fair to see,
An', careless o' the cares o' time,
    Wi' happy herts gaed we,
To speel wi' dawn the broomy braes,
    An' range amang the heather ;
An' oh ! but they were happy days,
    When we were boys thegither.

Tho' spring is back amang the braes,
    Wi' a' her flow'ry train,
Yet, oh, the hert o' ither days
    She bringsna back again !
Still sings the lintie in the bush,
    The lav'rock in the blue,
An tho' the burns in gledness gush,
    There's something wanting noo.
Creation's harp has tint ae string,
    Oor herts hae tint anither ;
In harmony they canna sing
    Since we were boys thegither.

The simmer days were langer then,
    Mair sweet the evening's fa',
And gloamin' linger'd in the glen,[33]
    As laith to gang awa';
An' laith were we the glen to lea',
    An' a' the green domain,
Till up abune the leddy mune
    Led forth her starry train.
There's something wrang wi' Nature noo—
    What ails our darling Mither?
The glory's faded frae her broo
    Since we were boys thegither.

There's suirly nae sic sunshine noo
    As there was in the days
When we were chasing the cuckoo,
    'Mang Barchan's bonnie braes;
A something nane can understaun'
    Has faded frae oor sight,
And earth's na mair a wonder-laun'
    O' evergreen delight.
There's something wrang wi' Nature noo—
    What ails oor darling Mither?
The glory's faded frae her broo
    Since we were boys thegither.

THE FISHERMAN'S WIFE

OH, they hae mony ills to dreed,
    A weary weird to dree,
The folk ordain'd to snatch their breid
    Frae oot the angry sea.

The mune is wading 'mang the clouds,
    Wi' face sae wan and pale;
They gather round her like death-shrouds;
    The sad winds weary wail.

And there's a moaning 'mang the rills,
  The seafowl clang and cry,
And a' the great auld Arran hills
  Are leaning 'gainst the sky.

I fear the look o' low'ring lift,
  The plash o' angry sea ;
The gurly winds, that sough and shift,
  Bring waefu' thoughts to me.

For a' the bairns and the guidman
  Are on that troubled sea :
I gie them a' the help I can
  By praying, Lord, to Thee !

Yet aye on sic a fearfu' nicht,
  Altho' it's but a spark,
I keep the cruisie burning bricht
  To guide them in the dark.

Oh ! hoo that wild wind soughs and raves
  Abune the angry sea !
And while they're wrestling with the waves,
  I'll wrestle, Lord, with Thee.

Oh ! little do the big folk ken
  The struggles o' the poor,
The battles o' brave fishermen,
  Or what their wives endure.

On sic a nicht my brithers three
  Did venture oot alane,
To brave for breid the angry sea,
  And ne'er cam' back again.

Tho' sic heart-break has always been,
  Oh ! must it ever be ?
I ask not, Lord, what it does mean,
  But bring them back to me !

Then lift, O Lord ! lift up Thy voice,
    And still the raging sea,
Bid thou my troubled heart rejoice,
    And bring them back to me.

THE DEATH OF EVAN DHU

THEY place the Chieftain in his chair
    Beneath the aged yew;
And is this all that now remains
    Of mighty Evan Dhu ?

The plaided clansmen gather round,
    And gaze upon his face ;
They fear that Death will soon lay low
    The hero of their race.

Vainly they tend and talk to him
    In friendship's soothing tone ;
The old man sits, with drooping head,
    Unconscious as a stone.

" Go, bring the minstrel of our tribe
    To sing the mountain strain—
The strain he lov'd—'twill bring him back
    To consciousness again."

And, leaning on his staff, at length
    The aged bard appears,
But, gazing on him while he sings,
    He scarce can sing for tears.

" A cloud hangs o'er Lochaber's wilds,
    Her vales are fill'd with woe,
The shaft has started from the string
    To lay her hero low.

" Behold the mountain warrior,
　The chief of sounding fame,
Whose claymore in the battle flash'd
　Like a consuming flame.

" But where, ah ! where's the princely air,
　The step so firm and true,
The eagle eye, the lordly brow,
　Of mighty Evan Dhu ?

" Are these the very hands which laid
　The Sassenach giant low,
Who dared invade Lochaber's wilds
　Full fifty years ago ? "

He heeds him not, he hears him not;
　The weeping clansmen seem
Like floating shadows hov'ring round,
　Or phantoms in a dream.

Anon he sings the mournful song
　Some exiled heart of yore
Sang when he thought that he would see
　Lochaber's hills no more.

Anon he wakes the battle-cry,
　The Cameron's gath'ring strain :
The light of battle flashes in
　The old man's eye again.

He clutches by his side, as if
　To draw his ancient brand,
And, starting from his couch, aloft
　He waves his wither'd hand,

And shouts, " Advance, sons of Lochiel ! "
　With all the fire of yore,
And seems as waving in his hand
　The terrible claymore.

Great Chieftain of the mountain race !
  It was thy last adieu ;
For clansmen clasp the lifeless form
  Of mighty Evan Dhu.

———

PAST AND PRESENT

Consider it warilie : read aftener than anis.
           —*Gavin Douglas.*

IT was about the midnight hour :
  The dew was heavy on the flow'r,
The winds were hushed, the weeds were still ;
And silence hung upon the hill.
Afar upon the white-walled town
The waning moon looked sadly down,
And all was quiet by the rill,
Save when the wand'ring whip-poor-will
By fits sent forth its weary wail
To pity in the greenwood vale.

The busy world to sleep had gone,
Yet I sat musing all alone.
I heard the bat's wing rise and fall,
The cricket chirp upon the wall.
The cat was watching by the seams,
Old Towser hunting in his dreams,
While I was rapt in admiration
Of this our age's elevation ;
And drawing many a queer contrast
Between the present and the past.

Said I, " We've reach'd a height sublime
Ne'er dreamt o' in the olden time,
Where we may safely sit at last,
And look wi' pity on the past.

Old Superstition's dead and gane;
She dee't wi' mony a dreary grane,
For Knowledge, the regenerator,
Fought wi' her till he fairly beat her.
O' sic a feat we weel may brag;
We've fairly kilt the gruesome hag!

" Our fathers, sure, were silly fools,
Wi' ghosts, and jougs, and cutty stools;
And then they lived in sic like biggins,
Wi' nocht but strae raips for the riggins!
Could they but frae the graves be brocht,
To see the wonders we hae wrocht,
How they would marvel at the sight,
And think their bairns had a' gane gyte!
Wadna' they gape, and stare, and staumer,
And talk o' witchcraft and o' glaumer?

" I'd like to hear my great-grandsire
Commenting on th' electric wire,
And on our ship, o' ships the wale,
That snoove on without wind or sail;
And then our modes to test and scan
The working out o' Nature's plan;
Our proofs, frae shells and moss-grown stanes,
Frae mastodon's and mammoth's banes,
How hills are carried here and there,
How worlds evaporate like air!
He'd think the de'il was in the lan',
The judgment day just close at han'."

" Hush!" said a deep voice in my ear,
And, looking up, I shook wi' fear,
For there I saw before me pass
Gaunt forms that ance were men, alas!
Whole generations o' the dead
Were passing, yea, without a tread!
I saw the Celt and Saxon come,
All marching to a music dumb.

A spectre led the ghastly crew ;
It motion'd, and they all withdrew,
Save ane auld man, o' aspect stern,
Like some old covenanting kern :
Upon his head a bonnet blue,
And in his hand a staff o' yew ;
His shepherd's plaid was checker'd three,
His breeches buckled at the knee ;
His stockings, rig-an'-fur o' blue,
Set aff a sturdy shank, I trou ;
His coat, a kind o' woolsey stuff,
Wi' leather buttons, flap and cuff ;
A dirk was dangling at his waist,
A Bible peeping frae his breast.

Tho' I was in nae mood for daffin,
Yet I could hardly keep frae laughin'.
As he approach'd wi' solemn pace,
I smirkit richt within his face ;
Says I, " Guidman, gif ane micht speer,
Wha are ye ? and what want ye here ? "

" I'm ane o' your ain auld forebears,
Wha's deid mair nor a hunner years.
Nae won'er I appear in anger :
I've borne, till I can bear nae langer,
Wi' a' the scorn and lies ye tell
On folk far better than yoursel'.
To think a set o' puir wee creatures,
Wi' scrimpit shanks and heartless natures,
Wad heap contempt on them wha brang them
Ocht guid that yet remains amang them ! "

Says I, " Your wrath is out o' season.
This age will list to nocht but reason :
We scorn a' foolish old pretences,
Things must be vouch'd for by the senses.
Look to the progress we hae made,
Our halls o' science, boards o' trade ;

We're better, and we're bigger, too,
And wiser, that I will avou.
The very infants in our schools
Might teach some sense to doitit fools."

" As for your progress, I must say
Ye're far ahead o' honesty ;
And then your teachers tak' such pains
To mak' ye men afore ye're weans,
That ony sense that nature gies ye,
By everlasting pourin' lea's ye.
Infants ye are, infants remain ;
Ye're ane o' them, or I'm mista'en."

Says I, " Stick till't—there's naething like it—
Folk's aye conceited when they're doitit ;
But will ye really now defend
Your crimes and follies without end—
Your fauseness a' the fowk deceivin',
Your border ridin' and your reavin',
Your faith in stabbing wi' the dirk,
And ilka kind o' bluidy work ;
Your strange belief in wicked e'en,
Your clues to mak' a foe a frien',
Your cures for witch-bewilder'd bairns,
Wrocht 'neath the moon at dead-men's cairns ?
Is't possible you would bring back
Your fire, your fagot, and your rack ;
Your hunts o' heretics and limmers,
Your doukin' o' uncanny kimmers,
Your magic words to lay the Deil,
As up the pulpit stairs he'd speel ;
Your bringing o' the holy book,
And shakin't at him till he shook ?
And ye wad hae us to exchange
Our boundless intellectual range,
Our wisdom and humanity,
For your auld dead insanity ? "

" For ane wha thinks a' men are brithers
Ye're guid at fin'in' faut wi' ithers.

Look nearer hame, and there, I trou,
Ye'll fin' ye hae eneuch to do—
Look to your list o' black transgressions,
Deceits, heart-burnings, and oppressions ;
Look to your hordes o' helpless paupers,
Your mighty army o' street-walkers.
Starvation and tyrannic pride
Are ever walking side by side.
Your working men, alack-a-day,
God pity them, I weel may say !
How many dree an awfu' doom,
Condemn'd forever to the loom ;
And some in fact'ries and in mines,
On whom the blessed sun ne'er shines.
Frae year to year they onward grope,
Poor creatures, without heart or hope,
Wi' pale, wi' melancholy features,
Ye scarce can think them human creatures.
Ere ye our ancient ways condemn
Say what has Science dune for them ?
For ev'ry ill ye've pointed out
Ye've ten that we kent nocht about.
And where our ancient virtue ?   Where
The big hearts that would do or dare ?
Wi' a' your outside things o' art
Ye're bankrupt both in head and heart ;
Your life's a game at hide and seek,
Like laddies playing at bo-keek ;
And then, ye're a' sae nice and gentle,
Sae milky and sae sentimental ;
My blessings on your mealy mouth,
Ye're always chokit wi' the truth."

" Whist, whist," says I, " Upon my conscience,
Nae mortal ever heard sic nonsense !
It's fause ! besides, I canna bear it,
Nor will I langer sit and hear it ! "—
And starting up in anger deep
I found I'd been an hour asleep !

PROVOST JOHN M'RAE

" WEEL, Kirsty, since we've got a coo
    We maun turn Tories, lass;
We maunna speak to puir folk noo,
    But snoul them as we pass.
We'll get in wi' the muckle folk,
    An', min' ma words this day,
Ye'll see I'll be nae langer Jock,
    But Mr. John McRae.

" I've tried to please baith rich and puir,
    Ca'd Whig and Tory brither,
But little cause hae I to care
    For either ane or ither.
Frae baith what insults I hae borne
    Mair than my tongue can say :
I've had to answer nicht and morn
    To vulgar Jock McRae.

" An' there's that Chartist, Patie Fleck,
    Wha gibes and jeers me noo,
In spite o' 's sowl he maun respec' [18]
    The man wha auchts a coo.
He ca'd me ' Hunk, time-serving tool,'
    And had the spite to say
' There couldna be a bigger fool
    Then silly Jock McRae.'

" But wha kens yet but I may sit
    In Provost Tamson's seat ?
And wha may staun afore me yet
    But this same jeerin' Pate ?
Wha kens but I may rise to be
    As big as Bailie More,
And a' the toun may come to see
    A chapper on ma door ?

" That chapper keeps ma spirits up,
  I see it ev'ry day—
Ay ! even while ma brose I sup,
  There's Provost John McRae.
Nae doot I ken there's twa or rhee
  Will sicken at the sight,
An' oh, what fun 'twill be to me
  To see their harmless spite !

" Then, when I'm walking up the street
  I'll hear the laddies say :
' Keep quait !' as soon's ma face they see't,
  ' There's Provost John McRae !'
An' then whaur dignities are met,
  Gin I but show ma face,
They'll a' gie way that I may hae
  The very heichest place.

" Ye needna shake your heid atweel !
  Didna the spaewife say,
' Cock up your bonnet ! surely ye'll
  Be Provost John McRae ? '
And didna ma ain mither say,
  As I sat on her knee,
' Its prophesied that in your day
  A michty man you'll be ?

" ' For on the nicht when ye were born
  The moon it shone sae clear,
Folk could hae seen to shear the corn,
  The rye and barley-beer ;
An' owre the hoose sic lichts did hing,
  A' dazzlin' gowden yellow,
That oor auld toop danced sic a spring
  The like was ne'er heard tell o'.'

" Sae what's ordaint to be maun be,
  The very planets say ;
The day will come—ye'll leeve to see—
  I'm Provost John McRae.

The sword's conferr'd by God abune!
I'm thinkin' in ma reign
Some blackguard radicals 'll fin'
I wear it not in vain.

" An' pride, an' poverty, an' spite,
That flourished in this toun,
I'm death upon the three, and quite
Resolv'd to put them doun.
Folk here hate merit, weel I wat,
For to this very day
The de'il a title e'er I got
Save vulgar Jock McRae.

" I'll lea' the Free Kirk, that I'll dae!
The auld ane I will try;
I should hae been an' elder tae,
And yet they passed me by.
To get that office hoo I focht,
An' learn'd masel' to pray;
Yet a' ma labor cam' to nocht,
I'm still mere Jock McRae.

" Hoo earnestly I gaed to work,
An' studied the divines,
Made for the auld wives o' the kirk
Sic tea and cookie shines;
An' bleart ma e'en owre many a text,
Made family worship tae;
An', tho' I pray'd till I was vex'd,
I'm still mere Jock McRae.

" They put Tam Tamson on the list—
I saw the cloven foot;
Wi' hauf an e'e a wean could see
'Twas a' to keep me oot.
No won'er I did stamp an' fyte,
An' swear revenge to hae,
Or that I pray'd through perfect spite
When I was beat that day.

" An' whan I'm Provost, then ye'll see
   A' the ill-wully pack ;
Whan they're brocht to be tried by me,
   Hoo I will pay them back !
Tam says a pray'r that's no his ain,
   Like bairn its lesson saying ;
I spout mine aff, no' like a wean—
   I beat him far at praying.

" Hoo ye'll rejoice to hear ma voice
   Pronounce them low and vile !
A speech I'll mak to Pate Fleck's pack,
   Ere them I sen' to jile.
I'll rise up slowly from the bench,
   Put on a dreidfu' face,
An' in this way ma nieve I'll clinch,[18]
   An' roar, ' Shame an' disgrace !

" ' For ye had ev'ry chance I had,
   Yet leuk at me the day :
While ye hae a' gaen to the bad,
   I'm Provost John McRae.'
Lord, in ma presence hoo they'll shrink !
   An' willna auld wives say
Ma very leuk it gart them think
   Upon the judgment day.
An' if I dinna dae for Pate,
   An' the Free Kirkers tae,
An' ev'ry leivin' soul I hate,
   Ma name's no' John McRae."

20

AULD HAWKIE [34]

I'VE hearkened to mony a lang-lippit chiel,
   Frae wee birkie Roebuck to slee Robbie Peel,
But I've heard only ane wha could instantly start
Ony tone that he lik'd frae the strange human heart.
Tho' but an auld beggar, wi' sair rauckle tongue,
Yet oh ! he enchanted the auld and the young.

I min' when a laddie hoo anxious I ran
To hearken wi' awe to that wonderful man.
'Twas no' what he said, nor the way that he said it, [18]
But a strange nameless soul that each sentence pervadit.
The past and the present were standing before you,
Or hung like the web of immensity o'er you.

He had a strange e'e, in a far stranger heid,
O' wonderfu' meaning, and ill, ill to read.
When you'd fixed on its meaning beyond a' dispute,
Some new ane was sure to flash instantly oot.
Now clear as a sunbeam, now dark as despair,
Anon it was flashing wi' lightning's wild glare ;
And fouk look'd and listen'd, and never grew tired,
For Hawkie aye spoke like a being inspired.
Without a set form of strict logical plan,
He aye threw some new licht on nature and man.
How he'd swing on his crutch as a big thought was born,
While words, like the Scots Greys, cam' gallopin' on !
At corners and crossings he'd take up his stan',
And test and try those wha bore rule in the lan';
And woe to the great anes wha waken'd his wrath,
For a torrent o' tongue he let loose on their path ;
The tombs o' their fathers he'd houk and ransack,
And, laden wi' crime, come triumphantly back.
His was not a roar, nor an Indian yell—
'Twas the laugh o' a demon tormenting in hell.

He had the haill annals summ'd up in his face,
O' the wand'ring, unsettled, improvident race.
In the Pauper Republic he ruled the haill time,
For his great love o' freedom approach'd the sublime.
He ruled undisputed o'er legions o' rags,
Commanded haill regiments o' auld mealy bags ;
His word was as law 'mang the gangrel folk,[35]
Wi' the lame and the lazy he aye had his joke.
E'en schule-weans ne'er tried to pelt Hawkie at a'—
He was nae common beggar, they understood a'—
And when he was drunk an' he couldna weel gang,
They would carry his bachles and help him alang.

I min' ae dark nicht, when I helpit him hame,
Mair drunk than was usual.   His tongue wasna lame,
And, aye as he swagger'd, he spoke against drink,
And aye he said, " Laddie, behold me and think—
Had my heart no' been harden'd 'gainst a' things divine,
With my auld mither's tears 'twad hae melted lang syne.

" I see hoo the land lies, my laddie, wi' thee ;
There's something I like in your bonnie blue e'e.
Ye may be a man yet, gin ye'll aye keep frae drink,
But I doot, my wee laddie, ye'll soar but to sink ;
I see something in you that's owre like mysel',
Sae it needs nae auld spaewife your fortune to tell.

" I canna weel bless you, that's no in my line—
I was better at cursin' since e'er I can min'—
But mark what I tell you, auld rake tho' I be,
May ye lang cheat the deevil, the gill-stoup, and me !
I ken that your heart hates the worldling's cold creed,
But virtues turn vices when heart maisters heid.
If ance ye let reason gie up the comman',
Ye may rin to the deil wi' your heart in your han' !
And this I wad hae ye to bear aye in min'—
For I'm thinkin' ye fain 'mang your fellows would shine—
That talent's a curse if it wiles us awa'
Frae the God o' salvation, wha reigns abune a'.

" My pride and my passion ance spurn'd at His yoke ;
Noo they hang roon' my neck in the waefu' meal-pock.
I'm a wreck ! I'm a ruin ! but ance in this breast
E'en love had a corner where she built her nest !
Could Jeannie hae thocht this, ah, ance in a day !
When oor prospects were heich, and oor young hearts
    were gay,
Oh ! could she noo see me, what, what wad she think ?
An auld gaberlunzie deleerit wi' drink,
And a wee raggit laddie conveying him hame,
Wha, if it were daylicht, wad maybe think shame.
Ah, ance I was big wi' ambition for fame,
And noo its a' ended in naething but shame.
I still hae a hanker for virtue and truth,
But they ill, ill agree wi' this damnable drooth.
I've done nocht but show, in the Auld Hawkie way,
How little true sense a real genius may hae.

" It's still at your option, my laddie, to be
A man, or an auld drucken beggar like me.
Decide while ye may, or your end will be mine,
And 'chief o' the beggars ' is far frae divine."

THE KNIGHT OF ELLERSLIE *

Supposed to be written at the monument on Abbey Craig, Stirling.

'TIS holy ground on which we tread !
   Uncover'd be each pilgrim's head
In honor of the mighty dead—
   The Chief of Ellerslie !

Hail, sacred shrine of Wallace wight !
Who in oppression's darkest night
Was ever foremost in the fight,
   That Scotland might be free.

---

* Or Elderslie, near Paisley, Renfrewshire.

When Freedom's flag was soil'd and torn,
Here Wallace blew his bugle-horn,
Which waken'd up on summer's morn
    Old Scotia's chivalry.

With hearts of fire, and souls of flame,
Our country's fierce avengers came,
While thus the Chief in freedom's name
    Cried, " On, and follow me !

" On, on ere Scotland breathes her last !
And answer to my bugle's blast,
For where the fight is thick and fast
    There shall my good sword be.

" Yonder the Saxons' banner waves,
Which soon shall float above their graves,
For Scotia's sons shall ne'er be slaves,
    Then, on and follow me ! "

And, with the light of battle flush'd,
Then like the tempest down they rush'd,
And Surrey and his host were crush'd,
    And Scotland still was free.

And still our ancient legends say
The Chief's sword made a roomy way,
Till rank on rank the Southrons lay
    On yonder bloody lea.

On many another battle plain,
Where Freedom's foemen strove in vain
A footing on our hills to gain,
    That bugle sounded free.

It echo'd like a dying knell
Where rose the battle's loudest swell,
And where the death-show'r thickest fell
    The foremost still was he.

Still Scotia hears that bugle-blast,
And still her hills are standing fast,
And sooner shall they be o'ercast,
          And sunk into the sea,

Than she'll forget the hero brave,
Who freedom to his country gave,
And found a martyr's bloody grave,
          Great Knight of Ellerslie !

While heather on a hill remains,
While thistle waves upon our plains,
While Scottish blood leaps in our veins,
          Great Chief ! we'll honor thee.

And patriot heroes yet unborn
Shall start up at thy bugle-horn,
Which raised our sires that summer's morn,
          And Scotland aye be free !

THOMAS CARLYLE

THE world reserves its honors for
          The smooth accommodator,
But trembles when the gods send forth
          The stalwart innovator.

There stands the Luther of our age,
          The soul that smiles at fear,
The scorner of the idols which
          The multitudes revere.

A Saul among the people, how
          He tow'rs above the crowd,
And stands alone, like Teneriffe,
          Enwrapt with mystic shroud !

An individuality !
  A great embodied will !
The non-conforming principle !
  A soul that can't be still !

He bears the stamp of character—
  No written one he brings ;
He's Rectitude, ordain'd to sit
  In judgment upon kings !

He throws a living energy
  Around him like a zone ;
He conquers, or he fascinates,
  By virtue all his own.

For him the prophets prophesy,
  For him the poets sing,
And messengers from higher worlds
  Are ever on the wing.

A soul of love and reverence,
  A spirit that adores ;
And yet there is a height to which
  That spirit never soars.

A heart imbued with holy awe,
  A spirit that can bow ;
And yet the pride of Lucifer
  Sits on that cliff-like brow.

Kingdoms may flourish, or may fade,
  And thrones may sink or swim ;
Great battles may be lost or won,
  It matters not to him.

And politicians, with their strife
  And little party spleen,
They but appear to him like geese
  That gabble on the green.

Think ye, poor fools, the great God can
    Be voted out or in?
Or human laws give permanence
    To virtue or to sin?

A moody man! now dogg'd to death
    With spectres gaunt and grim;
And now the fiend himself has got
    Dominion over him.

" This world is all a dance of apes,"
    And love and hope are vain;
And now he roars and bellows like
    A god become insane!

" Attend, ye Miserables all!
    Let heav'n and earth be still!
I issue all my oracles
    By virtue of my will!

" Come, Priesthoods, Popedoms, Lit'rateurs,
    And prove to me your worth,
Or with destruction's besom I
    Will sweep you from the earth!"

Anon he's on a wide, wide sea,
    With wrecks all drifting round;
Grim Death's the steersman of the ship,
    And for his shores they're bound.

This solid world is all afloat,
    The stars around him spinning;
Deep under deep, height over height,
    The end is the beginning.

A phantom ship, a phantom shore,
    All's fleeting and unstable,
A panorama of the soul,
    Her fancywork, her fable!

But of this strange, erratic soul
'Tis little we can know,
For greatness never wore a garb
That was put on for show.

On Being's path he glares aghast,
And utters but a scream ;
His dream of life, tho' dark indeed,
Is still a giant's dream.

TO HUGH M'DONALD

Author of " Rambles Round Glasgow," " Days at the Coast," etc.

I LOVE to look upon thy face,
And dote on ev'ry feature,
Thou humble, unassuming soul,
Thou simple child of Nature !
Thou lover of all lovely things,
With thee 'tis always May ;
For love has kept thy spirit young,
Altho' thy locks are grey.

Thou wert not made for cities vast,
Nor for the strife of gain ;
For thee 'twas joy to steal away
To Nature's green domain ;
To hie thee to the harebell haunts,
And to the glades of green,
Where wildwood roses hang their heads,
And hoary hawthorns lean ;

To hear the cuckoo's joyous shout
Come welcome o'er the lea ;
And listen 'mong the heather blooms
The bumble o' the bee ;

To hide thee in the hazel howes
  Of some lone cushat glen,
Or scale the Alpine summits hoar
  Of some old Highland Ben.

We love thee for the love thou bor'st
  The flow'rets of the wild ;
Thou lov'dst them with the artless love,
  The rapture, of a child.
Thou lov'dst them as the lover loves,
  And from no sense of duty ;
Thou lov'dst them as the poet loves,
  And only for their beauty.

Thy " flow'ring fern " shall never die,
  Thy gowan's aye in bloom ;
The lark is always in thy sky,
  The linnet in thy broom.
For Poesy hath touch'd thy heart,
  As with a living coal,
And Nature's voices evermore
  Keep singing thro' thy soul.

The wail of winds among the rocks,
  The laughter of the rills,
The silence of the dreary moors,
  The thunder of the hills—
Thy spirit was a cell wherein
  They lov'd to linger long,
And, baptized in its living font,
  They started into song.

The bridegroom on his bridal day
  Dotes not upon his bride
With look of deeper love than thou
  On our romantic Clyde.
Her Highland and her Lowland haunts
  Are dear unto thy breast,
But dearer far than each, than all,
  Our green glens of the West.

And led by thee once more we see
   The green haunts of the gowan ;
Again we dream beside the stream,
   Beneath the haw and rowan.
And lov'd ones that are now no more
   From out their graves will start,
And wander with me as of yore
   Upon the banks of Cart.[5]

And how thou lov'dst to linger round
   The ruins old and hoar,
Where mighty chiefs and warriors dwelt,
   And minstrels sang of yore.
Old Crookston Castle's[9] mould'ring walls,
   And Stanley's turrets grey,
And hoary Garnock,[10] telling tales
   Of glories passed away.

And how thou lov'dst the ruin'd shrines
   Where sits grey Melancholy,
Still calling to the passer-by,
   "Pause ! for the place is holy."
Is not our Paisley's Abbey hoar
   An old-world, weary moan,
A solemn chant, a holy hymn,
   A prayer that's breath'd in stone ?

Ah ! with what joy thou'dst linger round
   Our fields renown'd in story !
And how thine eye burn'd in the light
   Of Scotland's ancient glory,
As with unwearied feet thou'dst trace
   Her scenes renown'd in song ;
The streams that gush and leap and rush
   In deathless strains along.

And how thou lov'dst to treasure up
   The snatches of old rimes,
Quaint epitaphs and legends old,
   The tales of other times.

And many a pilgrimage thou'st made,
　As if thou fain wouldst number
The moss-grown, the forgotten graves,
　Where Scotia's martyrs slumber.

Thy feet shall tread those haunts no more,
　And Spring with all her train
Shall miss her pilgrim of the moor,
　The mountain and the plain.
Dear heart, farewell ! we cannot tell
　Where thou art laid to rest ;
But may the flow'rs thou lov'dst so well
　Aye bloom upon thy breast !

———

MY OLD SCHOOLMASTER [36]

HEROES there are unknown to fame,
　Who live and die without a name,
And yet whose lives might put to shame
　　The proud of birth.
Meek, humble, unassuming ones,
Ye are the spiritual suns
　　That gladden earth !

My old schoolmaster, upright John,
Tho' to the world but little known,
Was one who might have fill'd a throne.
　　Well would it be
If only all earth's thrones were fill'd,
And men were taught, and train'd, and drill'd,
　　By such as he.

Wide was his spiritual ken,
One born to guide with tongue and pen,
A leader--yea, a king—of men,
　　A soul upright.

Meanness and malice, lust and greed,
And all their hungry, heartless breed,
    Quail'd in his sight.

A bulwark to the mild and meek,
A staff was he to all the weak,
A voice for all who could not speak ;
    And sorrow lone,
With none to succor, none to cheer,
Had aye thy sympathetic tear,
    Great-hearted John !

Many there are could look on death,
And willingly resign their breath,
But few like him could face men's wrath,
    And nobly dare.
The bigot's frown, the tyrant's snoul,
The pointed finger of the fool,
    How few can bear.

But, throwing oft such things apart,
He found in Music's melting art
A solace for his weary heart.
    Music, ah, me !
Amid a world of sin and strife,
Thou art the very bread of life
    To such as he.

Oh, how he sang old Scotia's lays !
Of love in long forgotten days,
Of Freedom's battles 'mong the braes—
    Heroic strains
That thrill'd my heart, and sent the blood
All leaping like a roaring flood
    Along my veins.

E'en ballads old to him were dear,
And still the wailing strains I hear
That cost me many a sigh and tear
    Long, long ago.

Those little dramas, void of art,
Those heavings of the Scottish heart
        In joy or woe.

Tho' men were his peculiar care,
He lov'd all things of earth and air,
The bounding deer, the timid hare ;
        And he would say :
" Range, pretty creatures ! range at will !—
We lie not here to watch and kill—
        In freedom stray ! "

Like living things, fondly caress'd,
Each little wilding was a guest—
The gowan nestled on his breast,
        And blossom'd there—
Their loveliness his spirit caught,
And in his web of life he wrought
        The jewels rare.

By valleys green, by mountains hoar,
And on old Ocean's sounding shore,
He studied Nature's mystic lore,
        And learn'd her tongue.
Creation widened till he saw
All objects thro' the veil of awe
        Around her hung—

Saw matter's forms from spirit spun,
This rock-built world, yon regal sun,
But types of the Eternal One ;
        With awe-struck mien,
Beheld in the stupendous whole
The grand procession of the Soul,
        Which is not seen.

But, leaving speculations high
For other things that round us lie,
Things that our inmost spirits try,
        He spake words fit—

Yea, living words, all void of art,
The very coinage of his heart,
    I hear them yet :

" Falsehood may flourish for an hour,
And sit within the seat of pow'r,
And Virtue in her presence cow'r "—
    'Twas thus he spoke—
" But surely she'll be downward cast,
And weary Earth be free at last
    From her vile yoke.

" We see the just man vilely treated,
But God and Nature are not cheated,
He still is victor, tho' defeated
    Times ninety-nine ;
For who can put the truth to rout ?
Or who can ever trample out
    Aught that's divine ?

" When once thy duty's plain and clear,
Then do it thou, and never fear
Tho' friends may pity, fools may jeer,
    And cowards flee ;
Yea, what tho' all the world disdain ?
While God and Nature thee sustain,
    What's that to thee ?

" We issue from a bright abode,
But, weighted with this earthly clod,
We crawl thro' matter back to God,
    The glory gone ;
While all the hosts of angels' eyes—
No, not in anger, but surprise—
    Are looking on.

" Oh ! why will men not walk erect,
Their brows with native glory deck'd,
And feel the joy of self-respect,
    And moral worth ;

And throw aside their castes and creeds,
And make their standard noble deeds—
    Not blood and birth?

" Cast selfishness from out thy mind,
Feel for and with all humankind,
Leave nothing to regret behind,
    And death shall be
A summons to a higher state,
Where all thy lov'd and lost shall wait
    To welcome thee."

———

AULD GRANNY BROON

SOME say there's nae witches ava,
    That it's only an auld-world dream,
Or that they've been frighten'd awa'
    By science, by knowledge, and steam.
Some say sic a thing canna be
    As selling ane's sel' to Mahoun ;
But ye've only to hearken to me
    And the story o' auld Granny Broon.

Oh, she was a gruesome auld dame !
    And she howff'd by the Locher's lood fa'—
Ye couldna just ca' it her hame,
    For granny was aften awa'.
She'd talk of the planets, I voo,
    And show ye the way they swing roun' ;
There's few been as near them, I troo,
    As that wrinkled auld witch, Granny Broon.

As sure's there was wreck on the Firth,
    Auld Granny was aff frae her hame ;
She was riding the clouds in her mirth,
    Or lashing the sea into faem.

Her howe voice the fishermen kent,
   That the win's and the waves couldna droon,
But they daurna gie ill wishes vent
   On that wicked auld witch, Granny Broon.

And when in a riddle she'd float
   On the darksome, rouch ocean her lane,
She was sure to coup some hapless boat
   And mak' aff for the mountains o' Spain.
She was oot a' that wild windy night
   When the bell in the steeple fell doun,
For the Session had wauken'd the spite
   And the anger o' auld Granny Broon.

An' when she wad tak' to the shape
   O' a pyat, and flee owre the kirk,
The Session was sure o' a scrape—
   Some awfu' sculduddery work;
An' when there was death i' the cup,
   She wad come like a dog and coor doun;
In terror the kimmers look'd up,
   For they kent it was auld Granny Broon.

Her man gaed to skin and to bane
   Wi' her changin' him into a mare,
For wi' saddle an' bridle an' rein
   She rode him a' nicht thro' the air.
When auld Sturdy's mare took a fricht,
   And ran till it ran itsel' doon,
Wha think ye was ridin't a' nicht
   But the deevil an' auld Granny Broon.

An' to it auld Sturdy wad stick
   That he saw the queer couple astride.
" Noo, grip to the tail," quoth Auld Nick,
   "An', ma certie, but we'll hae a ride!"
He follow'd thro' moor and thro' dale,
   And chased them the Hie Craig aroon',
But he only could see the mare's tail,
   And the nicht-mutch o' auld Granny Broon.
  21

An' didna Kate Clurie ae nicht
  Catch her playin' at cards wi' the deil?
By the time Kate got ben to the licht
  He had changed himsel' into Will Steel.[37]
When the peddler was foun' in the snaw,
  Wi' an awfu' deep clour on his croon,
A hare was seen snoovin' awa'
  Wi' the hirple o' auld Granny Broon.

An' didna the sailor declare
  That she follow'd him thro' ilka place?
In ocean, in earth, and in air,
  He kent ilka screw o' her face.
An' oh! at Vesuvius black,
  It's wha does he see fleein' doun,
Wi' guid Elder Barr on her back,
  But the wicked auld witch, Granny Broon?

Jean Ferly cam' on her ae day—
  She was boiling hert's bluid in a pat—
" Guid guide us ! " was a' Jean could say,
  When she changed hersel' into a cat.
For mysel', I was sittin' ae nicht
  Wi' my lugs to the win's eerie soon,—
Ye may think that I got a gey fricht
  When I heard it cry, " Auld Granny Broon ! "

But Death got auld Granny at last ;
  She sleeps in the mools wi' her cat.
That the last o' her cantrips is cast,
  I'm no juist sae certain o' that !
Tho' some folk, that fain wad be wise
  Abune a' that in history's laid doun,
Will threep that it's little save lies
  I've been telling o' auld Granny Broon.

OLD ADAM

OLD Adam was a character,
   Old Adam was a sage ;
Ye'll hardly find his marrow noo
   In this degen'rate age.
He wore abune his raven locks
   A braid Kilmarnock bonnet,
A ham'art coat upon his back,
   Wi' big horn-buttons on it.

A plaid out owre his shoothers hung,
   The en' fell owre his sleeve ;
A crookit, knotit hazel rung
   Was in his wally nieve.
His breeks were side, sae were his shoon,
   His legs they were nae rashes,
And button'd upward to the knee
   Wi' great drab splatter-dashes.

A ringing laugh, a hearty shake,
   A bright eye beaming o'er you,
Ahint him Towser wags his tail,
   And there he stands afore you.
And yet the inner man was form'd
   On Nature's model plan ;
The dress but hid a heart that lov'd
   A' Nature, God, and Man.

He was nae thing that stood apairt
   Frae universal nature,
But had a corner in his hairt
   For ev'ry leevin' creature.
And after him, owre a' the toon,
   The dogs delichted ran ;
The very kittens kent fu' weel
   He was nae common man.

His hairt was just a leevin' spring,
　With sympathy owreflowin',
And roon' its brim the sweetest floo'rs
　O' Love and Hope were blowin'.
To see him, and to hear him speak,
　To look but in his face,
It made you fa' in love somehoo
　Wi' a' the human race.

A secret chairm, a hidden spell,
　A mystery, had boon' him ;
An atmosphere o' calm delicht
　Was always hinging roon' him.
'Twas even in the dress he wore,
　For tho' his coat was clootit
Ye never saw't, or, if ye saw,
　Ye thocht nae mair aboot it.

I ne'er could solve the mystery ;
　By words that drappit frae him
I felt, but couldna fin' the way,
　He carried conquest wi' him.
And weel I liked to sit and read
　The language o' his e'e ;
And try to sound the hidden deeps
　O' that untroubled sea.

The maist o' folk wha would be guid,
　And keep frae doing evil,
Maun aft hae battles wi' themsel's,
　As weel as wi' the deevil :
For some are guid by grace o' God,
　And some hae to be skelpit ;
But he was good and just because
　He really couldna help it.

His joy was in the woods to rove,
　To loiter by the burn ;
He lov'd wild Nature, and she loved
　Her lover in return.

He socht her green retired bit nooks,
    And nae ane better knew
The secret haunts, the fairy howes,
    Where a' the wild-flowers grew.

Aft would he follow in the track
    Whaur spring had newly been,
To see the primrose peepin' forth
    And blewarts ope their e'en.
The gowan didna better lo'e,
    Nor did the foxglove ken,
The hazel howes, the fairy knowes,
    O' bonnie Calder glen.

Ilk strange wee bird o' wood and wild,
    By learned men disputit—
Its name, its nature, and its sang—
    Weel kent he a' aboot it.
And when the wee grey lintie cam'
    Aroon' his cot to sing,
He wouldna let the vagrant touch
    A feather o' her wing.

And oh ! how he would sing the sangs
    O' lang syne's happy days,
'Till we were wafted back again
    Amang the bonnie braes.
We felt the magic o' the wood
    As we were wont to do
When we would hush our hearts to hear
    The voice o' the cuckoo.

Ance mair the flow'rs were leevin' things
    That round about us sprung ;
It wasna dew, but siller drops
    That round their bosoms hung.
The sky again was bonnie blue,
    Where no' a speck was seen ;
And oh ! the grass was green again—
    I canna tell how green.

We felt the breath o' meadows sweet,
  Ere yet the dews depairt ;
And oh, ance mair the gowans fair
  Had crept into our hairt.
And tho' he's lain him down to rest
  Frae a' earth's guid or ill,
His memory is fragrant yet—
  He's singing to us still !

AULD HAWKIE'S DREAM [34]

'TWEEN midnicht an' mornin', that eerie hour when,
  As Scripture says, " Deep sleep fa's doun upon men,"
When the wild winds are a' lockit up in their caves,
An' the ghosts o' the deid venture oot o' their graves,
To dauner aboot 'neath the bonnie muneshine,
Or bide aroun' places they likit lang syne.
Then, somehoo' or ither, I dreamed I was deid—
Guid kens what could put sic a thocht in my heid !
I was borne thro' the lift, an' awa' 'yont the mune,
And a' the wee stars that were rowin' abune.
At last I was loutit richt down at the gate,
Where holy Saint Peter's appointed to wait ;
But tied on my back was a burden o' sin,
Sae I thocht I'd hae trouble ere I could get in.
There were things on my conscience that heavily sat,
Sic as dribblin' an' drinkin', an' waur things than that.
Ah ! ye may believe me, I felt unco blate,
An' couldna tak' courage to rap at the gate.
Sae I crept in a corner to watch for a chance,
Whan wha does I see like a trooper advance,
But Granny McNab ! Haith ! I trummelt wi' fear !
What the deevil, thinks I, brings the auld viper here ?
I dootna she comes just to clype upon me,
An' feth, the auld lass winna stick at a lee !
I only could mutter, " Guid guide us frae skaith,

A lost sowl am I if it's left to her aith ! " "
Oot at her I keekit, a' sweetin' wi' fricht,
An' thankfu' was I to be oot o' her sicht ;
But up she comes bauldly, an' raps at the gate,
An' cries, " Open quickly, for I canna wait ! "
Says I to mysel', " Lass, if they'll tak' you in
There's hope for me yet wi' my burden o' sin."

Then oot cam' Saint Peter—an' there did he stan',
The keys at his girdle, a sword in his han'—
An' says, rather snelly, " Wife, wha may ye be ? "
When Granny says, smilin', " Ye suirly ken me ?
I'm Mistress McNab, frae the East Neuk o' Fife—
Ye'll fin' my name's doun in the Lamb's Book o' Life.
I've focht the guid fecht, an' the battle I've won,
Sae lead me in-by to the Faither and Son.
I claim the reward—naething less than the croun,
Wi' the gems and the jewels a' buskit aroun' !
Upon His ain shoulders I laid a' my sin,
Sae stan' here nae langer, but juist tak' me in.
I can say a' my questions, I've lines frae the Session,
For ne'er was I catcht, sir, in ony transgression ;
I believ'd the haill Book frae beginnin' to en',
Its' a' richt wi' me, Saint, sae juist tak' me ben."

" Hoot, hoot ! " quo' the Saint, and he seem'd unco brief,
" We carena a bodle aboot your belief ;
But juist let me hear o' some guid ye hae dune,
For it's only by guid works ye'll ever get in."

" The guid works I've done ? " quo' she, " hear to the man !
I'm tellin' ye o' them as fast as I can.
The foremaist was I, man, in ev'ry guid work—
The pillar an' prop o' the auld Burgher Kirk.
I ne'er could put up wi' the claver an' clash
O' the Baptists an' a' the mere Methody trash :
Wi' their wun' an' their water, I haena a doot,
If there's licht amang them they'll sune put it oot.
An' then wi' new notions I ne'er could agree,

I stuck to the auld anes, whate'er they might be.
Jean Tamson insisted on common Salvation,
But, heth! I preferr'd universal Damnation.
Jean gangs to nae kirk, an' she tell't me atweel
Sectarianism's the wark o' the deil!
' Ah, Granny,' says she, ' when we leave this auld frame,
An' the spirit, unfetter'd, mak's aff for its hame,
We'll never be speert to which kirk did we go,
Were we sprinkled, or plowtit,—ah, no, Granny, no!
It's the lives we hae led, the guid or ill we hae dune,
That mak's us or mars us wi' them up abune.'

"She tried to convert me to Mercy an' Grace,
   An' the natural guidness o' a' Adam's race,
   An' spak' o' the caum o' the bonnie blue sky,
   An' the fountain o' Mercy that never rins dry.
   Noo, Saint, did ye e'er hear sic havers as thae?
   Should she be alloo'd to lead young anes astray?
   They're awfu', the doctrines that she does advance—
   Thinks swearers and cut-throats may a' hae a chance;
   She couldna catch me! for I threw in her mouth
' An e'e for an e'e, an' a tooth for a tooth.' "

The Saint shook his heid, and said, " Woman, begin
And tell me at last o' some guid ye hae dune! "[18]

"But still," she continued, "od! am I no sayin',
   'Tween huntin' down heresy, plottin' and prayin',
   An' haulin' the ne'er-do-weel backsliders up,
   An' them wha unworthily drank o' the cup,
   I had a big han'fu' o' wark to get thro'.
   Oh, wha's to look after the licht limmers noo? "

"Hoot! hoot!" quo' the Saint, " wife, for guidsake begin
An' tell me at last o' some guid ye hae dune! "

"Do ye mean to tell me, sir, I did nae guid,
   When I for the kirk an' the cutty-stool stuid?
   When I was reviled by the licht an' profane,

And bore the haill brunt o' the parish my lane,
An' focht wi' Auld Hawkie—the warst o' a' men—
Wha said 'twas a farce frae beginnin' to en'.
Oh, he's an auld blackguard, an' has a vile tongue !
His words aye fell on me like strokes frae a rung.
He said my religion was a' a mere sham ;
Tell't me to my face, sir, I likit a dram ;
An' tho' I had gotten the faith o' assurance,
That I was a Jezebel past a' endurance ;
Tell't me to my face, in my auld flannen mutch,
In the days o' lang syne, I'd been burnt for a wutch.
' Ye're juist Mistress Grundy,' quo' he—the auld rake !
I'm sorry there isna a hell for his sake !
Ye'll min' when he comes here o' what he has dune,
An' ye'll no let the wicked auld blasphemer in."[18]

"Whisht ! whisht !" said the Saint, "wife, I've hearken'd
            owre lang ;
That ane ye ca' Hawkie was hardly far wrang.
Ye've come to the wrang place, my woman, I fear ;
Your kind o' religion's o' nae accoont here.
Ye ne'er were the woman to lichten the load
O' ony puir wretch on life's wearisome road ;
And, by your ain story, ye lived but a life
O' pious pretension, backbiting, and strife.
On mony a tender affection ye trod,
Tell't mony a lee for the glory o' God ;
Ye've weel earned your place in the great lowin' heuch.
Speak nae ither word, I've heard mair than eneuch !
To a' honest folk ye're a terrible fricht,
Sae aff, ye auld bissom, an' oot o' my sicht ! "

Dumbfounded, a moment the auld hizzie stan's,
Then up she rins at him, aclappin' her han's.
" A pretty-like story ! Is't you, sir," says she,
" Wha daurs to keep oot sic a woman as me ?
Ye were but a cooart, man, whan ye were tried !
I'm thinkin' the Maister I never denied.
Ye cursin' auld scunner ! ye leein' auld lout !

An' ye'd be for keepin' the like o' me oot !
Na, na ! Maister Peter, ere I gang to hell,
I'll hae twa-rhee words wi' the Faither himsel'."

For mair o' her clatter the Saint didna wait,
But in he slipt quickly an' bolted the gate.
An' oh ! sic a pictur' was auld Granny's face,
O' impidence baffled, o' shame, an' disgrace,
I burst oot a lauchin' !—I fairly did scream—
Which startled me out o' my won'erfu' dream.

———

THE WARLOCK O' GRYFFE

GRYFFE Castle, dreary, old, and lone,
   Look'd out from lichens grey,
And made its moan o'er heroes gone,
   And glories pass'd away.
It stood on an embattled bank,
   Beside a murm'ring stream,
Where waved some willows old and lank,
   Like spectres in a dream.

The moat's fill'd up, the drawbridge gone,
   Half hid in mosses grey ;
A fall'n old hero cut in stone
   Blocks up the narrow way.
The Castle had its secret nooks,
   And many a dusty den,
With parchments old, and steel-clad books,
   And skeletons of men ;

With crucibles, retorts, and jars ;
   And scatter'd round them lay
Stuff'd reptiles, coil'd among the spars,
   From regions far away.

There dwelt Sir William and his dog—
  The only friend he had ;
Folk said it was a friend *incog.*,
  That he himself was mad ;

That often they'd together walk,
  When there was work on hand,
And had their confidential talk
  None else could understand ;
That he was wrathful in his way,
  And fond of bitter oaths,
And talk'd of neighbors as if they
  Were just so many Goths.

" His talk," they said, " was all a maze
  No mortal could make out ;
There was a craze in all his ways—
  Ay, mad ! with ne'er a doubt."
Their story ran " that in his youth
  A jilt set him a-gley,
And losing faith in love and truth,
  A misanthrope grew he.

" When, lo ! the shout of Liberty
  Rang over Europe wide,
For France resolv'd she would be free,
  Whatever might betide.
And when he first heard of the fray,
  Like ane gane gyte was he,
And instantly he rush'd away
  To fight for Liberty.

" And many a long year pass'd away
  Ere aught was heard of him ;
E'en in this place, home of his race,
  His memory grew dim.
Then rumor said he tint his mind
  When Freedom's bubble burst ;
Then said that he was guillotined
  Among the very first.

" But 'twas believ'd he fled away
    From scenes he could not brook,
And serv'd in many a glorious day
    'Neath Britain's Iron Duke."
" It's best to let Sir Willie be,"
    Auld Elder Jamie said,
" For he's no canny—often he
    Has dealings wi' the dead.

" The leddy dee't repentin' sair
    That e'er his path she crost,
And noo she haunts the Castle stair,
    A lanely, wailing ghost.
Puir man, to hell he selt himsel',
    An' giet Heav'n in exchange,
For wealth his fill and pow'r at will
    Owre a' the world to range.

" He's very learned, too, they say,
    Amang the warlock tribe,
And winds and waves his word obey—
    He's baith their king and scribe.
And weel its kent that fearfu' dug
    Is no' the thing it seems :
When ye wad think it sleepin' snug,
    Or huntin' hares in dreams,

" It's rinnin' a' the worl' aroun'
    For a' shapes it can tak',
And noo it is a tinkler's loun,
    Broom besom on his back ;
And then an auld man wi' a beard
    That reaches to his waist,
And dauners roun' some auld kirk-yaird,
    An's neither man nor ghaist.

" Its whiles a traiveler late at e'en,
    Upon a weary nag ;
And then a bouncin' gypsy queen,
    Or some auld wither'd hag.

And when unlook'd-for death-ca's come,
    Amid the grief and din
O' that sad hoose, as quait's a moose,
    That dug comes slinkin' in.

" And when they foun' the waun'ert weans
    That perish'd in the sike,
Wha's sittin' on their blacken'd banes
    But that great towsy tyke?
When auld Curfufell droont himsel'—
    Guid keep us a' frae sin !—
Wha's watchin' by the open well
    But ' Lang Lugs,' leukin' in?

" Whan ma wee oe was near his last,
    And I was in a fyke,
I knelt to pray—when in my way
    There lay the gruesome tyke.
And up it cam' my han' to lick,
    As innocent's a lamb,
And oh, my bluid juist curdled thick
    When it join'd in the psalm !

" It tried to droun our voices doun',
    Which stopp'd us a'thegither ;
In deidly plicht we swat wi' fricht,
    And stared at ane anither.
When Elder John, that man o' God,
    Near to his en' did lie,
The winds were loune, and towers o' doun
    Were hangin' in the sky ;

" The sunbeam sleepin' on the lea,
    An' heav'n an' earth sae still,
The very silence ye could see
    On river, vale, and hill.
And hush'd was ilka bonnie bird,
    E'en craws had quat their din,
And no the faintest sooch was heard
    Owre Locher's roarin' linn.

" Ye wad hae thocht that angels bricht
     Were hoverin' roun' his bed,
For a' the time a heav'nly licht
     Upon his face was shed.
He seem'd to waun'er in his min',
     Kept talkin' to his wean
(That dee't, I think, in auchty-nine)
     As 't were alive again.

" Then cam' a chapman to the door,
     Wha suddenly took fricht,
Wheelt roun', and wi' a bark and roar
     Was aff and oot o' sicht.
Wha that was weel the watchers kent,
     For like a flame he flew,
As if the sword e'en o' the Lord
     In vengeance did pursue.

" The Castle's built on goblin caves,
     Where souls o' little worth,
Wha canna lie still in their graves,
     Come back to trouble earth.
And weel its kent to all aroun'
     That aye on Hallowe'ens
Sir Willie's there in his arm-chair
     Wi' his beheidit frien's.

" An' aye on that unhallow'd nicht,
     When a' that's guid's asleep,
The Castle's in a bleeze o' licht,
     Frae tower to donjon keep ;
An' ghaists, that ne'er hae been at rest
     Since auld saint-killin' times,
That waun'er roun' the worl' distrest,
     In penance o' their crimes,

" Wi' gruesome hags, to mak' their manes,
     Frae mony a hole come oot,
An' swarms o' wee unchrist'nt weans
     Are yaumerin' roun' aboot.

Its terrible—its waur than sin !—
　To hear the loud reports
Come thun'rin' frae the vaults wherein
　He keeps thae black retorts.

" An' ever at the fearfu' soun'
　The dug sets up its yell,
An' a' the craws come gabblin' roun',
　Like imps let lowse frae hell.
Owre lang they've kep' the laun' in dreed,
　And muckle ill they've dune ;
Judgment is hinging owre their heid,
　An' canna come owre sune.

" Something to set the world agaze
　Maun soon owretak' the twa—
Its like the haill howff in a blaze
　Shall pass from earth awa'.
I wadna be surprised to see
　Fire rain'd doun on the bike !
Ay ! there's be news, afore they dee,
　O' him an' o' his tyke."

DAFT JAMIE

DAFT Jamie dwelt in a cot-house
　Beside a wimplin burn,
Which, like a snake, crept thro' the glen
　Wi' mony a crook and turn.

Upon its banks some hazels hung ;
　A foxglove flow'r sae tall
Was looking thro' the rents time made
　In an auld ruin'd wall.

The truant school-boy shunn'd the spot,
   And there no trav'ler came,
For oh ! it was a dreary place,
   And had an ill, ill name.

A lang, dreigh muir on the ae han',
   Wi' no a hoose in sicht ;
A settled gloom hung owre the place,
   Tho' by the sun alicht.

Close by, a breaker-beaten coast,
   White wi' the saut sea-faem,
Whar mony a vessel had been lost,
   And never reach'd its hame.

Yet there a lonely woman dwalt
   Wi' her puir silly son,—
They'd soucht a quiet hermitage
   The jeering world to shun.

And there for mony years they lived,
   Forgotten by mankin',
Yet He wha doth the sparrows feed
   Had borne them still in min'.

To gather burdens o' auld sticks
   Puir Jamie likit weel ;
Heat was, he thocht, the greatest bliss
   A mortal man could feel.

For hours he'd sit and watch the lowe,
   And mutter to himsel',
Then lauch and croon, tho' what he meant
   Nae mortal man could tell.

But ae dark, dreary winter nicht
   This thocht cam' in his heid :
To place a beacon on the heicht
   Wad be a manly deed.

Sae Jamie started frae his seat,
    And clapt his han's wi' glee :
Oh, 'twas a blink o' sunshine on
    A dark and dismal sea !

"Ye've often tauld me Christ's a licht
    The wanderer to save ;
He's needed up upon yon heicht
    That's ca'd the sailor's grave."

That very nicht he clamb the steep,
    Ken'lt a beacon-fire,
And twirl'd his han's in wild delicht
    To see the flames rise higher.

And thro' long years this wark o' love
    He carried on wi' joy,
And mony a lonely mariner
    Had bless'd the idiot boy.

Yes, there upon the lonely rock,
    Tho' winds their voices raised,
And waves rush'd headlong to the shock,
    The beacon-fire still blazed.

They saw, who journey'd on the deep,
    At the deid hour o' nicht,
His form, increas'd to stature vast,
    Watching the beacon-licht.

While great men toil'd on flood and field,
    A selfish joy to reap,
I turn'd from all to that humane
    Puir idiot on the steep,

And sigh'd to think how many strive
    But to increase dark nicht,
And hide in everlasting gloom
    Each mental beacon-licht.
    22

Crounless Napoleon on his rock
 Can only make us weep ;
Humanity, whose hert is Hope,
 Crouns Jamie on the steep.

MY GRANDFATHER AND HIS BIBLE [38]

Inscribed to James L. Morrison, Esq., Toronto.

THIS sketch I dedicate to you,
 For in your early youth
Such characters full well you knew,
 Great souls that stood for truth.
The Scotland o' our younger days
 It will reca' to min',
And guid auld worthies and their ways—
 The heroes o' lang syne.

Yes, this is the volume ! I knew it of old.
 Such a vision of long-vanish'd years
The ancient Haw' Bible again has unroll'd,
 That I scarce can behold it for tears.
Creation lay then in life's glorious dawn,
 And love, hope and wonder were new,
And my young spirit bounded as free as the fawn,
 And bathed in the beautiful dew.

Again my rapt spirit is thrill'd as of yore
 With a gleam from the Fountain of Light ;
Across the wide gulf—yea, the gulf of three score !—
 What scenes flash again on my sight !
Ah, there in his bonnet and old coat of blue
 The hoary old patriarch stands ;
His face, tho' careworn, has the stamp of the true,
 And horny and hard are his hands.

The hair on his high, ample forehead is thin ;
  Compassion looks out from his eyes,
As if they had long look'd on sorrow and sin
  With a sad and a solemn surprise.
There is force in the face, and decision and power,
  There is weight in the air and the tread ;
He looks not like one who would tremble and cower,
  Or like one to be easily led.

As I look at that old man, in righteousness bold,
  Who fearless his faith did maintain,
The saints and the sages, the heroes of old,
  Assemble around me again.
With old Covenanters who bled for the truth
  His spirit communion did hold ;
They were his familiars, e'en up from his youth,
  And the saints and the martyrs of old.

This book was the deep mine of treasures untold
  To sojourners under the sky,
The well in the desert more precious than gold,
  The fountain that never ran dry.
It taught him the mere fleeting nature of time,
  And to strive for the spirit's high goal ;
And it gave him the wisdom, the knowledge sublime,
  Of the grandeur and worth of the soul ;

And what is the knowledge men prize so much here
  To the knowledge that comes from on high,
Which keeps the heart humble, the spirit sincere,
  And fits us to live and to die.
And, morning and evening, in boyhood I saw
  This volume before him outspread,
And my young bosom thrill'd with a joy and an awe
  At the wonderful things that he read.

And, then as he pour'd out his spirit in prayer,
  All earthly thoughts fled the abode—
Creation had vanish'd, and nothing was there
  Save the deep voice ascending to God.

And when by some grand or some terrible thought
   This poor peasant's spirit was fired,
To a loftier region his spirit seem'd caught,
   And he spake like a prophet inspired.

What to him were the crowns and the kingdoms of time,
   But mere passing things of a day?
Was he not the heir of a kingdom sublime,
   That knows not of death and decay?
Was he not appointed a great work to do—
   Appointed e'en by the Most High—
The dark pow'rs of evil to stem and subdue,
   The greatest work under the sky?

Then Potentates, Princes, and Pow'rs of the earth,
   Your gems and your jewels grew dim;
In presence of goodness and meek, humble worth
   Your sceptres were baubles to him.
And were not the gauds which the vain mass adore
   But trifles the faithful despise;
And the idols the multitudes bow down before
   But a refuge of folly and lies?

This old man was dow'r'd with invincible will—
   E'en tho' misdirected, 'twas grand;
In his presence rude natures grew silent and still,
   Or shrank like bond-slaves at command.
I've seen the bold braggart, the boaster and rake,
   In dudgeon away from him fly;
Beheld, too, the titled fool tremble and quake
   'Neath the scorn of that poor peasant's eye.

But virtue will grow into vices, I ween,
   And even the righteous will fall.
How few of us keep the straight balance and mean;
   But God is the judge of us all.
A deep sense of duty—however deceiv'd—
   Like an atmosphere over him hung,
And all that he either thought, did, or believ'd,
   From duty—stern duty—it sprung.

E'en human affections had all to give way—
   Was he there to think or to feel ?
His orders were *there*, he had but to obey,
   And his bosom 'gainst nature to steel.

.   .   .   .

He sleeps with his fathers ; his battles are o'er,
   The toil and the trouble are done ;
Disappointment and heart-break—ah ! no—nevermore
   Shall vex him here under the sun.

He was one of the last of a loyal old race,
   Who were simply yet grandly sincere,
Who look'd all temptation to sin in the face,
   And trampled on doubt and on fear.
But still in the heart of the sternly severe
   There were gleams of the spirit divine,
And, with all of our knowledge, we're forced to revere
   Those sternly great souls o' lang syne.

———

DAFT MAGGIE

LIFE'S a' a haze, a dreary maze,
   Oh, would that it were dune !
Oh, weary me ! would I could dee !
   What keeps the leddy mune ?
I lang for nicht, for this daylicht
   Rives a' my hert and brain,
But whan it's dune, oh, then I'm in
   A dear worl' o' my ain.

Day was a joy till that blin' boy
   Oor cottage enter'd in ;
Then peace and rest flew frae my breast ;
   He left a grief behin'.

When bleerie moles creep frae their holes,
    The bat is on the wing,
An' owls too-hoo the croodlin' doo,
    An' nae wee bird daur sing ;

The taid creeps oot the auld tree root,
    An' mounts his ain door-stane,
Like wee auld man o' some lost clan
    Left in the world alane ;
When puddock-stools by sleepin' mools
    Loup up in clear muneshine,
'Neath sill'ry wabs, wi' dewy blabs,
    An' fairies come to dine,

I mount my mare, and thro' the air
    I gallop to the sea,
Whaur mermaids fair, wi' dreepin' hair,
    A' gather roun' wi' me.
Then a' the nicht, wi' herts sae licht,
    We skim the munelicht sea
(Ye never saw sic leddies braw,
    Or sic blithe company) ;

Or sit us doun an' that sang croon
    Nae mortal e'er can learn,
We rock asleep the waukrife deep,
    As mither rocks her bairn.
Then to the caves aneath the waves,
    At vera streak o' dawn,
Thro' regions fair, 'mang pearls sae rare,
    We wan'er han'-in-han'.

Then, too, we hear, 'tween joy an' fear,
    The great sea-organ's swell—
Sic heaving moans, sic tempest-tones,
    Earth's language canna tell ;
An' while they ring the great wind's wing
    Is faulded on its breast,
While, sabbin' sair on oor breasts there,
    They lay them down to rest.

To hear the sang the sea-dogs thrang,
  An' water-sprites draw near,
While mighty waves are still as slaves
  An' hush their herts to hear.
Oh, weary me! what ills I dree!
  Will daylicht ne'er be dune?
There's something wrang, the day's owre lang!
  What keeps the leddy mune?

There was a psaulm aye drapt like baulm—
  Ma faither sang 't to me—
Ma heart-strings crack when it comes back,
  Awa' it winna glee.
I canna beir that psaulm to hear!
  It wafts me to the days
Whan peace cam' doun in great white goun
  T' oor cottage 'mang the braes.

The still loch lay in Sabbath ray,
  The hills sae solemn stood,
The waterfa', wi' souch o' awe,
  Gart phantoms roun' me croud;
The Sabbath bells, wi' saintly swells,
  Far up amang the braes—
Hoo frae ma hert they gart ootstert
  Some holy hymn o' praise.

At times we lea' the midnicht sea,
  An' a' the dancing waves,
An' thro' the mirk mak' for the kirk
  Amang the grassy graves.
The deid in crouds cam' in their shrouds,
  An' oh, they leukit braw!
An' spak' o' death aneath their breath
  Until the grey cock craw.

'Mang the unblest wha canna rest
  I'm sure last nicht I saw
The wee blin' bairn, oh, hoo forfairn!
  But noo I maun awa';

For see ! the mune comes peekin' in,
    An' sae I canna bide ;—
Hark to the sea ! it cries on me,
    Sae I maun up an' ride !

————

ON RECEIVING A PORTRAIT OF
AULD HAWKIE [34]

THAT'S Hawkie as he look'd lang syne !—
    In ev'ry feature to the Nine—
The stilt, the staff, the crookit spine,
    An' creeshy claes ;
The hat, a sair forfochten plug,
Aye shining like a pewter mug
    On dreepin' days.

Ah, well I mind that e'e o' blue !
The restless spirit keekin' thro' ;
Oh ! when it fasten'd on to you
    It held you fast,
As by some cantrip fascination,
As if some lang'd-for revelation
    Were come at last.

And then his voice—'twas something rare !
By lang exposure to the air,
It rispit maybe rather sair,
    But didna' skirl ;
For it was manly, tho' 'twas hoarse,
And with a kind o' bullet force
    Gart a' hearts dirl.

You see he's in a deep debate ;
That whisker'd fop wi' empty pate
He hammers hard, wi' words like fate,
    Yet slee and pawky :

While all aroun' the gaping crowd,
In roars o' lauchter lang and loud,
   Cry, "Weel done, Hawkie!"

For rich and puir would gather roun'
To hear him lay the gospel doun',
Or lash some wicked, graceless loun,
   In some high station,
Wha ground the faces o' the poor,
And obstinately, dowff and dour,
   Misruled the nation.

He placed the culprit in your sicht,
And gart you lauch wi' a' your micht—
Nae wee bit snicker, but ootricht,
   Wi' sides a' shakin';
Or made your heart heave like a sea,
For oh, an orator was he
   O' Nature's makin'!

Whiles like a fountain, gently gushin',
Whiles like a mighty torrent rushin',
The words cam' oot, ilk ither pushin'
   Wi' thund'ring pow'r;
For 'twasna by mere clever chaffin'
He gart folk greet, or kept them lauchin'
   Hour after hour.

Oh, he was great on burning wutches,
Oor grannies in their flannen mutches!
Wi' some inimitable touches
   Upon the kirk;
But bless'd the Lord religion true
Looks back wi' shame and sorrow noo
   On things sae mirk.

Some thocht him but a raucle deil;
And tho' perchance "nae quiet chiel,"
Yet Hawkie had a heart to feel,
   And hated wrang;

And his queer stories, dreams, and jokes
Serv'd but to licht the fearfu' rocks
    He'd got amang.

He'd lauchin' say : " This life's a muddle ;
To me it's a' a perfect puddle ;
Exceptin' when I'm on the fuddle
    A' 's dull and wae ;
But whiskey hides me frae masel',
And a' the deevils oot o' hell,
    An' them in 't tae.

" Oh, it's the cure o' a' distress,
The shortest cut to happiness,
The last remainin' well o' bliss [18]
    Left since the Fa',
Whaur a' the wretched, ere they sink
'Mang God's forgotten, come to drink
    Their waes awa'.

" I'm fautit aft for gettin' fu',
But let faut-finders sail my crew,
The very thocht wad mak' them grue
    O' bein' sober ;
It's the maist dreadfu' thocht I hae,
Be 't in the merry month o' May,
    June, or October."

For a' sic jokes, ae winter day,
When bluid was thin, an' cheeks were blae,
Full solemnly I heard him say :
    "Oh, it's infernal—
This fechtin' against wind an' tide,
Wi' passion, poverty, an' pride,
    An' drouth eternal !

" Is this the promise o' my prime ?
A wreck amang the shoals o' time,
Whiles stickin' 'mang the sand an' slime,
    An' then, O Lord !

The rudder gane—the compass, too—
An' oh, sic a rebellious crew
 I've got aboard !

" The maist o' them are bleart an' blin',
A' drench'd an' stupefied wi' gin,
An' then they keep up sic a din,
 Fechtin' thro' ither—
I'm tempted whiles to leave the ship,
To scuttle her, an' end the trip
 Noo an' forever !

" It's easy on a simmer sea
To navigate—but oh, waes me !
Whan rocks are lyin' on the lee,
 The ballast gane,
Encompassed roun' wi fogs and shoals,
An' like a log the vessel rolls,
 A' steerin's vain."

We saw in him a soul misplaced,
For, ne'er a doubt, he would hae graced
A parliament o' sages chaste,
 Despite the cup.
We saw his genius run to waste,
And not a single soul made haste
 To help him up.

Hard was his battle to the last,
And tho' he was at times douncast,
He's managed noo to jink the blast,
 Sae let it rave !
For a' his frailties, at this hour
There's few wha wadna cast a flow'r
 On Hawkie's grave.

THE SEMPILL LORDS [39]

H ERE let me sit at midnight hour,
  Where Sempill lords are sleeping ;
While moonbeams show'r thro' ruin'd tower,
  The stars their watch are keeping,
And wand'ring winds, like weary things,
  Thro' long rank grass are wailing,
Like shadows lone of warriors gone
  On misty moonbeams sailing.

Now Ruin haunts these lordly halls,[40]
  Where Mirth and Joy resounded ;
Where warriors dwelt, and captives knelt,
  And harps to Glory sounded.
Proud Eliotstoun's a ruin grey,[41]
  With none to tell her story,
Save winds of eve that come to grieve
  O'er wreck of ancient glory.

Where are the minstrels old and grey,
  That sung to Beauty's daughters ?
They've past away with list'ners gay,
  Like music on the waters :
The jocund bard of old Belltrees[16]
  In moss-grown grave is lying ;
The songs he sang till Scotia rang
  Are echoes faintly dying.

And lowly lies that warrior lord,[42]
  Who oft so gaily bounded
On dapple grey in war array,
  While trump to battle sounded.
There's no one left of that proud race
  That climb'd the steep of glory ;
Their might's a tale of grandame frail,
  A ruin old and hoary.

A LANG-HEIDIT LADDIE

HE'S a lang-heidit laddie, that Sannock o' mine,
  And sometime or ither that laddie maun shine ;
It needs nae auld spaewife his fortune to ken,
He'll be seen and heard tell o' amang muckle men.
But bairns are no' noticed by big folk, ye see,
That belang to a puir widow woman like me.
But he'll gar them notice, ere mony years go,
And listen to him, be they willin' or no ;
And to his decision he'll mak' them a' boo—
He's a lang-heidit laddie, and like him are few.

Alane by the burn-sides he reenges for hours,
And he kens a' aboot the wee birdies and flow'rs ;
He's aff ere the cock craws, awa' to the braes,
And he stays oot amang them for haill simmer days,
To talk wi' the peesweep and lane cusha-doo—
He's a won'erfu' laddie, and like him are few.

There's no' an auld castle that too'rs on the steep,
Nor a field whaur oor auld fechtin' forefaithers sleep,
Nor a bonnie wee burnie that wimples alang,
In the licht o' its gladness immortal in sang ;
There's no' an auld kirk whaur the grey hoolets cry
To the deid congregations around them that lie ;
There's no' an auld abbey that sits in the rain,
In widow's weeds sighing owre glory that's gane,
But he kens mair aboot them than antiquars do—
He's a lang-heidit laddie, and like him are few.

Auld Birsie, the bodie that lives by his craft,
Ance hinted to me that my laddie was daft ;
I bang'd up, and tauld him that he or his weans
Wadna likely gang daft by the wecht o' their brains,
Or their honesty either ; I gied him my min',
And the body can hardly endure me since syne.

The spite o' the crattur was easy seen thro'.
Mine's a lang-heidit laddie, and like him are few.

It's lang been my notion, and prood wad I be,
My wee freen'less laddie a preacher to see;
I'd sheer for the siller, I'd dae ony wark,
To see my wee laddie a licht in the kirk;
But he lauchs in my face, when he sees me sae fain,
And he says that he'll preach in a way o' his ain.
" There are preachers," he says, " ne'er ordaint by the kirk,
Wha dae a far greater, a far better work."
I whiles think his doctrines are really no soun',
But he lays them sae like oor auld minister doun,
It's a perfect delicht juist to hear him gang thro'—
He's a lang-heidit laddie, and like him are few!

He'll talk o' ane Plato, a great man, nae doot,
And heathens that folk here ken naething aboot;
When but a wee tot he would sit by himsel'
And speer at me quastions 'boot heaven and hell.
And oh! but it was a great quastion, he said,[18]
To ken hoo this yirth oot o' naething was made;
Hoo three could be ane, and ane could be three,
Was a thing he insisted that never could be;
Or why should we suffer for auld Adam's fa'?
Or for what God had made ony deevil ava?
I was fairly dumbfoun'er'd, and puzzled to learn
Hoo sic thochts could get into the heid o' a bairn.
But I haena a doot they cam' into his heid
Like the mumps, or the measles, or grew like a weed,
That's sune rooted oot by the Gard'ner o' Grace,
And flow'rs a' the fairer spring up in their place.
I aye haud the hope that I'll yet leeve to see
Him waggin' his pow in a poopit sae hie:
I haena a doot but that won'erfu' pow
Will set the haill country-side a' in a lowe.

AHEAD OF HIS TIME

Inscribed to Robert Kerr, Greenock, Scotland.

AULD Saunders the Great was a mere bonnet-laird,
    And o' riches but sma' was his share ;
Contented was he wi' a cot-hoose and yaird,
    Wi' wisdom, wi' knowledge, 'and lair.
And he was a character in his ain way,
    That to no common idol would bow ;
And the things that he did, and the words that he'd say,
    Kept the haill parish aye in a lowe.

A plain, unpretending apostle was he,
    Wi' a tourie-tapt, twa-storey heid,
And under each arch'd brow a double-ring'd e'e,
    In the centre a bonnie blue bead—
An e'e that was never intended to leer,
    That tauld o' a spirit high-toned,
Yet seem'd half unconscious of things that were near,
    And always seem'd looking beyond.

At times there was something would keek thro' the blue,
    Wi' a strange and a weird kind o' gleam,
And as you approach'd him it seem'd as if you
    Had waken'd him oot o' a dream.
'Twas hard to decipher the lines of that broo,
    Or to read what was writ on his face,
Yet his air and his negligent manner somehoo
    Had a naitural kind o' a grace.

But when he was roos'd, oh, how chang'd was his look !
    And what terrible things he wad say !
He wad get to his English, and talk like a book
    For the length o' a lang simmer's day.

When charged wi' some mean thing his spirit did spurn,
   A deevil look'd out o' his e'e,
And the bead in the middle, the way it wad burn
   It was worth gaun a lang gaet to see.

Wi' what rapture in boyhood I heard him discourse
   On man and on ither strange things;
For his thoughts had a grandeur, a power, and a force,
   That bore me aloft on their wings.
They bore me to regions undreamt o' before,
   And then, what a rapture was mine!
For I felt that on pinions my spirit did soar
   From the human up to the divine.

For great men he seem'd to care little ava,
   Their systems he lov'd to confute;
Save Shakespeare and Bacon, and some ane or twa,
   He cared na a bodle aboot.
" Napoleon the mighty was waur than a wean,
   And hadna the wisdom to see,
Despite his big intellect, and his coarse brain,
   That naething can stan' on a lee.

" Owre earth like a terrible tempest he pass'd,
   Loving naething ootside o' himsel';
And sae his card-castles a' vanish'd at last,
   As doun to destruction he fell.
But still when to earth some great conqueror comes,
   And fools offer homage profound,
'Mid the blaring of trumpets, the beating of drums,
   The calm voice of wisdom is drown'd.

" The prophets, the priests, the Messiahs of earth,
   The sad-eyed and lone, weary ones,
No heralding trumpets blare forth at their birth,
   No shouting, nor thunder of drums;
But the world grows sick of the drum and the fife,
   Of the wreck and the ruin they've wrought;
And here in the great battle-field of our life
   Henceforth shall our battles be fought.

" Here bloated wealth rears her palatial abode ;
　　E'en where the starv'd laborer dies,
And our pray'rs and our praises, ascending to God,
　　Are mix'd with his curses and cries.
Then boast not of what fighting forefathers did ;
　　From your crest wipe the dark bloody stain ;
In charity let their achievements be hid,
　　But boast of them never again.

" Go forth to the great battle-field of our time,
　　'Tis there you are called on to-day ;
Go, shelter the weak from temptation and crime,
　　And your heart's better instincts obey.
'Gainst fraud and injustice the battle shall be,
　　And all the iniquities old ;
The hero-to-be must humanity free
　　From the terrible fetters of gold.

" The angel of warning o'er Britain now floats—
　　Hearest thou what the spectre doth say ?—
Hush ! stern oaths are mutter'd in grim, dusky throats,
　　To rend from the spoiler the prey."
While frankly and fearlessly Saunders foretold
　　The wrath and the evil to come,
He look'd like a seer, or a prophet of old,
　　Who could not, or would not, be dumb.

The schulemaister, tho' little else than a fule,
　　When he heard o' sic doctrines, did glower :
" Thae precepts," quo' he, " wouldna dae in the schule,
　　Od, I wouldna be maister an hour ! "
The Bailie, wha aye was juist stovin' wi' drink,
　　His wrath oot on Saunders did pour :
Said he, " Civilization he'd turn to a sink,
　　A thing I could never endure."

" Na, na ! " said the Provost, " wise folk maun take care,
　　And no let the rabble comman' ;
Keep healthy distinction atween rich an' puir—
　　That's the bulwark and stay o' the lan'.
　23

Let the pot but ance boil owre, wi' scum an' wi' ase,
  We'll no' can see ither for soot,
And then in the hubbub, a' heids an' a' thraws,
  E'en the vera fire's sel' will gang oot."

Sir Tammas pronounced Saunders waur than an ass :
  " For, the creature, he seems unaware
That God in His mercy provided a class
  Baith to guide and to govern the puir.
Sic doctrines," he said, " wad sune ruin the state,
  Workin' folk wad sune rise in revolt ; "
Sae for safety he'd shove Saunders oot o' the gaet,
  And keep it 'neath key, lock, and bolt.

PART II.

Unheeding their clatter, auld Saunders for hours
  Would sit in contemplative mood ;
While his e'en would be fix'd on the bonnie wee flow'rs,
  'Twas thus he wad mutter and brood :
" We're puir little creatures all building for time—
  Thro' pride and ambition we strive—
But Truth is the only one temple sublime,
  That shall all other temples survive.

" The splendors of titles, of rank, and of power,
  That isolate men from their kind,
The pure human spirit they rob and deflower,
  And dwarf while they fetter and blind.
While high, haughty mortals, unsocial, austere,
  And cold to the very heart's core,
To whom no one living thing ever was dear ;
  With self the one God they adore—

" What millions are living a meaningless life,
  And know neither friendship nor love ;
And never once felt, in the tumult and strife,
  The warm brooding wings of the dove ;

Whose lives are a fiction—mask bowing to mask—
    Who know not what 'tis to be free—
Rich bond-slaves, who go thro' their pitiful task,
    That dare not to think and to be !

"They meet but as strangers—as strangers depart,
    All wrapt in a triple disguise—
Nor know they what's meant by communion of heart,
    And life is a commerce of lies.
How God-like this same human nature can be,
    When free from the worm at the core ;
How grand the communion of souls that are free,
    And mutually love and adore !

"We live upon sympathy, kindness, and love ;
    Each other we never can know,
Till the spirit of kindness descends from above,
    And the wells of affection o'erflow.
Beside human nature's pure, glad living fount
    What great golden harvests have grown,
Lang, lang, or ere Moses gaed up to the Mount,
    Or commandments were written on stone.

"Who has not met beings of high moral worth,
    That stept with a carriage sublime,
Who were rais'd far above the ambitions of earth,
    And the fleeting distinctions of time—
With spirits as pure as the sun's golden ray,
    That illumines the swamp and the fen ;
Still scattering blessings along their life's way ?
    Yes, such are the monarchs of men !

" And there is a sister with meek, modest grace,
    And eyes that are fix'd on the ground :
Where'er there's affliction that pitying face
    Is sure to be hov'ring around.
Whene'er I encounter those pitying eyes,
    A draft of pure glory I get,
And I cry, "Tho' surrounded by folly and lies
    There's hope for Humanity yet ! "

PART III.

" Sic doctrines were contra to natur'," folk said,
  And it was agreed thro' the toun,
That "tho' they micht dae weel to mak' a parade,
  In the market they wadna gang doun.
Sic doctrines micht suit vera weel wi' them a',
  Wha' hae riches and siller galore,
But the auld proverb says that love aye flees awa'
  When poortith comes in at the door."

The Bailie, he said, wi' a nicher and smile :
  "This love doctrine never will dae ;
It's the fear o' the gallows, o' hell, and the jile,
  Or I micht e'en mysel' gang astray.
He's only juist trying himsel' to deceive,
  There've been wars since the worl' it began,
Sae this turtle-dove doctrine I dinna believe,
  For I feel there's a deevil in man."

But Saunders paid little attention, for a'
  On Faith and on Hope he did lean ;
He believ'd far owre muckle—aye, that was the flaw,
  Baith wi' jiker and pitying frien'.
Yet his was a grand, a magnificent faith,
  That robs e'en the grave o' its gloom—
That bridges the great gulf that yawns over death,
  Yea, glorifies death and the tomb.

" Our forefathers' faith is a' past," he wad say,
  " The fire on the altar's gone out,
And nothing is left save the cold ashes grey,
  And darkness and terrible doubt.
Sad-eyed, weary ones, who bade farewell to Hope,
  When the last fitful glimmer had gone,
Encompass'd with darkness, they stumble and grope
  In the vast and the vacant unknown.

" Look up, weary ones, for the first streak of day
    Descends on the mountain and lawn ;
The mists of the midnight are passing away,
    And here are the ' Heralds of Dawn ! '
Hush ! hearken ! it is the great trumpet of change
    That's filling the earth and the air,
And new forms of beauty surpassingly strange
    Are starting to life ev'rywhere.

" While faithless and hopeless, at this very hour,
    As all undecided ye stand,
A Spirit gigantic—a new living pow'r—
    Is stalking abroad thro' the land ;
Proclaiming earth's sorrows are passing away,
    By the pow'r of the Spirit outcast,
And ancient iniquities hear and obey
    The summons to judgment at last.

"Before it the errors of ages give way,
    The old idols tremble and fall,
And the temples of selfishness sink to decay,
    And the Christ-spirit looms over all.
The air is alive, yea, with beings unseen,
    Who once dwelt in mansions of clay,
And o'er us, in joy or in sorrow, they lean,
    And walk in our streets in mid-day.

" We mortals are mere rudimentals of man,
    While passing thro' sense into soul ;
Nor can we conceive of the Spirit's vast plan,
    Till death forms us into a whole :
With faculties broaden'd, brute instincts rubb'd out,
    And freed from the passions of clay,
To a region where never comes darkness or doubt,
    The spirit soars singing away.

" Not dead are the dear ones that left us lang syne,
    Ah, no ! they have only withdrawn,
And still round our hearts their affections entwine
    In the land of the beautiful dawn.

Each high aspiration, each prayer sincere,
　　Each true deed without earth's alloy,
To the friends gone before us they straightway appear
　　As pure, living fountains of joy.

"They sit down beside them, and muse on the past,
　　On dear ones still left in the night,
And dream of the time when they'll join us at last
　　In the evergreen land of delight.
The height which the greatest can ever attain,
　　In this murky planet of ours,
Is but the initial of heart and of brain,
　　The germ of humanity's powers.

"But their intuitions have hardly a bound :
　　E'en the growth of the grass on the lea
To their delicate organs would heave with the sound
　　And the roar of the fathomless sea.
With senses unknown to the children of earth,
　　Those beings majestic are fraught ;
They breathe in the air where ideas have birth,
　　And bathe in the fountains of thought."

E'en according to him, folk in some o' the stars
　　Exist on a glorious plane ;
And to them wha inhabit the planet ca'd Mars
　　E'en Shakespeare wad seem but a wean.
And often he wonder'd why folk spent their time
　　On mere little tales of the past,
While here in our presence God's working, sublime,
　　On a scale overwhelmingly vast.

His miracles were not all wrought in the past :
　　The same sun is shining to-day,
And the stars ev'ry night, from infinitudes vast,
　　Come to herald the moon on her way.
All, all is a wonder, this soul and this sense,
　　From dust unto Deity, all ;
And the wonder of wonders, the wonder immense,
　　Is that we are living at all !

PART IV.

The villagers hung on ilk word that he said,
　For they kent he was upricht and true ;
Yet deep in their souls was an undefined dread
　He was prompted by some demon crew ;
And the story, it ran, that on ilk Sabbath e'en,
　At the meeting o' nicht and o' day,
To the far-off death region by beings unseen
　Auld Saunders was wafted away.

'Twas there, they mainteen'd, that he got a' his lair,
　Learn'd to prophesy what wad befa' ;
O' this they were perfectly positive sure
　That he wasna owre canny ava.
He spak' o' ane that he ca'd Swedenborg aft,
　And wise Willie often wad say :
"The twosome are red-wud, aye, perfectly daft,
　And to Bedlam are straught on their way !"

And aft to his comrades he'd laughingly say,
　Wi' a wink and a leer in his e'e,
"I won'er what bee's in his bonnet the day?
　Let's in, lads, and sune wull we see."
But somehow puir Willie aye got the warst o't ;
　His wutty things never wad tell ;
In presence o' Saunders they stuck in his throat,
　Or still-born and flat doun they fell.

And aft as he wended his way awa' hame,
　Rather huff'd at the fate 'o his jokes,
"He's mad ! yet to match him," wad Willie exclaim,
　"Wad amaist take anither John Knox."
His sayings kept ringing the haill kintry roun' ;
　E'en the king o' the shoemakers' craft,
A lang and a lean-looking infidel loun,
　Pronounced him decidedly daft.

"They're wun'erfu', truly, the things that he says,
　And ingeni'us, there's never a doot,

But for him to believe them, ah, there is the craze—
    It's the last spark o' reason gaun oot !"
There was ane wha could catch something very like sense,
    And he e'en gaed so far as to say
He could see gleams of grandeur and glory immense
    Until he grew blin' wi' the ray.

And some ithers thocht that nane should be alloo'd
    To blaspheme in sic a like way :
" He deserv'd a tar barrel," they bauldly avoo'd,
    " For leading young laddies astray."
The haill toun agreed he was cloored in the pate,
    And nae doot wad end wi' some crime—
It never cam' into their pows he was great,
    An' leevin' aheid o' his time.

And aften I thocht that the deils in the hells
    Maun hae lauch'd, wi' a lauchter sae grim,
At the puir silly bodies, sae prood o' themsels,
    A' sittin' in judgment on him.
For he lack'd but ambition, that vice o' the gods,
    To set the worl' a' on a blaze ;
When tauld sae, he only said, " What is the odds
    If I couldna make men change their ways ?

" Ambitious ! for what ? For the wreath that adorns
    The bard's or the scientist's name ?
Believe me, the green laurel covers but thorns,
    And Heart-Break's the hand-maid of Fame.
Yet I am ambitious—ambitious to see
    Still more of the Spirit's vast plan,
From sin and from sorrow to set myself free,
    And live the true life of a man."

THE RADICAL

WILLIE FULTON leev'd up 'mang the Gleniffer braes,
    In a wee flow'ry spot o' his ain ;
Peculiar he was in his words and his ways,
    Yet surely he leev'd not in vain.

His stature was sma', but his heart was real big,
    And upright the race that he ran ;
And tho' for long years he'd to delve and to dig,
    Yet he leev'd the true life o' a man.

His look had the real apostolical grace,
    That's pleasant e'en now to recall ;
And maist o' folk said, when they look'd in his face,
    That they couldna help thinkin' o' Paul.

The same kind o' spirit that dwelt in John Knox—
    The true martyr spirit—was there,
That wad hae gaen oot to the deserts and rocks
    For freedom to dae an' to dare.

I couldna tell a' that was writ in that face ;
    'Twas a volume to study and scan—
A guide to oor incomprehensible race
    On a new and original plan ;

A kind o' judicial, synoptical face,
    Closely written and a' underlined—
A living comment on the haill human race,
    By Faith, Love, and Hope countersigned

A face unco far frae the common, I ween ;
    Nae doot ev'ry word o't was true ;
And a' lichted up by the fathomless e'en
    O' calm, deeply beautiful blue.

His garments were russet, braid Scots was his talk,
  Wi' pith in each word as it fell;
His air and his manner, aye, even his walk,
  Were as guid as a sermon itsel'.

His words had the real gowden ring o' the richt—
  The thing that he thocht he wad say;
Ilk word bolted oot, no' afeart o' the licht,
  And into a' hearts found a way.

And he had a heart tae, as weel as a heid,
  That wi' kindness o'erflow'd to the brim;
And somehoo his ilka word, action, and deed
  Had a living resemblance o' him.

For nae sentimental bit body was he,
  Wi' little else in him than talk,
Nor was he forever ambitious to be
  The big " Bubbly Jock o' the walk."[43]

He focht wi' misfortune for mony a day,
  But triumph'd wi' courage and skill;
He put a stout heart to a stey staney brae,
  For michty was wee Willie's will.

He was nane o' the kin' that wad sit doun and greet
  When a stumbling-block cam' in the way;
"That gart me," said Willie, "but spring to ma feet
  An' meet e'en the deevil hauf way."

When fortune at last foun' oot Willie's abode
  His struggles he still bore in min',
And thocht the best way to be gratefu' to God
  Was to lessen the woes o' mankin'.

And sic a big heart as the wee body had!
  Its sympathies never gaed dune—
A fountain o' mercy to guid and to bad,
  Like the Faither o' mercy abune.

The truth for its ain sake to Willie was dear,
    And by it he'd stan' or he'd fa' ;
What *he* said or *she* said, in jest or in jeer,
    He simply cared naething ava.

Nae bigot was he aboot things o' the past,
    He cheerfully welcom'd the new :
" If this thing is true it will triumph at last
    Despite a' this hullabaloo."

Whate'er was the matter, whate'er the dispute,
    He saw the true point o' the thing ;
And straucht to the centre his arrows he'd shoot,
    That kilt mony lees on the wing.

And oh ! what a pith in the Doric he threw
    When he spak' o' the serfs o' the lan' !
Wi' the Genius o' Manhood enthroned on his brow,
    He look'd like ane born to comman'.

That he had his fauts, and his failings, nae doot,
    For ocht that I ken, may be true ;
But yet while he liv'd, I could ne'er find them oot,
    Sae I'm no gaun to look for them noo.

He had his ain crotchets, as maist o' folk hae,
    But little the waur was for that ;
For instance, when titled folk cam' in his way,
    He sturdily kept on his hat.

Willie didna believe that the hauf o' oor race
    Ready saddled and bridled were born ;
The ither hauf, booted and spurr'd, by God's grace,
    To ride them and lauch them to scorn.

But was he religious ?   Decidedly so !
    For rev'rence was writ on his face—
For ev'rything sacred abune or below,
    For God and the haill human race.

Religion wi' him was a thing o' the heart,
Whaur a' living virtues combine ;
His God was nae being frae nature apart,
But Love, which alone is divine.

Sae thus he was truly religious indeed,
And when a' religions he'd scan,
He placed that ane aye awa' up at the heid
That had maist love to God and to man.

THE CRINGER REBUKED

Willie Fulton's Address to a Time-Server who stood uncovered
in his presence

MAN, put your bonnet on your heid,
Gin ye hae ony brain !
Hoo daur ye gie a thing like me
What's due to God alane ?

I'd rather that the very earth
Would ope and swallow me,
Than I should stand wi' hat in hand
To ony lord I see.

Are ye o' Robin Burns's line,
A countryman o' Knox,
Wi' nae mair harns than yon auld cairns,
Green kail, or cabbage stocks ?

Can ye no' honor worthy folk
(And some deserve it well),
Yet stan'na like a barber's block,
Dishonoring yersel' ?

It's time that potentates and kings,
  And men o' ev'ry station,
Should learn that honor never springs
  Frae human degradation.

No, never throw your manhood doun,
  Whatever may befa';
Aye see, 'yont sceptre and 'yont croun,
  God's universal law.

He sets the highest dignity
  Upon the human brow;
To our puir frail humanity
  Baith King and Pope maun bow.

It's time indeed that all should know,
  Tho' titles may look braw,
Such things are but a passing show,
  And worth's abune them a';

And manhood is abune a' price
  To shield us frae the wrang—
Gin ye are wice, tak' my advice,
  And never let it gang!

Gie honor to the brave and good,
  To them, and them alone;
E'en tho' inspired by gratitude,
  Man, keep your bonnet on.

Hey! there's a shilling, ye leuk wae!
  Hey! tak' it and begone!
But min', my lad, whate'er ye dae,
  Aye keep your bonnet on.

Be eident aye; aye speak the truth
  And dae the best ye can.
Nae thanks to me—but henceforth see
  And try to be a man.

POVERTY'S CHILD

Willie Fulton's Address to a Wee Raggit Laddie

WEE destitute, deserted wean,
  Cast on the world thy leefu'-lane,
To fecht wi' poverty and pain,
    And nane to guide thee ;
Nae ane to lead thy steps aricht,
Or back thee in the weary fecht—
    What's to betide thee ?

Oh ! it micht mak' a heathen greet
To see thee chitt'rin' 'mang the weet,
Wi' hungry sides and shaeless feet,
    A' bare and blae ;
Yet ev'ry door's slamm'd in thy face,
As thou belang'dna to oor race,
    This winter day.

We boast aboot oor Christian lan',
And o' the wealth at oor comman',
And yet there's no' a helpin' han'
    Stretch'd oot to thee ;
And a' thae crouds o' thrifty folk
Pass thee as if thou wert a brock
    They hate to see.

My wee neglected, helpless creature,
Starvation writ on ev'ry feature,
What thou canst think o' God and Nature
    Beats me to ken.
This earth maun seem to thee a hell,
Whaur mony heartless demons dwell
    In shape o' men.

Frae ither bairns thou'rt kept apart ;
Nae words o' kindness ever start
The deep emotions o' thy heart,
    My puir, wee bairn :
Rear'd amang dirt and degradation,
Vile slang and horrid imprecation
    Is a' ye learn.

Hoo desolate thy heart maun be !
Nae mither tak's thee on her knee,
To sing old Scotia's sangs to thee,
    Baith air and late ;
But drucken dyvours tease and trick thee,
And swearin' carters cuff and kick thee
    Oot o' their gaet.

Ye canna spen' the simmer days
In rambles 'mang the broomy braes,
Or flow'ry haunts by lonely ways,
    Whaur burnies rin ;
But in dark cellars thou maun battle,
'Mang drucken swabs—vile human cattle—
    An' fumes o' gin.

Ye never heard the blithe cuckoo,
Nor croodle o' the cusha-doo,
Nor lav'rock singin' in the blue,
    Nor blackbird clear ;
But curses deep, and words o' hate,
And ribald sangs in filthy spate,
    Salute thine ear.

The glory o' the dewy dawn,
The purples o' the hill and lawn,
On thee, my child, hae never fa'n,
    Like gleams frae God,
To wauken in thee thochts sublime,
And show, ee'n thro' the chinks o' time,
    His bricht abode.

Ah ! dae we juist gang to the kirk
To pray for heathen, Jew, or Turk,
That a' oor duties we may shirk
    To sic as thee ?
I scarce daur look thee in the face,
For it's a shame and a disgrace
    Thy plight to see.

O Lord ! what time and siller's spent
On savages we never kent,
An' coaxin' heathen to repent !
    Here is a sample
Which should be lent to let them see
What oor religion's done for thee,
    Thou great example !

It's no' in singin' nor in sayin',
It's no in preachin' nor in prayin',
But it's in workin' oot, and daein'
    A' these in deeds
O' love an' mercy to ilk ither,
It's helpin' o' a helpless brither,
    That crouns a' creeds.

Miscellaneous

TRADITIONS

HURRAH for great Diana!
  And, whatsoe'er ye do,
Be sure to prop the old up
  And sacrifice the new.

Ye lean on old traditions,
  (To question them's a sin!)
And stifle holiest promptings—
  The God that speaks within.

Ye clog the soul of Nature
  With wretched little creeds—
Then lift your hands in wonder
  At dearth of noble deeds.

Ye pray the gods to guide you,
  Yet when the God appears,
You'll have no gods but old ones,
  And pierce His side with spears.

Ye boast of your achievements,
  Your feats with tongue and pen,
Till gods look down in wonder
  At little sons of men.

Hurrah for great Diana!
  And whatsoe'er ye do,
Be sure to prop the old up
  And sacrifice the new.
  24

WILSON'S GRAVE [44]

THEY should not have buried thee here !
   Oh, they should have made thee a bed
Where flow'rs at thy feet would appear,
   And the birds would sing over thy head.

Oh, they should have laid thee to rest
   From the smoke of the city away,
Where the dew would fall bright on thy breast,
   And the green turf would cover thy clay.

Afar in the forest's green shade
   The tall pine above thee should wave,
Where the bluebird would perch o'er thy head,
   And the whip-poor-will [25] sit on thy grave ;

Where Spring would come forth with her smiles,
   And the birds, that to thee were so dear,
Would sing 'mong the green leafy aisles
   The songs thou delightedst to hear.

And the red man would marvel to meet
   A grave in the green forest shade ;
And the hunter, at evening, would sit
   And weep where thine ashes were laid.

They should not have buried thee here,
   With no forest above thee to wave ;
But have borne thee away on thy bier
   Where the birds would sing over thy grave.

ODE ON THE DEATH OF ROBERT
TANNAHILL[45]

L AY him on the grassy pillow,
   All his toil and troubles o'er ;
Hang his harp upon the willow,
   For he'll wake its soul no more.
Let the hawthorn and the rowan
   Twine their branches o'er his head,
And the bonnie little gowan
   Come to deck his lowly bed.

Let no tongue profane upbraid him ;
   Here is nothing now but clay :
To the spirit pure that made him,
   Sorrowing, he stole away.
Let the shade of gentle Jessie,
   From the woods of old Dumblane—
Innocence he clothed in beauty—
   Plead not for the bard in vain.

Let the braes of grey Gleniffer,
   And the winding Killoch Burn,
Lofty Lomond and Balquither,
   For their sweetest minstrel mourn ;
And the Stanely turrets hoary,
   And the wood of Craigielee,
Waft his name and mournful story
   Over ev'ry land and sea.

Let the lily of the valley
   Weep her dews above his head,
While the Scottish muse sings waly [46]
   O'er her lover's lowly bed.
Lay him on the grassy pillow,
   All his toil and troubles o'er ;
Hang his harp upon the willow,
   For he'll wake its soul no more.

POOR DONKEY

POOR hapless, wretched, injured creature,
    With mis'ry stamp'd on ev'ry feature,
Was scorn for thee ordain'd by Nature,
        Poor donkey?

How lamentable is thy case !
Men jeer if thou but show thy face ;
Thy very name is a disgrace—
        Poor donkey !

And thou'rt the sport, alas ! alas !
Of all the low unreas'ning class ;
Thy crime is being "but an ass"—
        Poor donkey !

Thou'rt stupid, and thine ears are long ;
Thou'rt stubborn, and thy neck is strong ;
To cudgel thee can ne'er be wrong—
        Poor donkey !

Where shalt thou fly, where canst thou hide ?
The wretch's refuge, suicide,
Is even unto thee denied—
        Poor donkey !

'Twould do thee little good to know
There's sorrow wheresoe'er we go,
And thou art not alone in woe—
        Poor donkey !

Of sorrow's children thou'rt but one,
That for no evil they have done
Are wretched underneath the sun—
        Poor donkey !

My heart is sad, poor thing, to trace
The silent sorrow of thy face.
What's thine opinion of our race,
   Poor donkey ?

I well may blush to ask it thee,
For in thine eyes, ah, woe is me !
What cruel demons we must be—
   Poor donkey !

It needs no deep insight to guess
Thou canst believe in nothing less
Than in our " perfect cussedness "—
   Poor donkey !

Tho' thou art not accounted wise,
Thou must at times philosophize
On what goes on before thine eyes—
   Poor donkey !

How useless dogs are richly fed,
While Industry's in want of bread,
With scarcely where to lay her head—
   Poor donkey !

Or why yon puppy is carest
And pamper'd on the very best,
While thou'rt a drudge with want opprest—
   Poor donkey !

What compensation for thy groans,
Thy bleeding feet among the stones,
Thy hungry sides and weary bones,
   Poor donkey ?

It seems a lack of common-sense,
Or of intelligence gone hence,
To tell thee all's beneficence—
   Poor donkey !

Or what good will it do to know
For ev'ry needless curse and blow
Thy persecutors shall have woe,
      Poor donkey?

There's some wise end, I do not doubt,
Tho' it is hard to find it out :
God's ends are strangely brought about—
      Poor donkey !

No doubt thy fate seems most unjust,
From sympathy for no crime thrust,
But we've to take a deal on trust—
      Poor donkey !

GO INTO DEBT

WOULDST thou have sorrows manifold,
    And prove that friendship can grow cold,
And love itself be bought and sold,
      Without regret ;
And feel the great world's god is gold ?
    Go into debt.

Wouldst thou lose faith in human worth,
Have no one left to love on earth,
And be to callous souls for mirth,
      In mock'ry set ;
And curse the hour that gave thee birth ?
    Go into debt.

Wouldst bid adieu to pleasure's rays,
And find the world a weary maze,
And wander on through crooked ways,
      With thorns beset ;
Have sleepless nights and weary days ?
    Go into debt.

Wouldst bid adieu to honor's beam,
And see depart fame's happy dream,
Be slave to creatures low and mean,
   Whose creed is *Get;*
Be fallen in thine own esteem ?
  Go into debt.

And wouldst thou be the very slave
Of any selfish, sordid knave,
From morn till night to sit and rave—
   Within a net—
And find peace only in the grave ?
  Go into debt.

Wouldst thou forswear man's soul and stature,
Renounce thy very name and nature,
Have coward stamp'd on every feature,
   Thyself forget,
And live a crawling, creeping creature?
  Go into debt.

But if thou'dst know of no disgrace,
And look the whole world in the face,
And have 'mong men an honor'd place,
   A watch thou'lt set,
That pride nor passion e'er shall chase
  Thee into debt.

SCOTLAND

O CALEDONIA, can it be
 A wonder that we love thee ?
Tho' we be far removed from thee,
 We place no land above thee.
For tho' in foreign lands we dwell,
 A sacred tie has bound us ;
Our hearts can never lose the spell
 Thy mountains threw around us.

And tho' thy breath is cold and keen,
  And rugged are thy features,
Yet, O my country ! thou hast been
  The nurse of noble natures,
Who left us an inheritance—
  A world of song and story,
A wealth of sturdy common-sense,
  And doughty deeds of glory.

But Scotland ! 'tis thy sense of worth
  And moral obligations
Which makes thee mighty on the earth,
  A ruler 'mong the nations.
Does not thine humblest peasant know
  The truth of truths supernal—
That rank is but a passing show,
  But Moral Worth 's eternal ?

Scotland ! the humblest son of thine
  Is heir to living pages—
Heir to a lit'rature divine,
  Bequeathed to all the ages—
Heir to a language void of art,
  And rich with human feeling—
Heir to the language of the heart,
  Its sweetest tones revealing—

Heir to those songs and ballads old,
  Brimful of love and pity,
Which fall, like show'rs of living gold,
  In many a homely ditty.
Oh, sing us songs of other days,
  Of ruins old and hoary ;
Oh, sing of lang syne's broomy braes,
  And freedom's fields of glory !

Ah ! we may leave our mountains high,
  Our grand old hills of heather,
Yet song's the tie, the sacred tie,
  Which binds our hearts together.

WE LEAN ON ONE ANOTHER

OH, come and listen while I sing
    A song of human nature;
For, high or low, we're all akin
    To ev'ry human creature:
We're all the children of the same,
    The great, the " mighty mother,"
And from the cradle to the grave
    We lean on one another.

It matters little what we wear,
    How high or low our station,
We're all alike the slaves of sin
    And sons of tribulation.
No matter what may be the coat
    With which our breasts we cover,
Our hearts within are of one stuff,
    And link'd to one another.

The earth beneath's our common home,
    The heavens bending o'er us,
And wheresoever we may turn
    Eternity's before us.
Thro' pride and envy we have been
    But strangers to each other,
But Nature meant that we should lean
    In love on one another.

With Adam from the bow'r of bliss
    We all alike were driven,
And king and cadger at the last
    Must square accounts with heaven.
We're all in need of sympathy—
    Tho' pride the fact would smother—
And it's as little 's we can do
    To comfort one another.

A fool's a fool, the wide world o'er,
    Whate'er may be his station ;
A snob's a snob, tho' he may hold
    The sceptre of the nation
And Wisdom was ordained to rule—
    (Tho' knaves that truth would smother)—
That all the human race might live
    In love with one another.

A king may need our sympathy,
    For all his great attendance ;
Among all men there's no such thing
    As perfect independence.
Tho' great is mighty England's heir,
    Poor Paddy is his brother,
And from the cabin to the throne
    We lean on one another.

WHAT POOR LITTLE FELLOWS ARE WE

WHAT poor little fellows are we !
    Tho' we manage to make a great show,
Yet death has a claim on us all,
    And the king and the beggar must go.
How vain the distinctions we make !
    Neither wisdom nor wealth can us save,
But the prince and the peasant alike
    Are journeying on to the grave.

Then why should we listen to aught
    Which pride or which vanity saith ?
We're all on the current of time,
    And bound for the narrows of death.
The shafts of misfortune and fate
    Know neither the high nor the low ;
We're brothers to sorrow alike—
    And the king and the beggar must go.

A SONG OF CHARITY

COME, sing a song of Charity !
 Oh, may she ne'er forsake us !
For, good or bad, we're all what God
 And circumstances make us.
What's clear to me is dim to thee ;
 Opinions are divided ;
'Tis hard to judge what's wholly fudge,
 For things are many-sided.

I have a few thoughts of my own,
 With no one would I niffer ;
On such points both may be mista'en,
 So let's agree to differ.
We'll sing a song of Charity,
 And may she ne'er forsake us !
For, good or bad, we're all what God
 And circumstances make us.

Yet men will sigh, and wonder why
 The bigot's hither sent—
Such solemn fools are but the tools
 To work out God's intent.
So may we never do them wrong,
 Such still has been our prayer,
For had our lot been theirs, I wot,
 We'd just been such as they are.

But tho' so mad the wars we've had,
 When Death shall send us thither,
For all that's past we hope at last
 To meet in light together.
Then sing a song of Charity !
 And pray for truth to aid us ;
For, good or bad, we're all what God
 And circumstances made us.

WORTH

I CARE not for country, I care not for creed;
We're all sons of Adam, the best poor indeed.
I care not for station, I want but to know
If thy heart can with pity and love overflow?
With country and kindred I've nothing to do;
If thou hast a heart that is honest and true,
Then come to my bosom, whatever thy creed,
For thou art my friend and my brother indeed.

Oh, boast not to me that thou'rt above need,
But tell me, my friend, art thou far above greed?
Oh, talk not to me of thy pow'r and estate,
I'd ask thee, my friend, art thou far above fate?
How far art thou raised above sorrow and woe,
To look with contempt upon aught here below?
With vanity's prompting, oh, be not elate!
For death's pains and sorrows thou canst not abate.

Away with the bosom, tho' cover'd with gold,
If the heart that's within it be callous and cold;
Oh, show not your garments to me if they hide
But hearts all polluted with passion and pride.
And talk not to me of your delicate food
If ye love not the banquet prepared for the good.
If the great joy of sorrow thou never hast known,
Thou still art a slave, tho' possess'd of a throne.

Oh, give me the man that has triumph'd o'er self!
Who feels there are some things far, far above wealth;
Who chooses the truth, and will by it abide,
And deems it a treasure above aught beside;
Tho' in roughest homespun that mortal is dressed,
The heart of a man's beating under his vest;
Tho' poor and tho' humble may be his abode,
He bears the true stamp of the image of God.

Then let us believe that the time's coming round
When worth will be honor'd wherever 'tis found,
When men will be tested, no, not by their creeds,
Not the length of their purse, but the worth of their
    deeds !
The hand be exalted, tho' hard as the horn,
If the full cup of Mercy it ever hath borne ;
And virtue and goodness, the measure of worth,
And Truth, Love and Mercy abide upon earth.

IF YOU WOULD BE MASTER

THIS life is a struggle, a battle at best,
    A journey in which there's no haven of rest ;
And craggy and steep is the path you must tread
If you would be master and sit at the head.

The gods had their battles—they fought for their thrones,
And mounted up to them with struggles and groans ;
E'en so the frail mortal must soar above dread
If he would be master and sit at the head.

Be humble and lowly, be upright and brave,
Be often the servant, but never the slave ;
Submit to be bullied, but never be led,
If you would be master and sit at the head.

The laws of creation insist on respect ;
Believe in the virtues of cause and effect ;
Trust only to truth, and you'll ne'er be misled,
If you would be master and sit at the head.

Renounce all deception, all cunning and lies ;
Let truth be the pinion on which you would rise ;
Believe all deception is rotten and dead,
If you would be master and sit at the head.

WE'RE ALL AFLOAT

WE'RE all afloat in a leaky boat
  On Time's tempestuous sea ;
Death at the helm steers for his realm—
  A motley crew are we.
Through waters wide on ev'ry side,
  Away to sunken shoals,
He steers us o'er to Passion's roar,
  The heave of living souls.

We hear the splash, the heavy dash,
  The weary, weary moan ;
Embark'd in woe, we only know
  We sail the great unknown :
Some telling tales of happy vales
  That lie beyond the gloom ;
While Greed and Spite are at their fight
  For one more inch of room.

And Fraud and Pride, they push aside
  The weak ones and the old ;
While curses deep from mad hearts leap,
  They've huddled in the hold.
'Tis sad to hear 'mid tempest drear
  The selfish crew go on :
They curse and swear, all snarling there,
  As dogs do o'er a bone.

Anon, in brief but sweet relief,
  Amidst the fighting throng,
Some poor waif starts to cheer our hearts
  In blessed voice of song :
He sings of peace, the heart's increase,
  When Love o'er th' crew shall reign ;
The rudest hear with willing ear,
  Each heart cries out "Amen!"

THE HERO

WHILE hosts of cowards in our time
　　Round idols old are falling,
I hear a voice from realms sublime
　　To ev'ry true man calling :
" Up and despise time-honor'd lies ;
　　The reign of terror, end it ;
Bring forth the true, the fair, the new,
　　And manfully defend it.

" Men hide their ignorance with gilt,
　　And call it education ;
And halls and colleges are built
　　To stamp out innovation.
Despise the bigot's vile behest
　　That to his faith would pin you,
And utter thou the soul's protest
　　Which rises up within you.

" For he to whom the truth is true,
　　The very heavens adore him ;
Tho' men with thorns his path may strew,
　　Yet angels walk before him.
He marches on with ne'er a doubt,
　　And does the work assign'd him,
And what tho' all the rabble rout
　　Are barking on behind him,

" He's aye surrounded by a host
　　Of heroes, bards, and sages,
Who come to cheer him at his post
　　While Freedom's battle rages.
Then never fear the taunt and jeer,
　　But what is wrong amend it ;
Seize on the right with all your might
　　And manfully defend it."

THE PASSING OF JOLLITY

THE age, ah, me! of jollity
　　Is number'd with the past,
For our new world her lip has curl'd—
　　We've all grown good at last.

The joyous ways of youthful days
　　No more abroad are known;
With rock and reel and spinning-wheel,
　　They're gone, forever gone.
The Maypole gay has pass'd away,
　　The dance upon the green—
And Hogmanay, and New Year's Day,
　　And joyous Hallowe'en.

The legends old which then were told,
　　The fairy tales of yore,
The minstrel's lay, ah, well-a-day!
　　They're heard abroad no more.
The fairs of old, with joys untold,
　　Which young hearts doted on,
With puppet shows and dancing joes,
　　They're gone, forever gone.

We've nae bairns noo, with rose-red hue,
　　That romp in wood and glen;
But in their place we have a race,
　　Not weans, but wee, wee men;
Wha calculate at nae sma' rate,
　　And are always taking stock,
For, saving cash, all else is trash
　　To our won'erfu' wee folk.

What have we got our sires had not,
　　In our intellectual march,
Save vain conceit, the way to cheat,
　　With our stiff'ning and our starch?

Oh, give to me the spirit free,
   The ringing laugh and roar,
The simple heart, devoid of art,
   As 'twas in days of yore.

Lament with me, for jollity
   Is number'd with the past;
Our prudish world her lip has curl'd—
   We've all grown good at last.

LANG SYNE

HOW oft in life's gloaming in mem'ry I'm roaming
   That dear land for which still in spirit I pine;
Once more a young rover, in joy wand'ring over
   The green fields all hallow'd with mem'ries divine.

The lark gladly soaring, his anthem down-pouring,
   As if from the fountain of music divine;
The whole air is reeling with jubilant feeling,
   More deep than the rapture that flows from the vine.

Once more in life's morning young Hope is adorning
   The future with treasures that never can tine;
Her sweet song she's singing, her magic she's flinging
   Around a fair creature—oh, were she but mine!

Love's rapturous feeling thro' ev'ry vein stealing,
   How joyful we pour out the spirit's red wine;
Life all an emotion of love and devotion,
   How changed, oh, how changed since the days o'
     lang syne!

Life's day is declining, a' nature is dwining,
   And ev'rything wearing an aspect forlorn;
Tho' dark is life's setting, there's yet nae forgetting
   The glory that gilded the breaking of morn.

25

CLAMINA

A WAEFU' weird I noo maun dree ;
   A weary, weary wight I'll be ;
For oh, my heart has died wi' thee,
   My loved, my lost Clamina !

'Tis mony a year since we were wed,
And mony a couch for me ye spread ;
Noo I maun mak' for thee a bed,
   Thy long, thy last, Clamina !

How dowie will our ingle be !
For a' its licht's gone out wi' thee ;
And henceforth there is nocht for me
   But dark, dark days, Clamina !

Oh, thou art changed, as changed can be ;
'Tis not my own belov'd I see !
And thou canst be nae mair to me
   What thou wert aye, Clamina !

These lips that I sae aft hae prest ;
That head which hung upon my breast ;
My loved, my beautiful, my best !
   Farewell, farewell, Clamina !

Our treasures we are laith to tine ;
We deem our jewels all divine ;
But thou canst never mair be mine,
   My loved, my lost Clamina !

Abune thy head the birds shall sing,
From out thy grave the flowers shall spring,
And morn her clearest dew-draps bring
   To deck thy turf, Clamina !

And spirits of the viewless air,
And ev'rything that's good and fair,
At ev'ning hour shall linger there
   To weep for thee, Clamina!

A waefu' weird I noo maun dree;
A weary, weary wight I'll be;
Oh, would that I had died with thee,
   My loved, my lost Clamina!

I LONG NOT FOR RICHES

I LONG not for riches, I long not for wealth—
   The goddess I worship is rosy young health;
For wealth, it but deepens the wrinkles of care,
And oft steals the bloom from the cheek that is fair.
In gathering wealth some are gathering woe,
For the more that they get all the poorer they grow;
They lose life's enjoyment in holding it fast,
Till it either leaves them or they leave it at last.

A fig for your scholar who puzzles and looks,
And sees Nature's ways but in musty old books!
Can Greek or can grammar, can science or art,
Confer on a fool e'er a head or a heart?
And what's all this digging and hoeing about?
If genius is in, it will find its way out.
'Neath great loads of learning they stagger and groan—
Oh, let me have little, if that is mine own!

I'm sick of refinement, I'm weary of art,
I hate all refinement that withers the heart;
Away with your dandies, your creatures of steam,
With nothing but buttons where hearts should have been.
Still give me the laugh of the children at play,
For where is the monarch as happy as they?
Away with all tinsel—'tis foolish, 'tis vain—
Like them let us live with old Nature again.

REIN AULD ADAM IN

TO gather gear is all the rage,
   By ony crook or wile;
No legal dodge seems to our age
   Intolerably vile.

But ne'er by giving way to greed
   True happiness we'll win;
Alas! the maist o' us hae need
   To rein auld Adam in!

To us the money-getting art
   Is but the one thing real;
We seldom cherish in our heart
   A holy, high ideal.

Alas, alas! to a' beside
   Yon puir rich man is blin';
When tempted, never has he tried
   To rein auld Adam in.

He never strove to rise above
   Mere little paltry pelf;
No, never had he aught to love
   Beyond his shabby self!

Poor man, he's always on the hunt
   O' profitable sin,
And far awa' beyond affront
   To rein auld Adam in.

The social heights he's reached to here,
   Through mony a snub and thraw,
One loving-kindness wi' a tear
   Would far outshine them a'.

He plots and schemes to filch the puir,
   With ne'er a sense o' sin,
Altho' a wee bird in the air
   Sings, " Rein auld Adam in."

And yet, for all that he is worth,
   His moral manhood's rotten,
And soon as he's laid in the earth
   Then he'll be quite forgotten.

Then always, when we're on the brink
   O' some delightful sin,
Pause for a moment, stop and think,
   Then rein auld Adam in.

With self the battle must be fought,
   That right may wear the crown,
And never, never cherish aught
   To drag our manhood down.

Still let us cherish faith and hope
   That heart at last shall win,
And give the God within us scope
   To rein auld Adam in.

JOHN FRASER'S FAREWELL TO THE CHURCH
OF SCOTLAND [36]

FAREWELL to the Church of my fathers,
    With thee I no longer can dwell,
Constrain'd by the Spirit to bid thee
    A sad and a solemn farewell.
Yet many and dear recollections,
    From which I can never get free,
And hearts that are sleeping beside thee,
    Still bind me, old temple, to thee.

For oh! to my heart thou still bringest
    The far away, old happy times,
The long summer days of my boyhood,
    And Scotia's old ballads and rimes.
No doubt that the age has outgrown thee,
    For faults of the spirit are thine,
And yet thou didst nourish affections
    That surely had something divine.

Ah, many a simple-souled peasant
    Grew great on thy terrible faith,
And, fearless 'mid flames or the torture,
    Walked into the valley of death.
But tho' thou couldst teach man to suffer—
    To suffer and even to die!—
Yet poor human nature had longings
    And wants that thou couldst not supply.

And tho' thou hadst gleams of true grandeur,
    And struggled to reach the divine,
The heart had a higher ideal,
    A holier hunger, than thine.
Farewell to the Church of my fathers,
    With thee I no longer can dwell,
Constrain'd by the Spirit to bid thee
    A sad and a solemn farewell.

OLD SKINFLINT'S DREAM.

MY frien's, I've had a hasty ca',
    I'm summoned hurriedly frae a';
There's scarce been ony time at a'
    Gien to prepare,
For ere the shades o' evening fa'
    I'll be nae mair.

I've been sae bothert nicht and day,
I ne'er had time to learn to pray,
But some o' you perhaps wad say
    A word for me,
And straught accounts and clear the way
    Before I dee.

I've orders that I maun fulfil,
I've grain unenter'd at the mill,
I've cash uncoonted in the till,
    Letters to write;
Then there's the making o' the will,
    And a' ere night.

This nicht, this very nicht, I lea';
Oh! how can I gie up the key?
Wha'll manage things as well as me
    When I'm awa?
Oh! its an awfu' thing to dee
    And leave your a'.

Ye see I'm in a sorry plicht;
Nae wonder that I sweet wi' fricht;
I saw and heard o' things last nicht
    That gar me grue—
Enough to mak' me mad outricht,
    They were sae true.

A' yesterday I spent in dunning,
And nickit some wha think they're cunning,
So I sat doun to coont the winning,
    And write snell letters
To those wha've lang been backward running,
    My doun-gaun debtors.

Says I, "My lads, I'll let ye see
Frae justice ye'll nae langer flee.
Nae mercy will ye get frae me ;
    Ye'll pay the cash,
Or else I'll houn' ye till ye dee,
    Ye worthless trash."

And then I swore by earth and sky,
And by the Ane wha reigns on high,
That tho' they micht o' hunger die,
    Whate'er they've got
They'd give me, or in jail they'd lie
    Until they rot.

I swor't again, but in a trice
A voice exclaim'd, "Thou hoary vice !"
And then it cried oot "Murder !" thrice
    Within mine ear,
While something rattled like the dice
    Amang my gear.

I saw a hand o'erturn the licht,
And in an instant a' was nicht ;
But, tho' my hair stood up wi' fricht,
    I closed my nieves,
And out I roar'd, wi' a' my micht,
    "Catch, catch the thieves !"

Tho' I was in a fearfu' state,
I made to shut and bar the gate,
But then a voice, like that o' fate,
    Cried three times, "John,

Prepare for death and judgment straight,
    And hell anon ! "

Nae frien', nae helping hand, was near,
And down I sank, o'ercome wi' fear ;
But still the voice rang in mine ear—
    Still it cried, "John,
Prepare for death and judgment near,
    And hell anon ! "

Oh ! how my heid ran roun' aboot,
And strange things wriggled in an' oot ;
I tint my senses, ne'er a doot.
    At last a light
Was brocht by creatures black as soot,
    Wha girnt wi' spite.

Away I vainly strove to flee,
While roun' an' roun' they danced wi' glee,
And oh ! what mouths they made at me,
    And scratch'd my face,
While one says, "John, we've kept for thee
    The warmest place."

While I sat sweetin', trem'lin' there,
The perfect picture o' despair,
Wha comes, and in my face did stare,
    But widow Young?
And then she opened on me sair
    Her tinkler tongue.

She gabbit for an hour or more
Aboot the things I falsely swore,
And o' the character I bore
    For cursed greed,
And telt that story o'er and o'er
    Aboot her deed.

She spak' o' a' my ac's unhallow'd,
O' a' the oaths that I had swallow'd,
And how in ill-got gear I wallowed,
          And, what d' ye think?
Cast up the hizzies that I follow'd
          And stov'd wi' drink!

I bore it lang.   At last thinks I
The best o' law is to deny;
It's no the first time—faith, I'll try,—
          Sae up I got,
But oh, the very infant lie
          Stuck in my throat.

For then my eye fell on a sign,
The very one that had been mine
When I was in the grocery line;
          I saw wi' shame
Light wechts, false measures, bogus wine,
          Stuck to my name.

Then the receipts that folk had lost,
For which I sued and put to cost,
Cam' roun' me like a mighty host;
          On each my name
Stood up before me like a ghost
          And cried oot, "Shame!"

Then a' wham I had e'er brow-beated,
And all that I had ever cheated,
And those I humbugg'd and defeated
          In Brampton court,
Stept forth, and each his tale repeated
          As if 'twere sport.

A' spak' o' my infernal greed,
Nae ane wad help me in my need,
But tied me to a stake insteid,
          Wi' three-inch cables,

While boiling gowd upon my heid
    They pour'd frae ladles.

I roar'd as loud as I was able,
An' wi' ae bound I burst each cable,
And struck my temples on this table;
    Then I awoke.
Oh, lauchna, frien's! nor ca't a' fable—
    It's nae a joke.

No, no! my frien's, I wasna' fu',
But sober as I am the noo;
I'll never see the morn, I trou;
    I sweat wi' fricht,
For a' thae horrors they'll renew
    This very nicht.

This nicht, this very nicht I lea';
Oh, how can I gie up the key?
Wha'll manage things as well as me
    When I'm awa'?
Oh, its an awfu' thing to dee
    And leave ane's a'?

————

JOHN TAMSON'S ADDRESS TO THE CLERGY IN SCOTLAND

ATTEND, ye rev'rend gentlemen,
    O' a' denominations,
For, as ye are sae guid yoursel's
    At giein' exhortations,
Ye'll surely hear me for a wee
    While I ca' your attention
To twa 'r rhee things nane but a frien'
    Would ever think to mention.

I wad be unco loath indeed
  To vilify or wrong you,
For there are heich heroic souls
  And Christian men among you.
I micht speak pleasant words, nae doot—
  The knave's aye geyan ceevil—
But gie's the man who speaks the truth
  And shames the very deevil.

I'll tell you, without makin' mou's,
  The things that hae incens'd me,
And ye wha find the bonnet fit
  Will first cry out against me.
Now, if the kirk we've lov'd so long
  Is falling into ruin,
Then let me whisper in your lug :
  " You're not the right pursuin'."

Just let me tell you, as a frien',
  Ye mak' an awfu' blunder
Whene'er ye lend yoursels as tools
  To help the rich to plunder ;
Ye lose the love o' honest men,
  And ope the mouths o' scorners,
Ye mak' your faithfu' brethren greet
  Like Zion's waefu' mourners.

The deevil's taken noo-a-days
  To selling and to buying,
And drives a thrifty, thriving trade
  In little legal lying.
He's pleading noo in a' oor courts,
  He's in amang the jury,
And even 'neath the judge's wig
  He's no' afraid to courie.

Lang, lang in councils o' the state
  He's dodged and he's dissembled,
And absent neither night nor day
  Frae Parliament assembled.

He's even in the pulpit, too,
    And turns the flatt'ring sentence,
And hauds your tongues when ye should ca'
    Fat sinners to repentance.

He mak's you turn in twenty ways,
    Yet aye stick to the strongest,
And mince your Bibles to suit them
    Whose purses are the longest ;
To heap the thunders o' your wrath
    Upon the poor transgressor,
But daurna for your souls attack
    His wicked, proud oppressor.

Ye needna preach to weary toil
    About the Christian graces,
As lang's ye wink at wickedness
    When seated in high places.
Ye canna get us to believe
    That poverty's nae evil,
And so ye say it's sent by God
    To keep us frae the deevil.

O' heathens and their horrid works
    Why gie us sic like doses,
And nae word o' the heathendom
    Beneath your very noses ?
Why prose about the slaves abroad,
    Bought, sell't and scourged to labor,
And ne'er a word o' sympathy
    About the slave—your neighbor ?

O' evils that are far awa'
    We canna bide your prattle,
Unless ye'll help our home-bred slaves
    To fecht their weary battle.
I wadna hae you fill your veins
    Wi' bluid like that o' Howard's,[47]
But that's nae reason why ye should
    Be arrant moral cowards.

Awake ! if ye wad longer be
  The pilots that would steer us ;
Attack the vices o' the age,
  Be up, be moral heroes !
Tell Sutherland's heich mighty duke,[48]
  Tell Athol, without fearing,
The deevil keeps a black account
  Against them for their clearing.

And dinna let Breadalbane slip ;
  Loch and his tribe, beset them ;
We've nae use for a deil ava
  If that he disna get them.
By fire and famine they have done
  The work o' extirpation,
And hounded out a noble race,
  The bulwark o' the nation.

Sadly they left their mountains blue,
  To go they knew not whither,
Or, far amid Canadian wilds,
  Sigh for their hills o' heather.
Tell county lairds ye'll tolerate
  Their bothies black nae longer,
Try whether Christianity
  Or Mammon is the stronger.

Explore the dreary vaults o' toil,
  Where fashion never centres—
The Saxon slaves in sweating caves
  Where daylight never enters ;
Tell tyrants ye are watching them ;
  Tho' ere so deaf they'll hear you,
And a' the lazy vampire crew
  Will baith respect and fear you.

And if ye canna humanize
  The heartless, purse-proud reavers,
Ye'll cheer at least the drooping hearts
  O' hungry, starving weavers.

Wherever there is Nicht and Woe,
　Bring tidin's o' the morrow ;
Oh ! let the kirk be, as o' auld,
　"The sanctuary o' sorrow."

Leave forms to flunkeys and to fools,
　They never made a true man ;
Preach Christianity as it is,
　A thing intensely human.
Be as your Lord and Maister was,
　The shield o' the forsaken,
And dying Faith will spread her wings,
　And into life awaken.

———

BURNS *

H AIL to the bard, wha did belang
　　To nae mere class or clan,
But did maintain, and not in vain,
　The Britherhood o' Man !
The King o' Herts ! wha did far mair
　To knit us to ilk ither,
Than oor lang line (some ca't divine)
　O' kings a' put thegither.

An' what although he may be puir,
　On Richt he tak's his stand,
An' bears him wi' the very air
　O' oor ain mountain land.
His mission is wi' wrang to cope,
　An' bid it to depart ;
Anew to kindle love an' hope
　In the despairing heart.

---

* This poem was awarded the Gold Medal offered by the Toronto
Caledonian Society in 1885.

Frae what plain common-sense c'as richt
  Nae sophistry can win him;
He daurs to speak wi' a' his micht
  The burning thochts within him.
His sense o' richt, his sense o' wrang,
  His love o' humble worth,
He poured in an immortal sang,
  That's ringing roun' the earth.

For, intellectually sublime,
  This humble peasant saw that,
Despite distinctions here, in time,
  " A man's a man for a' that ";
And if there was a man on earth
  Wha had his detestation,
'Twas he wha measured men by birth
  An' worshipped rank an' station :

For after honors he wad sneak,
  An' he'd defend the wrang,
An' he wad trample on the weak,
  An' truckle to the strang;
Stick ribbons in his button-hole,
  An' gartens at his knee,
An' his bit trifle o' a sowl
  Gang perfectly a-gley.

But still, despite o' a' the wrang
  That comes by human blindness,
The spirit o' the peasant's sang
  Is pity, love, an' kindness :
He pities e'en the warst o' folk;
  For even some o' them,
Wi' a' their flaws, he fin's mair cause
  To pity than condemn.

An' for the outcast everywhere
  He had a hert to feel,
An' had some sympathy to spare
  E'en for the very Deil.

Tho' in the grasp o' poverty,
    Wi' a' its wants an' fears,
His hert o'erflows for ither's woes
    As 'twere a fount o' tears.

E'en when he sees a needless pang
    Gi'en to the brute creation,
He wha inflicts maun bide the stang
    O' his roused indignation.
The thochtless youth cannot escape,
    Wha wounds the harmless " Hare,"
For Mercy, in the peasant's shape,
    Stands forth protesting there.

His sangs hae something in their soun'
    That fills the hert an' e'e ;
" Ye banks an' braes o' bonnie Doon "
    Are magic words to me.
O Doon ! thou'rt like nae ither stream ;
    Love's sacred spell has bound thee,
For a' the glory o' a dream
    The peasant threw around thee.

Thou sped'st unknown through ages lang,
    A little nameless river,
Till pity poured love's tears in sang,
    An' hallowed thee forever.
Lang as the human hert remains
    A fount o' hopes an' fears,
This simple little strain o' strains
    Shall stir it into tears ;

For by the Poet's magic art,
    Tho' but a moorland river,
Through the green regions o' the heart,
    It shall roll on forever.
Wi' him the birds forever sing,
    The gowans ne'er depart ;
He carries a supernal spring
    Forever in his heart.

26

The "modest flower" he crushed to earth,
  Wi' a' its snawy blossoms,
By him transplanted, blooms henceforth
  Forever in oor bosoms.
An' a' the streams may cease to flow,
  The sun itsel' may vary,
But down the ages he shall go
  Wi' his dear Highland Mary.

Anon the bard doth change his mood,
  And in the mirthfu' vein
What fancies flit on mother-wit,
  An' humor a' his ain :
Until his mirth-provoking strains
  Set daddie Care a daffin',
An' pit sic fun in his auld veins
  He canna flyte for laughin' :

Despite the thunder's dreedfu' soun',
  A' through the air sae mirk,
'Mang deils an' witches he's set down
  In Alloway's auld kirk.
He hears auld Nick play up a spring,
  Amang his crew uncanny ;
Sees a' the deevils dance an' fling,
  An' cross an' cleek wi' Nannie.

Hears Tammie, as his senses swim,
  Roar, "Weel dune, Cutty Sark,"
An' hears the hellish legion grim
  Rush on him in the dark ;
An' lang across the brig o' time,
  That legion, weird an' scraggy,
Shall chase triumphant Tam, sublime
  On his immortal Maggie !

An' lo ! aneath the cloud o' nicht,
  Despite misfortune's deggers,
Saw mortal ever sic a sicht
  As a' they "Jolly Beggars"?

E'en happiness, that shuns the great,
    Can nestle amang rags,
And even love an' joy can wait
    Amang auld mealy bags.

E'en wisdom gravely listens when
    His "Twa Dugs" tak a seat,
To get some licht on ways o' men ;
    But even dugs are beat.
Burns wasna perfect to a dot,
    An' wha amang us a'
But has some hole in his ain coat,
    An' maybe some hae twa ?

Let them tak tent wha think they staun ;
    God keep us humble a' !
The pride o' never having fa'en
    Itsel's a dreedfu' fa'.
Oh, never, never forward be
    The erring ane to blame,
For under like temptation ye
    Micht just hae dune the same.

Burns micht hae muckle to repent
    O' "passions wild and strong,"
But did he gie his soul's consent,
    Although he did the wrong ?
We love him, even wi' a stain,
    Nae matter wha may ban ;
We love him, for he did maintain
    The liberty of Man.

And till the ages a' are fled,
    And time shall cease to roll,
His "Scots wha hae wi' Wallace bled "
    Shall fire the freeman's soul.
Hail ! Minstrel o' the brave and true,
    Tho' Scotia's pride thou art,
In spirit thou belongest to
    The universal heart.

Sketches from the Wanderer

A PROSE POEM

Inscribed to W. T. Boyd, Teacher

THERE is no place, no spot of earth, though e'er so wild and desolate, but has its history. Though 'twere but the changes time writes on it, they become leaves of the mighty volume and will not perish. Man vainly tries to count the furrows in great Nature's face and fix her birthday thereby; but in his vain attempts he loses himself in æons, and the Infinite rushes upon him, till he stands transfixed in silent wonder.

There is no place where human beings lived, loved, and wrangled, but has its annals, uttered in some shape. The whole past is blended with the future; we the living links which bind the whole together. List to that ancient song, so full of human feeling. It is the voice of buried generations speaking to us through the long aisles of ages. They have not perished, though they've passed away; they commune with us still—yea, the dead are here, of ages most remote. Old Time is no destroyer; he has garnered all the past, and formed us of it.

We would speak of his works, for all his lines are of surpassing virtue; all his oracles divine, though but old men's grey hairs. Aye his dumb ministers—Change, Ruin, Death, Decay—are awe-inspiring preachers; even in their silence, eloquent, sublime.

I'm old and weary, and would sit me down and talk about the past.

In yonder vale I grew from youth to manhood, but long since departed from it, and, in my weary age, have sought it once again, to lay me with my forefathers. And yet I feel as though this were not the place of my nativity; for every face I meet tells me I'm a stranger here. The old are dead and buried, and the young have grown out of my recollection: even those I dandled on my knee are men and women grown; and if they do remember me, 'tis as an image in some half-forgotten dream.

Even Nature's face is changed! Yon mountains wear another aspect; the streams talk not to me as of old.

And you, ye woods, which half o'erhang that once delightful village! Though your green faces are familiar, yet somehow ye have acquired a melancholy meaning. Ye are not the green cathedrals where awoke spontaneous worship, glad as the sunbeams which streamed through your long dark leafy arches.

And you, ye flowers, clinging up there to the rough bosom of the rugged rock, like virtue to rough natures! Still ye are beautiful; but ye are not the fairy mirrors where the young heart's joy was imaged. Ye are not, as of old, Nature's delighted revelers: the livelong summer day spreading your honey bosoms to the bee; all the night long drinking the dews of heaven till they overflow your silken tresses. Ah! no, a joyous something has departed from you. There ye hang, like jewels on Death's bosom, mournful mementos of joys departed.

Even yon ruined tower, built in the days of old, where dwelt the long forgotten mighty! Still, as of yore, it looks down on the valley—but ah! how changed its look! Its lordly air is gone. It is still called the "Eagle's Eyrie," as in mockery of him who built it on the steep. His fame, his name, his race, have perished from the earth, and the old tower alone tells of what has been.

What secret sympathy still drags me towards it? Does its fate resemble mine? Oh! tell me, is there not some strange mystic affinity between old walls and our affections? Why can dead matter, on immortal mind, beget emotion infinite? Why can a moss-clad ruin, or a mouldering stone, touching some secret sympathy, attune the chords of our affections till the heart overflows in liquid melody;

melting down years to moments, making our whole lives, with all their good and ill, pass in review before us ; wafting us away to the death-realm—calling up the dead from their deep slumber, wiping their clammy lips, planting the rose of health on their pale faces, even while listening with a holy awe to the dread secrets of another world?

Turn which way we will, are there not eyes innumerable looking out on us? Stand we not in a mysterious presence? Is there not something sitting in yon tower—a face of sorrow looking through all its loop-holes? Does not yon blasted pine, by lightning riven, stretch out its naked arms in proud defiance of the element which wrought its ruin? Is not the yew tree melancholy? Does not the willow weep? All Nature's forms seem but spirit mediums. Ah, me ! what a world !

WHENCE COME WE?

WHENCE come we? Whither do we go? For what purpose sent into this wondrous world? Is this our final sphere, or is it but the mere bud of our being? Is death eternal sleep, or an awakening from a troubled vision? Is this decaying form moulded on an immortal? Are we but the outward shadows of an inner world—fleeting reflections of enduring things? Is the tree of knowledge unattainable? Can Science or Philosophy not aid us here? Science is mute, Philosophy is dumb. Vainly have we arraigned the elements of earth and air to interpret their voices ; transformed tyrannic matter to a slave ; dived to the depths of earth's foundations, and explored wrecks of a former world ; or soared from atoms to the ponderous worlds which roll forever through immensity. But, ah ! they cannot lift the veil which shrouds our future fate. With dead matter our triumphs cease.

Then wherefore are we finite things thus cursed with a desire to grasp infinity? Why are we thus bound bleeding to the wheels of fate, in doubt and darkness shrouded?

Why is all we know but an intimation of the things we know not? Why do our lights but make the "darkness invisible," if interests of eternal weight hang in the balance?

Wherefore, inquirer, but to teach presumptuous man a lesson of humility; to lean not on his own capacity, but on the Arm Omnipotent. Thou hast leaned too long on human knowledge. Has it scathed sin, or killed her brood of sorrow? Has it done aught but add to thy pride? Yea, pride has ever been thy most familiar demon. Ambitious worm, fain wouldst thou be a god, and by thy knowledge scale the heights of the empyrean. But knowledge and power were given thee, not for self-exaltation, but that thou mightest the deeper feel the need of a guide omnipotent; therefore, let faith ever be thine anchor and the evidence.

Neither art thou, as without chart or compass, thrown on life's vast ocean. When the winds and waves of passion lift their voices, when misfortune's thunder-cloud is o'er thee, a star still gilds the gloom; yea, though thy bark were a floating wreck, and spirits of the storm shrieking the death-dirge over thee, the sun of hope divine should light thee to a refuge from destruction.

MORNING IN SPRING

'TIS morning, and from the east the sun comes like a conqueror, driving night down the world. The mists have vanished in his presence; even those which sought a refuge in the valley are retreating. Now the scattered fugitives have made a stand on the brow of Ben-lomond, like a vanquished host gathered for a last rally!

Now they are gone, and morn is offering up her song of triumph. The lark is high in the heaven—the only speck in the azure immensity—and from it gladdest music gushes. Even the distant torrent has lost its midnight roar; its hum greets the ear with pleasing solemnity. From the sea the breeze is coming, and the pines nod to each other; the cuckoo calls like a spring spirit from the bosom of the woods, and, answering to her call, the leaves have burst to being. Even the blackbird on the bough has forgotten his long silence, startled into song by the general chorus.

And I, even I, old and aweary, feeling something of the flowery freshness of life's morn revive within me, instinctively join in Nature's rejoicing. Oh, Nature is as beautiful as on creation's dawn! 'Tis the gloom in ourselves which weaves her pall, for she is all unchanged, lovely as on her natal morn. Man and his institutions change, but Nature is eternal!

Ah, old Ocean! there thou art, the same in every feature; still, as of old, a deep unfathomed wonder. Even now I feel some tone of that strange feeling of delightful awe which thrilled my bosom when a consciousness of thine immensity first dawned upon me; when man and the world vanished, and I stood wrapt, lost, within the shadow of the Infinite.

Then I became a dreamer; and for hours would sit me on this spot, watching the heavings of thy breast, and listening to thy long, deep respirations; or in imagination dived to the secret depths, ransacked thy coral caves, and communed with thy mysterious spirits.

When from the Tempest's eye flashed the forked lightning—when at his awful voice the mountains shuddered and the winds rushed shrieking from their caves—then didst thou feel smitten with the madness, and didst howl and foam in concert, dashing thy bosom 'gainst the rocks, heaving thy crest up through the cloudy columns till they burst in torrents, and the affrighted sun looked through his bloody curtain.

I'm old and weary, and my soul longs but for quietude; yet thine angry voice, thy rage and uproar, still, as of old, are music to mine ear.

NOTES

Page 49 (^{1}), *Who knows?*

The critical reader (inclined to complain that McLachlan too often harps on this hopeless, plaintive, Jeremiah string) may care to have his attention directed to certain other lines less pessimistic, less agnostic, or more hopeful in tone, and which our poet appears to have had in mind as a possible antithesis to this piece.   Poets are seldom consistent philosophically.   As a sample we may point the reader to the lines (in *Awful Spirit*, page 165) :

> " Dreamer vain and Pantheist
> May define Thee as they list;
> As in childhood, we would rather
> Look up to Thee as ' Our Father.'
>
> .   .   .   .
>
> Where the light eternal flows,
> And no wand'rer asks " Who knows?""

Page 72 (^{2}), Serfdom in Russia.

In the days of the Crimean War, 1853 to 1855, serfdom was prevalent throughout the Russian Empire, a condition abolished by the successor of Nicholas I.   The reference to "serfs" is therefore not poetic imagination, but veritable history.

Page 73 and elsewhere (^{3}), Corrybrechtan.

Corrybrechtan, or Gulf of Brechan (also spelt Corrievrekin), is a whirlpool or dangerous passage a mile broad on the west coast of Argyleshire, in the strait between Scarba and Jura Isles.   It is caused by tides (often running twelve or fourteen miles an hour) meeting from north and west in the narrow passage into the sound of Jura, round a pyramidal rock, which rises from a considerable depth to some fathoms from the surface.   This rock forces the water in various directions.   In stormy weather, at flow-tide, vast openings form in the water, immense bodies of which tumble headlong as over a precipice, then, rebounding from the abyss, dash together and rise in spray to a great height.   The noise is heard over the isles around.   The water is smooth for half an hour in slack water.

Page 100 ([4]), "Canty auld Christopher."

John Wilson (born 1785, died 1854) was Professor of Moral Philosophy in the University of Edinburgh.   Born at Paisley, he was reared in Mearns parish, a wild moorland district in Renfrewshire.   Long afterward he commemorated his boyhood there in some of his most charming essays.   Under the pseudonym Christopher North, or Kit North, he was the soul of the success of *Blackwood's Magazine* for a quarter of a century from 1816.   *The Recreations of Christopher North* is a selection in two volumes from the mass of his essays furnished it.   His range of power was extraordinary : while a muscular Christian, he could give expression to the finest subtleties of feminine tenderness.   After Burns and Scott, he captured the heart of the Scottish people almost as effectually as they, and after the death of Scott, in 1832, became their accepted literary representative.

Pages 102, 214, 239, 313 ([5]), *Cartha Again.*

The Cart (poetic Cartha) is a stream in Renfrewshire falling into the Clyde.   (See Biographical Sketch, p. 20.)

Page 105, 136 ([6]), Foggy-bee.

The foggy-bee is a small species of bee that makes its cells among fog (that is, moss).

Pages 107, 195 ([7]), Chimley.

Chimbly, or Chimley, for Chimney, is not uncommon in Ontario. According to "Dialect Notes," (Vol. I., pp. 67, 375), this is widespread, being heard in Old and New England, and reported from Kentucky, Louisiana and Tennessee.

Page 111 ([8]), Balclutha.

Balclutha—Dumbarton rock—visible from the birthplaces of the poet and his friend.   (See Biographical Sketch, p. 21.)

Pages 114, 313 ([9]), Crookston Castle and Langside.

After Mary, Queen of Scots, escaped from her island-prison in Loch Leven, she soon found herself at the head of an army of 6,000 men. On 12th May, 1568, it was met by Regent Murray at Langside, near Glasgow, and defeated.   When Mary, from a place of safety (Crookston Castle) near the battle-field, saw what would be the result of the engagement, she took horse, made her way across the border, and threw herself under the protection of Elizabeth, only to become a captive for life.

Pages 114, 313 ([10]), Glengarnock, and Hardyknute.

The ruin, one of the most picturesque in Scotland, is well seen from the opposite bank of the river Garnock. It is alluded to in the grand old ballad (to be found in Percy's " Reliques ") of Hardyknute, beginning :

> " Stately stept he east the wa',
> And stately stept he west."

Page 114 ([11]), Largs.

Largs is a small town on the coast of Ayrshire, a favorite resort for sea-bathers, beautifully situated on the Firth of Clyde, on a pleasant strip of shore backed by hills, eighteen miles below Greenock. Here, in 1263, Alexander III of Scotland, in a war between that country and the Norwegian colonies of Man and the Isles, defeated Hacon, King of Norway, who, with 160 vessels and 20,000 men, had descended on the coast of Ayrshire. The result was the immediate withdrawal of the invading force and the abandonment within three years of Norwegian pretensions to the Scottish Isles.

Largs is to the Scot what Clontarf, near Dublin, is to the Irishman. There a national hero, Brian Boroimhe, in 1014, won a great victory over the Danes, expelling them from Ireland. In like manner, Alfred's overthrow of the Danes at Edington denotes a patriotic victory over foreign invaders. The Norwegians being a branch of Scandinavians included under the general term " Danes," it follows that each of the three kingdoms had its deliverance from a foreign yoke through a hero-king, followed by the firm establishment of self-government in each of the three kingdoms. These particulars it is thought worth giving that other Britishers may understand and appreciate the feelings of the Scot in the parallel case.

Page 129 ([12]), "The good old Queen."

Marjory Bruce, daughter of the hero of Bannockburn.

Page 130 ([13]), "a kingly shadow."

Paisley Abbey was founded by Walter, High Steward of Scotland, progenitor of the Royal Stuarts.

Page 130 ([14]), " good Saint Mirin."

Saint Mirin is the patron saint of Paisley.

Page 130 ([15]), " two wrathfu' spirits."

This is an allusion to the feuds of the Montgomeries and Cunninghams. (See Semple's History of the Lairds of Glen.) These feuds have a historic basis, not a mythical one, like those of the Montagues and Capulets of the great dramatist.

Pages 130, 346 (¹⁶), "bard of old Belltrees."

Robert Semple, of Belltrees, is meant. He was author of the celebrated song, "Maggie Lauder," also an elegy on Habbie Simpson, the
piper of Kilbarchan, and other poems.

Page 131 (¹⁷), "Jenny Geddes."

The story referred to is that of Janet Geddes, who kept a green stall
in High street, Edinburgh. Archbishop Laud, in the time of Charles I,
attempted the introduction of a service-book into the Kirk of Scotland.
Sunday, 23rd July, 1637, was fixed for this innovation, so very obnox-
ious to Scottish Presbyterians. An immense crowd filled the High
Church of Saint Giles, Edinburgh. When the Dean of Edinburgh began
to read, his voice was lost in a tumultuous shout. Jenny, rising from
the stool on which she sat, exclaimed, "Villain! dost thou say mass at
my lug?" and hurled it at the dean's head. Uproar and universal confusion followed. The dean threw off his surplice and fled to save his
life. The Bishop of Edinburgh, attempting to restore order, was assailed
by a volley of sticks, stones, and other missiles, accompanied by cries
and threats that effectually silenced him. This proved the death-blow
to the liturgy in Scotland.

Pages 136, 216, and elsewhere (¹⁸), McLachlan's Rimes.

Anyone examining McLachlan's rimes is apt to conclude that he
bent much that very flexible thing called poetic license. This is true
in but a small proportion of cases however. Most are due to his not
aiming at received pronunciation, but following his own ear rather than
the dicta of the orthoepist. (1) With him close o (ō) was often open o
(ŏ), *road* being pronounced much like *rod*. So the riming of *road*
with *God* (page 153) satisfied his ear, as did *on* with *throne* (p. 177),
code with *God* (p. 223), *smoke* with *shock* (p. 118). (2) Standard open
i (ī) as in *river* he pronounced, as is very general in Scotland, with e,
much like e in *let*, but closer and more tense (é); as *riv'n*, *Heav'n*,
driv'n, *heav'n* (p. 177), *merit*, *spirit* (p. 216), *striv'n*, *heav'n* (p. 217),
bench, *clinch* (p. 303). Campbell (in *Hohenlinden*) has *riven*, *driven*,
heaven, as is common with Moore and the North British poets generally. (3) The "mixed vowel" in *guid*, *abune*, *sune*, etc., is pronounced in Scotland, as elsewhere, in two ways: (i) As a "front"
vowel with tone of i in *sin*, but with the mouth as for u in *put*, which
might be marked *iu*; (ii) as a "back" vowel, with tone of u in *put*,
and the mouth as for i (*ui*). McLachlan used the first of these
ways, hardly ever the second: Witness *abune*, *sin* (p. 136), *inn*, *mune*
(p. 289), *begin*, *dune* (p. 326), *dune*, *in* (p. 327). (4) In ct, t is silent
in most cases; which explains *respec'*, *Fleck* (p. 300), *facts*, *tax*, *ax*
(p. 257). Besides (1), (2), (3), (4), which are classes of words, we may
specify (5) certain isolated words: *says* he would pronounce to rime
with *days*; *said* with *made* (p. 348), *said it* with *pervadit* (p. 304),

exceptionally with *head* (p. 228) and *tread* (p. 254); *wound* (noun) he rimed with *mound*, as was common early in the nineteenth century, not with *tuned*, which now prevails; *mourn* he thought a perfect rime with *burn*, as *again* with *strain* (p. 222), exceptionally with *then* (p. 227).

Page 141 ([19]), " Could I again see thee."

This love-song was a reminiscence, not a piece of imagination without foundation in fact. It commemorates some child-love among play-fellows. On his return to Scotland the author looked up and found that the subject of it did " ' mang the living still ' bide." But, alas for day-dreams! she had not the slightest recollection whatever of her boyish admirer!

Page 141 ([20]), *Sing Me that Sang Again.*

A recent Scottish poet of great merit, Robert Ford, in " Tayside Songs" (Gardner: Paisley and London, 1895), page 20, has " Oh, Sing Me that Sang Again, Lassie," of which the last stanza is :

> " Oh, sing me that sang again, lassie,
>   Sing a' that sang again ;
> Its ilka note is bliss the best,
>   Sweet, sweet's the auld refrain.
> It glints a gladness roun' my heart,
>   It wraps my soul in glee ;
> Oh, lassie, that's the dear auld sang
>   My mither sang to me."

Pages 143 ([21]), *John Tamson's Bairns.*

This piece and *The Cringer Rebuked* (p. 362) must be taken as McLachlan's voicing of the Brotherhood of Man. (The Fatherhood of God he has voiced in *Awful Spirit*, p. 165.) It is parallel to Burns's

> " That man to man, the world o'er,
>   Shall brothers be for a' that."

Or to Tennyson's " Parliament of Man," governed by consensus of public opinion, " the common sense of most."

> " Far along the world-wide whisper of the south-wind rushing warm,
>   With the standards of the peoples plunging thro' the thunder storm ;
> Till the war-drum throbb'd no longer, and the battle flags were furl'd
> In the Parliament of Man, the Federation of the world.
> There the common sense of most shall hold a fretful realm in awe,
> And the kindly earth shall slumber, lapt in universal law."
>   —LOCKSLEY HALL.

Pages 156, 166 ([22]), " *Million arms are swung.*"

The evergreen pine, with its lordly stature, when played on by the breeze, gives forth a sound as of a mighty rushing wind, but attuned by a million vibrating chords, the needles or leaves of the tree. These, or possibly the branches, are meant by our author's " million arms are swung." It is particularly noticeable in winter and from the height of

the tree. On approach of storms, when sounds are more readily trans-
mitted, this, with the creaking and groaning of the mighty trunk of the
stately tree (whose "great bosom shrieks"), gives a weird feeling,
probably felt strongly by the author.

Page 168 ([23]), *Mystery*.

A recent prose writer has given expression to what is tantamount to
the same thought :

" For whether we acknowledge it or not, the springs of our entire
existence are hidden. From the darkness of the womb to the darkness
of the tomb, the source of our every action is veiled from us. Mystery
is the beginning ; mystery is the ending ; mystery is the whole body of
our life. We cannot breathe nor sleep, nor eat, far less think or speak,
without exercising powers which to us are inconceivable, by means of
processes which are to us inscrutable. Who is so ignorant as not to
know these things ; who so learned as to make them clear ?"—
W. MARSHAM ADAMS, in "The Book of the Master," p. 21. London :
Murray, 1898.

Page 182 ([24]), *Bobolink*.

The Bobolink (*Dolichonyx oryzivorus*) is called, after moulting, the
reed-bird. It is also known in some localities as the rice-bird (*oryzivorus*). In summer it is a wild, ecstatic black-and-buff singer, soaring above meadows, leaving a trail of rippling music. In autumn it is
a brown striped bird, hunted by gunners, and voiceless but for a metallic
"clink." Mabel Osgood Wright, writing (in "Birdcraft") from the
latitude of Connecticut, says : "Of all our songsters none enters into
the literature of fact and fancy more fully than the Bobolink, and none
so exhilarates us by his song. Sit on the fence of an upland meadow
any time from early May until the last of June, watch and listen. Up
from the grass the Bobolinks fly, some singing and dropping again,
others rising, Lark like, until the distant notes sound like the tinkling
of an ancient clavichord. Then, while you are gazing skyward, from
the choke-cherry tree above your head will come the hurried syllables
in which Mr. Burroughs interprets the song : ' Ha ! ha ! ha ! I must
have my fun, Miss Silverthimble, if I break every heart in the meadow.
See ! See ! See !' Meanwhile, the grass is full of nests and brown
mothers, neither of which you see, for you are wholly entranced by the
song. Bryant's poem on "Robert of Lincoln" contains a good description of the bird's plumage, but is too precise and measured to express
the rapture of the song. It may describe a stuffed Bobolink, but never
a wild, living one. . . . Prose writers vie with the poets in singing
the Bobolink's praises ; their own words turning to music under his
spell. Listen to what Thoreau says of the song : ' It is as if he [the
bird] touched his harp with a vase of liquid melody, and when he lifted
it out the notes fell like bubbles from the strings. . . . Away he
launches, and the meadow is all bespattered with melody. . . .
He is the peerless musician whom no one should wittingly destroy."

Pages 188, 225 ([25]), *Whip-poor-will.*

The Whip-poor-will (*Antrostomus vociferus*) was better known in Ontario in its forest-covered days than now. It is still abundant in season in northern Ontario. As the present generation are not familiar with it, it may be in place to give a short account of it. The note "whip-poor-will" is usually repeated five times. Mrs. Wright (in "Birdcraft") tells us: "This weird bird, with its bristling, fly-trap mouth, who sleeps all day and prowls by night, . . . has not at any time even a transient home to abandon; like pilgrims of old, earth is his only bed. . . . Nature has taken great pains to blend the colors of its plumage with the browns and greys of the bark and rocks of the forest, and has given it the unusual habit of sitting lengthwise on the branch when it perches, so that it is invisible from below and so closely resembles the branch against which it is so flattened as to escape notice. The Whip-poor-will prefers forest solitude, but in nocturnal flights often comes near houses, and sometimes calls close to a window with startling vehemence. The breeding habits of this strange bird are not the least of its peculiarities; when its ground-laid eggs are hatched they are beset by many dangers from weasels, snakes, etc., but the young birds are almost invisible to the human eye, even if their location is known. The female is very adroit, and if she thinks her family has been discovered she will move them to another place, carrying them in her mouth as a cat does kittens."

Page 194 ([26]), "Ev'ry weeping slave."

Canada has the proud pre-eminence of having been one of the first to abolish slavery, which was done in 1793 by Act of Parliament. It appears that it was not immediately abolished, though importation of slaves was stopped, though those actually holding such were allowed to keep them, but not to acquire others. Black children were free on attaining the age of twenty-five; their children were free-born. It is one of the traditions of Toronto that when Miss Elizabeth Russell, sister and heir of Peter Russell, Lieutenant-Governor of Upper Canada (1797 to 1799), had her slaves freed, they with one accord declined to be freed. A full account of "Slavery in Canada" has been patiently collected by Mr. J. C. Hamilton, LL.B., Toronto, and published in the "Transactions of the Canadian Institute" for 1890-1897. It was not till 1st August, 1834, that Britain abolished slavery by paying an indemnity; and not till 1st January, 1863, that the United States did so by confiscation, by Lincoln's proclamation in the throes of civil war (1861-5), or the slaveholders' rebellion. Before that, this parody was common:

> "The star-spangled banner triumphantly waves
> O'er the homes of the free and—three millions of slaves."

Page 194 ([27]), "A refuge for the slave."

Canada was the northern terminus of "the underground railroad"—the pole-star being a "fire by night" to guide the southern Negro.

Pages 195 (^{28}), *Sparking.*

Sparking was a term equivalent to wooing or courting. It was the regular term in the middle third of the nineteenth century in Canada, but is now falling into disuse.

Page 200 (^{29}), "and antler'd herds."

This refers to deer, often seen singly and in herds by the pioneer.

Page 224 (^{30}), Rosa.

Salvator Rosa, a celebrated Italian landscape painter, of the Neapolitan School, lived 1615 to 1673.

Page 224 (^{31}), "songless, ev'ry one."

It was a frequent subject of remark with McLachlan that the birds of America are songless. British birds are far more tuneful. The brighter plumage of the birds of the new world seemed to him compensation for lack of song. British birds compare unfavorably with ours in plumage.

Page 234 (^{32}), "with its silver tassel."

In America, *corn* means maize, or "Indian corn." Our author refers to the long brilliant silk fringe or tassel at the top of the growing cob.

Pages 240, 291 (^{33}), "gloamin's hour is long."

The scene is in latitude 56. The higher the latitude the longer are summer days, and the longer is twilight. This is very noticeable in eastern Quebec, still more so in Manitoba, with its latitude of 51 or 52. The scene of the song is in the same latitude as the centre of Hudson's Bay. The statement in the text is sober fact.

Pages 304, 324, 342 (^{34}), *Auld Hawkie.*

William Cameron, "The King of Glasgow Wits," was "a gangrel buddy" (see next note), and was a celebrated character and street orator, familiarly known wherever he peregrinated, which was over most of the west of Scotland. He was called *Hawkie* from his burlesque prediction concerning the destruction of the "Briggate," and which prediction was announced by him as emanating "frae an Aberdour twa-year auld quey" ("quey" being a young cow, and "hawkie" being a Scots name for a white-faced cow, or sometimes for any cow, being frequently used as a pet name). Hawkie died about 1858. His biography has been published.

Page 305 (^{35}), "gangrel folk."

"Gangrel folk" (presumably *gangrel* is from *gang*, to go) are tramps, riff-raff, "great unwashed," Carlyle's *sansculottes.*

Pages 314, 388 ([36]), *My Old Schoolmaster.*

John Fraser, of Newfield House, Johnstone, was something of an ideal teacher, for, besides the instruction furnished, he could both inspire pupils and develop latent talent. He was an effective elocutionist and musician, as were the members of his family. As such, he gave entertainments in Britain, much as Kennedy did at a later date. He began an American tour, appearing in New York, Albany, and Boston, where, in August, 1852, the star of his troupe, a favorite daughter, Jeanie, contracted a cold, which resulted in death the following February, at Lanark, Ont. This stopped the tour. Fraser retired, half broken-hearted, to Johnstone. He died 3rd March, 1879, aged 85.

Page 320 ([37]), Will Steel.

Will Steel was a warlock (wizard) notorious in the west of Scotland.

Page 336 ([38]), *My Grandfather and His Bible.*

An old Haweis Bible (the "Haw' Bible" of the poem) is, along with a grandfather's clock, one of the heirlooms of the poet's family in Orangeville—a ponderous volume, larger than the 1623 folio Shakspear. It is a leather-bound book of 672 pages, measuring 10 by 18 inches, with notes, engravings and atlas of sacred geography, published at Edinburgh in 1825, and in regular use by the poet's grandfather, Alexander Sutherland. It is named "Haw'" from its compiler, Rev. Thos. Haweis, LL.B., M.D., rector of Aldwinkle, Northamptonshire, in 1765.

Page 346 ([39]), *The Sempill Lords.*

The estate of Castle Sempill, in Lochwinnoch parish, when seen from the heights around, is one of the most beautiful and picturesque in Scotland. Acquired by Col. Wm. McDowall in 1727, he demolished Castleton, one of the ancient castles of the Sempills, and built a modern residence on the site.

Page 346 ([40]), "these lordly halls."

The Peil, once a fortress of great strength, built by Lord Sempill in 1560, is now a complete ruin.

Page 346 ([41]), Eliotstoun.

Eliotstoun, the most ancient residence of the Sempills, built in 1280, with massive walls and arched fastnesses, is rapidly falling to decay.

Page 346 ([42]), "that warrior lord."

Lord Sempill was with Regent Murray at the engagement at Langside. (See note 9 above.) For valor, achievements and counsel he was called "The Great Lord Sempill."

27

Page 360 (^{43}), "Bubbly Jock."

This is a name popular in Scotland for the turkey cock, corresponding to "gobbler" with us.

Page 368 (^{44}), *Wilson's Grave.*

Alexander Wilson, the Scottish poet and American ornithologist, is buried in the cemetery of the Swedish Church, Southwark, Philadelphia. The Navy Yard refreshment rooms and a wharf are within a hundred yards of his grave. "Had I been at home when he died," said his friend George Ord, "I would have selected some quiet spot in the country, retired from the city, where birds would warble over his grave—such a spot as he himself would have preferred."

Page 369 (^{45}), Robert Tannahill.

Robert Tannahill (born 1774, died 1810) was a Paisley weaver. He was attaining some celebrity after publishing "Poems and Songs," in 1807, but while his modest fame was extending, morbid melancholy clouded with gloom the quiet and diffident poet, leading to suicide by drowning. He had a genuine lyrical gift, without force and passion, but with grace and sweetness. His best songs are : "Loudon's Bonnie Woods and Braes," "Jessie, the Flower of Dumblane," and "Gloomy Winter's Noo Awa'."

Page 369 (^{46}), "While the Scottish muse sings waly."

A beautiful old Scottish ballad, to be found in "Percy's Reliques," begins

> " O waly, waly up the bank,
> And waly, waly down the brae."

Waly is an interjection of grief. It appears to be allied to *wae* (woe) and *waefu'* (woful).

Page 396 (^{47}), Howard.

John Howard, the celebrated philanthropist and reformer of prisons in Europe, but especially in the British Isles, died in 1790, at Kherson, in Russia, infected by a fever patient for whom he had prescribed.

Page 396 (^{48}), "Sutherland's heich mighty duke."

The cruelties inflicted by the Dukes of Sutherland, Athol and Breadalbane on their poor clansmen were so revolting that the massacre of Glencoe appears merciful in comparison. For a full account of these barbarities, perpetrated under the eye of the British Government in the nineteenth century, see "Gloomy Memories," by Donald McLeod; a book without literary pretension, but which reveals a tale of horror at which Scotsmen must blush.

GLOSSARY

This glossary is not taken from any existing one, but has been made expressly for this volume. It professes to include such words only as were thought likely to cause difficulty to the reader unfamiliar with broad Scots.

McLachlan's dialect does not differ essentially from that of literary Scotland (Burns's Ayrshire). That differs from standard English (of which it is the northern variety) somewhat in *vocabulary* (as *lug* for *ear*, *gar* for *compel*), but chiefly in *orthoepy*. The reader will readily get "the run of it" by bearing in mind these general statements : (1) Verbs make their past in "it," as *descendit* for *descended;* the i of "it" is elided if practicable, as *ordaint* for *ordained;* which happens even with the word *it*, as "*A'll* no dae't" for "I will not do it." (2) D is elided after n: *en'* is *end*, *han'* or *haun'* is *hand*, *an'* is *and*. (3) *Ow* is *oo* generally: *noo* is *now*, *roun'* is *round*, *moo* is *mouth*. (4) Final l is dropped : *fa'* is *fall*, *ca'* is *call*, *won'erfu'* is *wonderful*. (5) It has a mixed vowel like French u, German ü : *guid* is *good*, *bluid* is *blood*, *schule* is *school*, *fule is fool*. (See note on McLachlan's Rimes, p. 406.) (6) The guttural, so common in our language in the Tudor period, still holds sway. However, it is the voiceless guttural (usually spelt ch), as *wecht* for *weight*, not the voiced one which gh in current spelling appears to indicate. (7) Open i (as in *ill*) shifts to tense e (é): *clénch* is *clinch*, or else open i shifts to u in but : *wull* is *will*, *runklt* is *wrinkled*. (8) Short o becomes short a : *lang* is *long*, *sang* is *song*, *thrang* is *throng*, *amang* is *among*. (9) Final long u (as in *Hindu*) is apt to shift to ae (like ey in *they*) : *shae* is *shoe*, *dae* is *do*, *tae* is *too*, *blae* is *blue*. (10) Ei or ey has the force of Latin ei : *gey* is geï. (11) The present participle ends in "in" : *roarin* is *roaring*. (12) After c, t is commonly dropped : *exac'ly* is *exactly*. (13) After m, b is commonly dropped : *trummelt* is *trembled*, *thummle* is *thimble*. (14) Most speakers speak with increased tension of voice, the syllables are uttered with "snap," the opposite of drawling speech. In this respect it resembles French.

The reader should understand that all the above differences have not been fully carried out, because to do so would spoil the

27*

volume for popular use. There is a convenient half-way house between what the above differences logically lead to and the forms of words in every-day use as sanctioned by custom. To wrack a dialect on the Procrustean bed of philologic precision is to spoil it for popular use. For example, on page 364 will be found "slamm'd" and "belang'dna," where remark (1) above requires *slamt, belangtna.*

A', all.
Abune, above.
Ac's, acts.
Ae, one.
Ain, own.
Air, early.
Aith, oath.
An', and.
Ane, one.
Ance, once.
Ase, ause, ashes.
Aucht, aught, to own, possess.
Aughty, eighty.
Ava, at all.

Bachles, old shoes down at the heels.
Ballant, ballad, song.
Bang, to spring or recoil instantly.
Baum, balm.
Beek, to bask in the sun.
Ben, the inner part of the house, the end away from the speaker.
Ben, a hill.
Bide, to brook, endure.
Bike, byke, a beehive.
Birk, a birch.
Birken-shaw, a level at the foot of a hill, and covered with birches.
Bissom, a jade.
Blab, a drop, a bleb.
Blae, blue, blue with cold.
Blewart, the germander speedwell (*Veronica Chamædrys*).
Blate, shy, modest, bashful.
Bleart, bleerie, watery about the eyes.
Blethers, nonsense, idle talk.

Blue-waup, blue-whaup, a species of curlew.
Bodle, a copper coin, one-sixth penny.
Bonnet-laird, a petty freeholder.
Bothie, a cot, a hut for servants.
Brae, a hill-face.
Brattle, a clattering noise.
Bree, Brie, liquid, juice, soup.
Breeks, breeches, trousers.
Brose, oatmeal porridge not thoroughly cooked.
Buskit, dressed.
Burn, burnie, a brook.

Canny, cautious, prudent, frugal.
Cantrips, tricks, charms, spells, incantation.
Canty, cheerful, happy, lively.
Chapper, a door-knocker.
Chiel (child), a man, male person, fellow.
Chitter, to shiver, chatter from cold.
Chuffy-cheekit, chubby-cheeked.
Claes, clothes, dress.
Clash (v.), to gossip ; (n.) idle talk.
Claver, to talk foolishly or persistently.
Cloot, a stroke, a patch.
Clootit, struck, patched.
Clour, to strike ; a bruise or dint.
Clype, to tell secrets, blab, betray.
Coor, cour, courie, to stoop, crouch.
Coup, to overturn, to buy.
Creashy, greasy.
Croodlin', humming, purring, cooing.

Crowdie, porridge, cold gruel or brose.
Crusie, a small iron oil-lamp.
Cushat, cusha, cushie doo, ringdove.
Cutty, short, low.
Cutty-stool, a low stool, stool of repentance.

Dae, do.
Daidlin', trifling, hesitating.
Darg, a day's work, task.
Dauner, dander, daunder, to walk leisurely or aimlessly.
Daud, dawd, a large piece, chunk.
Daur, to dare.
Dee, to die.
Deid, dead.
Deleerit, delirious.
Dirl, a sharp, tremulous blow.
Doitit, stupid, confused.
Douce, serious, sedate, modest, respectable.
Doukin', ducking, bathing.
Dour, hard, stubborn.
Dowff, dull, sullen.
Dowie, melancholy, languid, inclining to decay.
Dree, to endure.
Dreigh muir, tedious, tiresome moor.
> "O, the dreary, dreary moorland."
> —TENNYSON.
Dribblin', dropping, tippling.
Dug, dowg, a dog.
Dune, done.
Dyvour, a bankrupt, disreputable.

E'e (pl. *e'en*), eye.
Eerie, fearful, sad, dreary.
Eident, busy, diligent.
Eneuch, enough.

Fan', found.
Fasht, annoyed, bothered.
Fauld, fold.
Faur, far.
Fause, false.
Fautit, faulted, blamed.

Fecht, faucht, fight.
Flannin, flannen, flannel.
Fog, moss.
Forfochten, tired, fatigued.
Forfairn, hurt, injured.
Fraise, to flatter, commend.
Fule, a fool.
Fyke, commotion, trouble.

Gabbit, talked, prattled.
Gaberlunzie, a wallet.
Gaberlunzie-man, a beggar.
Gae, go; *gaed*, went; *gaen, gane*, gone; *gaun*, going.
Gangrel, a waif, tramp.
Gar, to compel, force.
Gar me grue, to make my blood creep.
Gart, compelled, made.
Gey, geyan, very, rather, somewhat.
Gill-stoup, a whiskey measure.
Girn, to grin; *girnt*, grinned.
Glaumer, glamour, a kind of hypnotism supposed to make us see the unreal.
Glee, gley, to squint.
Glint, a peep, glance.
Gloamin, darkening, evening twilight.
Glifft, alarmed, frightened.
Gowan, daisy.
Gowd, gold.
Gowdspink, a goldfinch.
Gowkit, foolish, dazed.
Greet, weep, cry.
Grun', ground.
Gurly, gurgling.
Gyte (to gang gyte), to act wildly, foolishly.

Haffet, side of the face, cheek.
Haill, whole.
Hained, saved, kept.
Hale, to heal.
Hameart, home-made.
Harns, brains (German, *gehirn*).
Haud, to hold.
Haun', han', a hand.

Havers, nonsense.
Heich, high.
Heugh, a steep hill, a glen, the shaft of a pit.
Hing, hang.
Hinny, honey.
Hirple, to limp, walk with difficulty.
Hizzie, a hussy.
Hoodie-craw, a carrion crow.
Hoolet, *houlet*, howlet, owlet, owl.
Howe, a hollow.
Howf, a haunt, favorite place.
Howkit, dug.
Huff, anger, vexation.
Hurdies, hips, buttocks.

I', in.
Ill-wully, ill-willed.
Ilk, *ilka*, each, every.
Ingle, the house fire.

Jile, jail.
Jink, to elude, cheat, dodge.
Jinker, *jiker*, *jouker*, an artful dodger.
Joskin, a bumpkin.
Jouk, to stoop and dodge, to avoid danger.

Keek, to look; *keekit*, looked.
Ken'lt, kindled.
Kimmer, a gossip, a married woman.
Kitlin, a kitten.
Knowe, a knoll.

Lair, *lear*, learning.
Laith, loath.
Lang-heidit, "long-headed," shrewd and far-seeing.
Lap, leapt.
Lauch, laugh.
Leefu'-lane, *lee-lane*, quite alone, singly, without company.
Leeve, *lieve*, live.
Leuk, look.
Lift, the sky.
Lilt, to sing sweetly.
Limmers, women (opprobriously used).

Linn, a waterfall, cascade.
Lintie, a linnet.
Lint-white, white as flax (lint).
Lo'e, love.
Loun, a scamp.
Loune, *lowne*, calm.
Loup, a leap.
Lout, to stoop; *loutit*, stooped.
Lowe, flame.
Lowin', burning, flaming.
Lowse, to loosen.
Lug, an ear.

Mahoun, Satan.
Mailins, farms.
Mane, moan, lament.
Maun, must.
Mavis, a thrush.
Mensefu', dignified, honorable.
Mirk, darkness.
Muckle folk, great folk, gentry.
Muir, a moor.
Mune, moon.
Mutch, a woman's cap.

Nickit, caught, observed instantly.
Nieve, fist.
Niffer, exchange.
No', not.
Nocht, nothing.

Ocht, ought.
Oe, grandchild.
Ootstert, outstart.
Owre, over.

Pat (n.), a pot; (v.) preterite of *put*; (adj.) suitable.
Pauky, *pawky*, discreet, sly.
Peesweep, the lapwing.
Plowtit, plunged, immersed.
Poopit, pulpit.
Poortith, poverty, want.
Pow, the head, the poll.
Puddock-stools, toad-stools, fungi.
Pyat, a magpie.

Quat, quit.
Quait, quiet.

Raip, a rope.
Rash, a rush.
Ratton, a rat.
Raucle, rash.
Reave, rieve, to rob, plunder.
Rax, to reach.
Red-wud, stark mad, crazy.
Reest, to dry (as in the sun), to smoke.
Reenge, range.
Riddle, a sieve.
Rig-an'-fur, ridge and furrow, ribbing on stockings.
Riggin', the roof.
Risp, to rasp.
Routh, plenty, abundance.
Rouch, rough.
Runklt, wrinkled.
Runnell, stream, rivulet.

Sabbin', sobbing.
Sae, so.
Sair, sore.
Saut, salt.
Scaur, untamed, wild.
Schule-weans, school-children.
Screed, a discourse.
Scrieve, to write.
Scrimpit, scrumpit, scanty.
Sculduddery, breaches of propriety.
Scunner, dislike, disgust.
Shae (pl. *shaes, shoon*), a shoe.
Shaughled, shaky.
Shaw, level ground at a hill-foot.
Shouther, shoulder.
Siccar, certain, sure.
Side, long downward.
Sike, sewer, drain.
Siller, money, silver.
Sill'ry, silvery.
Slee, sly.
Skaith, harm.
Skalp, to slap, run away.
Skirl, scream.
Smirk, a slight laugh.
Snash, arrogant speech, impertinence.
Snell, sharp, sharply cold.

Snoove, to sneak off.
Snoul, to overbear, snub, frighten.
Spaewife, a fortune-teller.
Spate, flood.
Speel, to climb.
Speer, to ask ; *speert*, asked.
Speerit, spirit.
Stance, status, footing.
Starn, a star.
Stey, steep.
Stoun, spasm, twinge.
Stoup, stowp, a measure, water bucket.
Stov'd, stovin' (wi' drink), heated.
Strae, straw.
Stuid, stood.
Swab, a fighter, bully.
Swat, did sweat.
Sweet, sweit, sweat.
Syne (as, since syne), after that.

Tae, too, (n.) toe.
Taid, a toad.
Tauld, told.
Tautit, matted.
Thack, thatch.
Thae, these, those.
Thrang, busy, throng.
Thraw, a twist, contradiction, cross.
Threep, to insist.
Timmer, timber.
Tine, to lose ; *tint*, lost.
Toop, a ram.
Totem, a toddling baby.   [ing.
Tourie-tapt, tower-topped, or taper-
Towsy, rough, unkempt.
Trummelt, trembled.
Twasome, twasum, two together.
Tyke, a dog.

Vera, very.
Voo, vow.

Wad, would.
Wae, woe ; (adj.) woful.
Wale, a choice.
Waly, waly, expression of grief (like " Wo is me ! "), large.

Wanter, a bachelor.
Wauken, to waken.
Waukrife, wakeful.
Waun'ert, wandered, astray.
Waur, worse.
Wean (wee ane), child.
Wecht, weight.
Weet, water, rain.
Whalpit, born, whelped.
Whan, when.
Whang, a lump, large slice.
Wheen, many.
Whinny-knowe, a knoll overgrown with whins (gorse).
Whist, hush !
Whunstane, granite.
Wice, wise.

Wimplin', purling.
Win (awa' hame), to get, reach.
Winnock, a window.
Witch-thummle, witch-thimble, witch-bells, flower of the foxglove.
Wrath-wud-hags, probably a form of *rig-wuddie-hags*, that is, women worthy the *rig-wuddie* (or rope) by which the shafts of a cart are held up across a horse's back.
Wutch, witch.

Yaird, yard, garden.
Yaumer, to complain whiningly.
Yirth, earth, ground.
Yorlin, the yellow-hammer.

INDEX TO FIRST LINES

Appendix

GOING TO THE BUSH

This settlement is getting old,
   And just a leettle crowdy;
I'll not loaf round this worn out ground,
   Like any idle rowdy.
There's few like me, can fell a tree,
   I'm bully at the axe;
I'm twenty-one, its time dad's son
   Was up and making tracks.

Dad says, that when he's dead and gone,
   I'll have this farm of his'n,
If I'll but stay, and work away,
   Since market stuffs have risen.
That's too onsartain, and besides
   I'll never wish him dead, —
Not fond of pelf — yet for myself
   I want to go a-head.

I'll chop a homestead o' my own,
   The first thing that I'll do,
And raise a shanty right away,
   With room enough for two.
I'll hunt me up some neighbour gal —
   For I wont live alone;
And there in joy, without alloy,
   Raise chickens o' my own.

425

Now, let me see — who will it be,
   To whom I'll give the call?
I'll surely find one to my mind,
   When I've the pick of all!
I'm a six-footer in my socks —
   Tho' tanned a leetle yeller;
Yet after all, what gals would call,
   A rather handsom' feller.

Well, there's that Buckley gal — but she's
   Too slow upon her feet;
She'd be no use, back in the bush,
   With nothing but conceit.
There's Laura Larkings — she won't do,
   For she's both cross and cranky;
I know she'd shirk all kinds of work,
   Like any down-east Yankee.

There's Mary Ann, smart gal I swan!
   And good too, I consider;
But, then you see, it cannot be
   'Cause I won't have a widder.
And there is Sal, a tidy gal!
   A favorite o' my mother's;
But then I would be eaten up,
   With all her loafing brothers.

And there's the Reeve's young daughter too
   That gal's got quite affected!

426

And O, what airs she always wears,
    Since her dad was elected.
And how she squalls, at what she calls
    'Her sacred songs so charming;'
But, O my stars! them heavenly airs
    Are really quite alarming.

There's Liz — but she won't do for me!
    For she's her mother's daughter,
Whose tongue has kept this settlement
    For years in boiling water.
A hansom' gal tho' she may be —
    And very few are smarter —
We went to school, but çould'nt pull,
    For she's a regular Tarter.

There's Nancy Ann, the gal I swan!
    Jist laughing ripe, and mellor;
A perfect brick! she'll do right slick!
    Lord, I'm a lucky feller.
I mind, when old schoolmaster frowned,
    And shook the blue-beech o'er me,
She took my part, and bless her heart!
    She lied like sixty for me.

Yes, Nan shall be the gal for me!
    A clever-handed gal!
I'll get her too, with small ado,
    I'm certain sure I shall.

Then here's for Nan! she's mine I swan!
   And we'll have no delaying,
Hitched right away! that's what I say!
   And start the first o' sleighing.

ELORA

Lovely Elora! thy valley and stream,
Still dwell in my heart like a beautiful dream;
And everything peaceful and gentle I see,
Brings back to my bosom some image of thee.
I've roamed this Dominion allured by the beam
Of wild woodland beauty, by valley and stream;
From lone Manitoulin all down to the sea;
But found ne'er a spot, sweet Elora, like thee.

There's lone rocky grandeur away at the Sound,
And down the St. Lawrence wild beauties abound;
Quebec, towering proudly, looks down on the sea,
And lone Gananoque there's beauty in thee;
And Barrie! the lady that sits by the lake,
O, would I could sing a sweet song for her sake!
But here in thy beauty a-list'ning the fall,
O, lovely Elora! thou'rt queen of them all.

If friends should forsake me, or fortune depart,
Or love fly, and leave a great void in my heart;
O, then in my sorrow away I would flee,
And hide from misfortune, Elora, in thee.

428

Away from the world, with its falsehood and pride,
In yon lowly cot where the smooth waters glide,
I'd commune with Nature till death set me free,
And rest then for ever, Elora, in thee.

ONTARIO

Far away from my forest home,
In the land of the stranger I must roam;
And sigh amid flowers and trailing vines,
For mine own rude land of lakes and pines.
And I long — O, how I long to be
In mine own Dominion of the free —
                              Ontario! Ontario!
In mine own Dominion of the free —
                              Ontario!

The old school-house, is it standing still?
Do the pines still hang o'er the old saw-mill?
Is the maple tree still fresh and green,
That over our old log-house doth lean?
Ah! back to them all, I fain would be
In mine own Dominion of the free —
                              Ontario! Ontario!
In mine own Dominion of the free —
                              Ontario!

And does the blue-bird, in the Spring
Come to it, as of old, to sing?

And 'mong its branches build her nest,
And rear its young ones in its breast?
O, had I wings like her, I'd flee
To mine own Dominion of the free —
                    Ontario! Ontario!
To mine own Dominion of the free —
                    Ontario!

And what, tho' many do forget,
There's still one there that loves me yet!
I see her form, I see her face —
I hear her voice in every place!
And backward still, she beckons me
To mine own Dominion of the free —
                    Ontario! Ontario!
To mine own Dominion of the free —
                    Ontario!

And still, as a knock comes to the door,
Tho' disappointed ten times o'er,
She runs — but to find her hopes are vain,
Of her wand'ring Billy back again:
And back to her breast, I fain would flee,
And mine own Dominion of the free —
                    Ontario! Ontario!
And mine own Dominion of the free —
                    Ontario!

THE DEATH OF THE OX

And thou art gone, my poor dumb friend! thy troubles all
  are past;
A faithful friend thou wert indeed, e'en to the very last!
And thou wert the prop of my house, my children's pride
  and pet, —
Who now will help to free me from this weary load of debt?

Here, single-handed, in the bush I battled on for years,
My heart sometimes buoyed up with hope, sometimes bowed
  down with fears.
I had misfortunes not a few, e'en from the very first!
But take them altogether, 'Bright,' thy death's the very worst!

My great ambition's always been, to owe no man a cent;
To compass that, by honest toil, my every nerve I've bent;
Not for proud Independence! no, of which the poets sing,
But for the very love of Right — the justice of the thing.

To clear accounts within the year, I saw my way so plain —
But losing thee, it throws me back, God knows, how far again!
Just when I thought within my grasp, I had success secure,
Here comes Misfortune back again, resolved to keep me poor!

I've no one to depend upon, to do my teaming now!
And there's ten acres to be logged! the fallow all to plough!
How can I ever clear the land — how can I drag the wheat?
How can I keep my credit clear — how can my children eat?

431

O, nothing in the shape of work, was e'er a scare to thee!
Thou wert the hero of the field, at every logging bee!
The drags, they might be double length, the maples monster
    thick,
Then give thee but a 'rolling hitch,' and off they went so slick.

Twas but a tug — the monsters seem'd to thee as light's a pin;
And how you wheeled them round about, and how you jerked
    them in;
The very crookedest of all, would hardly make thee strain,
And from the teamsters, every one, fresh laurels thou didst gain.

A gentleness, a beauty, too, within thine eye did dwell!
It seemed to me as beautiful as eye of the gazelle!
And, how thy hide of tawny-white lost every shade of dun,
And its brown streaks to velvet changed, all in the summer's sun.

And through the Indian Summer too, transfigured thou didst
    seem,
A great dumb giant looking through her hazy amber beam!
And how you loved in Spring-time oft, to browse beside the
    creek —
When all the air was laden with the odour of the leek.

How you would stand and ruminate, like sage in thoughtful
    mood;
Or listen to the children's shout, far in the leafy wood, —
While they were hunting flowery spots, where Spring had
    newly been, —
Or gathering lilies, red and white, beneath the maples green;

432

Or, far beneath the tamarac's shade — where many a hemlock
  leans
Above the salt-licks, in the dell, fringed with the evergreens; —
Or climbing the o'erhanging bank, or swinging from the tree;
Or starting with their ringing shout, in search, old friend, of thee!

And laden with the spoils of Spring, they'd follow up thy track,
And wreath thy horns superb with flowers, and mount upon thy
  back;
And how you shook your tawny sides, in absolute delight;
And I have stood, and looked unseen, in rapture on the sight.

It seemed a miracle to me — for thou wert never broke —
How willingly you always came, and bowed beneath the yoke;
And when Buck — as he sometimes did — would take a stubborn
  fit,
Then, in some language of thine own, you coaxed him to submit.

It's clear to me, that thou hadst got some kind of moral sense, —
For never didst thou sneak, and steal, nor ever break a fence, —
And when Buck would leap over one, for he was ne'er reclaimed,
How hurriedly you stole away, as perfectly ashamed!

And thou wert so sagacious too, so sensible and shrewd,
And every word I said to thee, was fully understood.
No whip was e'er laid on thy back, nor blue-beech,
  never never!
While slaves and tyrants wrought and fought, we lived in
  peace together.

433

I've no doubt, but you learned some things, my poor old friend
   from me,
And many a silent lesson too, I also got from thee;
I ne'er could think thou wert a brute, but just a silent brother!
And sure am I, to fill thy place I'll never get another!

THE OLD SETTLER'S ADDRESS TO
HIS OLD LOG HOUSE

My Old Log-House, I love thee still!
I left thee sore against my will;
My new house, finer tho' it be,
Can never be as dear to me;
For memory's spell is o'er thee cast,
And I must love thee to the last.
For life's first breath in thee I drew,
In thee from youth to manhood grew,
All early thoughts are twined with thee,
And thy o'erhanging maple tree!
It seemed to me no other place
Had ever half so sweet a face;
And on the winter nights and days,
No hearth had half so bright a blaze
Among the trees no taper shone
With half the welcome of thine own,
And when from thee I went away,
In sunny southern lands to stray,
'Mid all their bloom, my heart would flee, —
Mine own log cabin — back to thee!

Tho' now thy household gods are gone,
Still often I come here alone,
And, on thy hearthstone, cold at last,
I muse and ponder on the past!
Till parents, brothers, sisters dear,
In all their beauty re-appear,
Despite of death, the joyous train
Comes back to love me once again!
I see my father in his chair!
My mother with her knitting there!

The children crowding round, to hear
The stories that we loved so dear;
Or list'ning to that martial song
Which rushes yet my veins along,
Re-counting deeds of heroes bold,
In Britain's battles won of old.

And many a happy night I ween,
Beneath thine old roof tree I've seen;
For after every logging bee
The neighbours all would meet in thee;
For when the hard day's work was done,
The logging contests lost and won,
We gave ourselves to social mirth,
And banished sorrow from the hearth:
And ev'ry happy girl and boy
Danc'd till thy rafters shook with joy.
A thousand recollections rush,
And tears into mine eyelids gush,

435

When thinking of the manly race
Who first were settled in this place,
Uncursed with thought, which has destroyed
Our social joys, and left a void —
A dreary void within the heart
Which cannot be supplied with art!

And here, upon my wedding day,
No palace ever look'd so gay;
With evergreens and wild flowers dress'd,
You smil'd a welcome to each guest;
And well I mind the joyous cheer
Which welcom'd home my Mary dear;
And how the youngsters danc'd and sung
Until thy very rafters rung,
And all the world to me did seem
As floating in a blessed dream!

And here, while she remained on earth,
She was the sunlight of thy hearth;
And here — beneath thine old roof tree,
She nurs'd my children on her knee;
There, with the very smile she wore,
She comes up to me as of yore,
As if she still would cheer the mate
She left at last so desolate;
And all the children, as of yore,
Are romping round her on the floor;
There Mary! with her eyes of blue,
And heart so tender and so true, —

Who pass'd to brighter worlds away,
While yet her life was in its May:
And Charlie, with his face so fair,
His large blue eyes and shining hair,
And ringing laugh, which seemed to say, —
'O, life is all a summer's day!'
I hear him singing in the lane —
'Royal Charlie's come again!'
How strange! that he so light and gay,
Was called the very first away.

But, ah! the vision's past and gone!
And I am standing all alone
Upon thy hearth all desolate,
To sigh o'er the decrees of Fate.

Thy walls are mouldering to decay,
Like all things, thou shalt pass away.
And here, the grass shall flourish green,
And nought to tell of what has been.
But sacred thou shalt ever be —
No hand unfix thine old roof tree!
And here I'll often come and sit,
While evening shadows round me flit,
Till as of yore the joyous train
Are all around me once again.

SABBATH MORNING'S SOLILOQUY
OF AN OLD OX

Ah! times are chang'd, aye, changed indeed;
Hard work, ill usage, and scant feed,
Hae wrought a waefu' change in me:
I'm no' the beast I used to be.

O, they were times ere I was brought
Beneath auld Jawbaw's heavy yoke:
O, they were blessed times, I trow,
Wi' plenty and scarce ought to do;
For surely kindness and good feeding
Is the hale secret o' good breeding.

Who could believe me the same creature
So sleek in hide and great in stature,
So light o' heart, so free frae care,
That took the prize at Erin fair?
Then mony a body star'd at me,
And said I was worth gaun to see:
The judges said, in a' the fair
There was nocht wi' me could compare:
They stuck the riband on my heed,
And said I was of noble breed,
And sent a glib-tongu'd jockey wi' me,
To lead me roun' and let folk see me.

But, oh! these happy days are past,
And I'm reduced to want at last;

438

I'm wrocht to perfect skin and bane,
And aft maun thole a hungry wame:
It matters na tho' I'm discreet,
I'm but a *thing* wi' cloven feet,
And ony wicked blackguard knave
May goad me like a galley slave.

But Guid be thankit, this is Sunday,
And I'll hae peace and rest till Monday:
The very thought this day brings rest
Keeps up the heart o' the oppress'd;
A blessed day to a' the weary,
It aye returns to make them cheery.
Oh! but for this sweet happy time,
I had been dragg'd to death langsyne;
For its a great grief to some folk

That we should e'er get out the yoke,
For, oh! they grudge and spend the Sunday
Yawning and wishing it were Monday.
They'd do awa' wi't a' thegither,
And keep us in the yoke forever;
But, were the rascals in our skin,
They'd pray for twa instead o' ane.

They're born but to command, they say,
And we poor creatures to obey;
For we are of the working classes,
And sae we maun put up wi' lashes,
Maun cultivate the virtues humble,
And feed on thistles and ne'er grumble.

439

Ah! mony a time I've sadly thought,
When I've been ill used and hard wrought,
That 'tis our quiet disposition
Which keeps us in this sad condition:
We've no' eneugh o' spunk and Devil
To gar twa-footed brutes be civil:
Our kicking, our casting the yoke,
Has always ended but in smoke:
'Tis gentleness and want o' knavery
Which keeps us, as a race, in slavery.

You dog, wha's play'd me mony pranks,
A creature o' the upper ranks,
An ugly, biting, barking devil,
Wha hasna the sense to be civil

To decent, quiet, honest folk,
Even when they're let out the yoke,
But struts roun' wi' a face fu' sour,
To let them feel that he's in power;
Wi' collar large, that a' may see
A great dog in authority,
And rides, tho' but a dirty messin,
Aye on the tap o' his commission,
And a' his surly rude behaviour
Is just to get himsel' in favor.

I've seen him fawn and phrase and whine
Upon aud Jawbaws mony a time;

Aye, even after he wad kick him,
The messin wad crawl up and lick him:
The creature then I could hae crush'd
Wi' perfect contempt and disgust.

I hate, frae the depth o' my heart,
A creeping, crawling, sycophant:
It's muckle I hae got to bear wi'
Without a single hope to cheer me;
But I'd as soon walk to the knife
As lead that creeping creature's life:
And Guid kens my lot's far frae easy;
For, since I'm getting auld and crazy,
And canna draw the loads I used to,
By young and auld I maun abus'd be.

Had I been o' a thievish nature,
A sleekit, sloungin', sly fence breaker,
But I! who've walk'd in virtue's ways,
To treat me sae in my auld days!
To live in want, in hate and fear,
Is more e'en than a beast can bear.

And there is my young neebor Lyon,
He's better hous'd and fed than I am:
If Jawbaws didna feed him weel,
He'd break in through barn doors and steal;
The hichest fence he wad leap over,
And wallow to the wame in clover.

441

But mony a time I've hungry been,
Close by where oats were tempting green,
Tho' I'm but a four-footed beast,
I've had the virtue to resist.
Yet, in hard times, when a' are starving,
The bite's gi'en to the undeserving:
To be rewarded thus for merit,
Might even break an ox's spirit.

And, oh! there are twa-footed beasts
Wi' nae compassion in their breasts:
My master's one o' the vile brutes,
Waur not ocht that e'er walk'd on clutes;
Tho' he's a man, 'twould be a sin
To compare even me wi' him.
His heart's as cauld and hard as steel,

A cruel, drunken ne'er-do-weel,
Wha grudges me a moment's ease,
And gangs to a' the logging bees;
And if I dinna haw and jee,
And jump as gleg's I us'd to do,
O! then his wicked tongue gets loose
Wi' awfu' torrents o' abuse,
And blauds o' blasphemy and sweerin',
Till I've been horrified to hear him.

And O! I hae a sad foreboding
'Twill be my death this weary logging;
For when the heavy day is through,

And a' the hauns are bleth'rin' fu'
They'll keep a rantin' and a roarin'
A' telling their great feats and splorin'
While I for hours maun sadly wait,
Like sorrow at a tavern gate;
Wi' weary hide and hungry wame,
And haurel then the blackguard's hame.

As sure as Jawbaws taks a spree,
Wi' a' he meets he'll disagree,
Then I'm in terror o' my life,
He'll hae a quarrel wi' the wife;
For he's henpeckit in the main,
And daurna ca' his soul his ain,
And as sure as they disagree,
He'll out and vent his rage on me.

And after a' his drucken fits,
Especially if he's got his licks,
He'll gang about as quaite's a lamb,
Pretending he's an alter'd man;
And then he'll talk sic awful' nonsense
About the Bible and his conscience.
He little thinks that when he prays,
I'm watching every word he says:
He kens na that his puir auld ox
Regards him as a perfect hoax.
Did he but ken, to wrath 'twad move him,
What I, a puir dumb beast, think of him;
For, tho' my prospect dark and dree is,
Thank God, I'm no' the brute that he is.

YOUNG HOSS

Now here's a boss, that is a boss!
  Most folks are of opinion,
There isn't such another hoss
  In all our great Dominion.
See, how he paces like a prince!
  He's willing, and no schemer;
And at a race, or trotting pace,
  I tell you, he's a screamer!

To see me driving past the mail,
  To reach the railway station,
And leaving it both head and tail, —
  I tell ye, it's a caution.
And them old farmers, with their wheat,
  They're to the market teaming;
How hopefully they jog along,
  Of mighty prices dreaming!

I like to see them old coons riled —
  They're always plaguey bosses!
You may insult them if you will —
  But do'nt insult their hosses.
I drives up quietly behind,
  And if there's aught like sleighing —
I gives the whip, and like a ship,
  I passes them hurrahing!

A mighty swell came out from town,
  And boasted, O, tarnation! —
His mare would trot the township down,
  And gallop all creation.
And how he swaggered all around;
  Stumped everyone about him;
Thinks I, the clown, I'll do him brown!
  I'll take the conceit out him.

We tabl'd down a x a-piece,
  And started off like thunder;
Past him I flew, with small ado,
  Which made the critter wonder.
And there the miller's daughter stood,
  And how she laughed, O — cricky!
As she would bust, to see me fust,
  And roared out, 'well done Dickie!'

A gal so sensible as Sal,
  You'll seldom come across, sir; —
For ignorant's the most o' gals;
  But well she knows a hoss, sir.
And a tarnation handsom' gal —
  A regular romping filly;
And all the other gals in town,
  Beside her look so silly.

There's something in her, when she's rigg'd
  For 'Sunday go to meeting;'
I feels abash'd, for — O be-dashed —

She sets my heart a-beatin'.
And she knows how to hold the reins —
  Tho' Dandy's against her striving;
You have to see't, it's so complete,
  O Lord, to see her driving!

With saddle, or without it, she
  Can ride a hoss quite handy;
I tell ye it's a sight to see
  Her mounted upon Dandy.
We two would work in harness well,
  And that I often tell her;
And faith, I think, she likes it well,
  She loves a smart young feller.

Them fools of fellers up the town,
  They need not round her slaver —
For I've it fixed for April next,
  And I'm the boy will have her!

OLD CANADA; OR, GEE BUCK GEE

The country's goin' fast to ruin!
This edication's our undoin',
We're comin' to a pretty pass,
Our boys who scarce have been to grass,
Have all gone off, bound to the teachers,
Or city clerks, or peddlin' preachers;
Our darters too, are quite Sultanas,

All strummin' on them cuss'd pianos,
And try to trip us up with rules
They've learn'd away at Grammar Schools,
And look upon the likes o' me —
Who nurs'd them criters on my knee —
As far beneath them, — Gee Buck Gee!

And then they're all Book Farmers too!
And they would teach me what to do;
Manurin', ploughin', drainin', seedin',
All farmin's to be done by readin'!
O Lord! O Lord! it makes me mad,
When every striplin' o' a lad,
And every edicated ass,
Who scarce knows growin' wheat from grass,
Must teach the like o' me to farm,
Wi' Latin names as long's my arm;
Them criters teach the like o' me?
Who farm'd ere they could reach my knee,
Aint it presumption? — Gee Buck Gee!

I tell ye what! them and their books,
Are getting to be perfect pukes;
And sure enough this edication
Will be the ruin o' the nation;
We'll not ha' men, it's my opinion,
Fit to defend our New Dominion;
Not one o' them can swing an axe,
But they will bore you with the facts;
I'd send the criters off to work,

447

But that, by any means they'll shirk!
Grandad to some o' them I be,
O, that's what riles and vexes me!
Ain't it a caution? — Gee Buck Gee!